Radical Ambition

The publisher gratefully acknowledges the generous support of the Ahmanson Foundation Humanities Endowment Fund of the University of California Press Foundation.

Radical Ambition

C. Wright Mills, the Left,
and American Social Thought

Daniel Geary

UNIVERSITY OF CALIFORNIA PRESS
Berkeley · Los Angeles · London

University of California Press, one of the most
distinguished university presses in the United States,
enriches lives around the world by advancing scholarship in the humanities, social sciences, and natural
sciences. Its activities are supported by the UC Press
Foundation and by philanthropic contributions from
individuals and institutions. For more information,
visit www.ucpress.edu.

University of California Press
Berkeley and Los Angeles, California

University of California Press, Ltd.
London, England

Library of Congress Cataloging-in-Publication Data

Geary, Daniel.
    Radical ambition / C. Wright Mills, the Left, and
American Social Thought / Daniel Geary.
        p.   cm.
    Includes bibliographical references and index.
    ISBN 978-0-520-25836-5 (cloth : alk. paper)
        1. Mills, C. Wright (Charles Wright), 1916–
1962. 2. Sociology—United States—History—20th
century. I. Title.

    HM479.M55G43   2009
    301.092—dc22   2008035577

Manufactured in the United States of America

18   17   16   15   14   13   12   11   10   09
10 9 8 7 6 5 4 3 2 1

This book is printed on Natures Book, which
contains 30% post-consumer waste and meets the
minimum requirements of ANSI/NISO Z39.48–1992
(R 1997) (*Permanence of Paper*).

For Jennie

Contents

Acknowledgments

Writing a book is in many ways a lonely endeavor, but I was fortunate to receive the assistance of many people. Most young scholars are lucky to have the support of a single great mentor. I was blessed with four. As my dissertation advisor, David Hollinger guided this book from start to finish. At crucial junctures during this project, he offered wise advice and helped sharpen the book's methods and arguments. Perhaps more important, this book is deeply indebted to the approach to intellectual history that I learned from him. My work on Mills began with an undergraduate thesis completed in 1997 at the University of Virginia under the direction of Nelson Lichtenstein. Reading over my thesis recently, I saw that I thanked Nelson for his "intellectual and political guidance." That gratitude remains today. During the past decade Nelson provided continued encouragement and criticism, and our many conversations about Mills over the years helped shape this work. Time and again, Howard Brick offered me invaluable feedback on the manuscript. I am very grateful for his challenging comments, which inspired many a revision, and to his understanding of twentieth-century American social thought, which proved a crucial influence on my own. Finally, my distinguished colleague during my three years at the University of Nottingham, Richard King, was a vital source of encouragement and criticism as I transformed my dissertation into this book.

I also greatly appreciate the many friends and colleagues who commented on this project as it developed and who read drafts and offered comments. Those deserving of particular mention are Robert Adcock, Julian Bourg, Michael Burawoy, Healan Gaston, Van Gosse, Susan Haskell, Joel Isaac, Martin Jay, Andy Jewett, Matthew Jones, Saul Landau, Waldo Martin, Paddy Riley, Dorothy Ross, Doug Rossinow, the late Michael Rogin, Austin Senseman, and Jonathan VanAntwerpen. I would also like to thank the staff at the Center of American History at the University of Texas, where the Mills Papers are housed. I am also very grateful to the staff at the University of California Press, particularly to my editor, Naomi Schneider, who was an early and enthusiastic supporter of this project; to the readers of the manuscript, Daniel Horowitz and George Cotkin; and to my excellent production editor, Jacqueline Volin, and copy editor, Sharron Wood.

I am extremely grateful to the Mills family for all of their help. Yaroslava Mills generously offered me permission to view the Mills Papers. She also provided me with excellent tea, lunch, and information one afternoon during a visit to West Nyack. Acting on behalf of the Mills estate, Nik Mills promptly granted permission to publish quotations from Mills's unpublished manuscripts despite logistical hurdles. I owe a special debt of gratitude to Kate Mills, whom I continually consulted because of her expertise on the life and work of her father. Kate provided me with hundreds of photocopies of crucial documents. She also read the entire manuscript, correcting more errors that I would care to count. Kate's assistance was absolutely essential to the success of this project.

I am deeply grateful to my family and friends for their support. My parents, William and Susan Geary, have long encouraged and supported my intellectual endeavors as well as those of my brother, Patrick. Susan also provided invaluable copyediting assistance for the final manuscript version of this book. My passion for many of the issues that drove me to write this book were a result of discussions with many close friends I have had since adolescence, including Dave Barnett, Joe Bowers, Ben Fraser, John Hardenbergh, Lori Ito, Todd Ito, Kurt Newman, and Brishen Rogers. Andrew Blouet, Michelle DeTorie, Susan Haskell, Andy Jewett, Kurt Newman, Pamela Pollock, Brishen Rogers, and Healan Gaston offered me places to stay during research trips.

Most of all, I would like to thank my wife, Jennie Sutton. Around the same time that I discovered C. Wright Mills, I met Jennie. That summer before my senior year in college, I carried *The Power Elite* under my arm. I also fell in love. Jennie's contribution to this book was enormous. She read multiple drafts of each section and provided both enthusiastic support and editorial advice. She even typed the first chapter when severe tendonitis in my wrist prevented me from doing so. The sacrifices she has made for this book have been great. But it is because of her sweet love and devotion that I dedicate this book to her. Now that the book is finished, she can be secure in the knowledge that my commitment to her has outlived the one I made to Mills.

Though others deserve much of the credit for this book, any blame for errors of fact or interpretation rests solely with me.

Maverick on a Motorcycle?

The Thought and Times of C. Wright Mills

The sociologist, social critic, and political radical Charles Wright Mills (1916–1962) did not fit the 1950s stereotype of the "egghead" intellectual. Famous for riding a motorcycle, he dressed in boots and a leather jacket at a time when academic protocol dictated more formal attire. Over six feet tall and weighing more than two hundred pounds, he had an imposing physical presence. He was good with his hands as well as with his brain: he knew how to fix his motorcycle, he helped build two of his houses, and he chastised friends for not baking their own bread. He spoke with a noticeable Texan twang and could regale his New York acquaintances with tales of his grandfather, a rancher who had been shot to death. And, of course, he wrote a series of books—most notably *White Collar, The Power Elite,* and *The Sociological Imagination*— that broke with the postwar liberal consensus by offering sharp, radical analyses of American politics and society. These writings became influential in large part because of the authentic critical voice of their author, whose very name proclaimed that he was one who could "see right." They would have a particularly significant impact on New Left social movements of the 1960s era.

C. Wright Mills was one of the most fascinating personalities in recent American intellectual history. However, a full understanding of his ideas and their historical significance has been obscured by a captivating caricature of him as a motorcycle-riding maverick, a lone dissident from the conservative complacency of the cold war era. Scholars

generally have portrayed Mills as a rebel *with* a cause, the intellectual
equivalent of contemporary movie characters played by James Dean
and Marlon Brando. To Russell Jacoby, Mills was a "one-man show
from the hinterlands—a rebel in an American vein—he raged against
the apathy and conformity of post World War II society."[1] To Tom
Hayden, leader of the New Left organization Students for a Democratic
Society (SDS), he was a "radical nomad."[2] To James Miller, historian of
SDS, the moral of Mills's story is "how one lone-wolf writer, against all
odds, actually managed to make a difference."[3] The sociologist Harvey
Molotch recalled, "My first image of sociology was through the writing of C. Wright Mills, whom I . . . imagined as an album cover. He
merged with Jack Kerouac, Lenny Bruce, and Henry Miller in my
mind; they were all heroes who knew the world through its edges—
deviant, strident, and/or dirty-mouthed."[4] Mills's thought is often seen
as a natural extension of his personality: independent, tough, and subversive; as the sociologist and former SDS leader Todd Gitlin put it,
"His forceful prose, his instinct for significant controversy, his Texas
hell-for-leather aura, his reputation for intellectual fearlessness and his
passion for craftsmanship . . . seemed all of a piece."[5]

The notion of Mills as a lone rebel has persisted because it served
different needs in the decades following his death. Mills himself did
much to shape this image. Though he purchased a motorcycle as a
solution to the parking shortage near Columbia University, where he
taught, surely he knew that riding it would contribute to his outlaw
image. In his writings, Mills often presented himself as an intellectual
renegade: the antithesis of a bureaucratic social scientist and a model
radical intellectual who told the truth during a time of left-wing defeat.
Yet Mills's efforts alone did not create his legendary status; he acquired
that only after his death in 1962. To certain members of the generation reaching maturity during the 1960s, Mills became an important
symbol. New Leftists found inspiration to challenge the status quo in
Mills's persona as much as in his writings. As one SDS activist recalled,
"You had to know C. Wright Mills," which required familiarity not
only with his ideas, but also with his personal style and the anecdotes
told about him.[6] Mills appealed especially to male radicals as an icon
of masculine authenticity.[7] To many sociologists of the era, Mills was a
crucial symbol of rebellion against the limitations of their discipline. As
members of the 1960s generation came to prominence in both radical
politics and social science, they retained this idealized image of Mills.
Since the 1980s, Mills has also appealed to his proponents as a model

of the "public intellectual," often said to be a dying breed. Indeed, Mills is a central protagonist of Russell Jacoby's 1987 book *The Last Intellectuals*, which introduced the term *public intellectual* into widespread debate.[8]

The common interpretation of Mills as a maverick traces the critical power of Mills's writings directly to his personal iconoclasm, his refusal to work within the parameters of the political categories or sociological thought of his time. Yet Mills's thought was far more characteristic of his era than has been recognized. If we see his ideas as emanating primarily from his heroic personality, then we miss their grounding in larger cultural and political trends. In fact, Mills is a fascinating subject for historical study precisely because of his serial involvement with major developments of midcentury intellectual life. Such trends included the growing postwar prominence of the social sciences, marked by new empirical sophistication and an ambitious theoretical agenda to understand modern society; the postwar reception of German social thought in the United States, based on the emigration of intellectuals from Germany to the United States and the newfound interest in Max Weber's work; the impact of the cold war on intellectual life, which forced thinkers to take a clear stance on American foreign policy; the growth of popular social criticism during the 1950s; and the decline of the Old Left of the 1930s and 1940s and the birth of the New Left at the end of the 1950s. Although Mills often found himself in the minority, he nevertheless learned from others who shared his positions and frequently borrowed from mainstream discourse. Indeed, Mills's ideas resemble even those of the liberal political thinkers who were his primary targets and against whom scholars generally contrast him today.

AMERICAN REBEL?

The basic details of Mills's life are well known. He was born in 1916 in Waco, Texas. His father, Charles Grover Mills, worked for an insurance company. His mother, Frances Wright Mills, came from a family with deep Texas roots. A devout Catholic, she insisted that Mills be raised in the church. After graduating from Dallas Technical High School in 1934, Mills spent an unhappy year at Texas Agricultural and Mechanical College before transferring to the University of Texas at Austin, from which he concurrently received a bachelor's degree in sociology and a master's degree in philosophy in 1939. He earned his

Ph.D. in sociology from the University of Wisconsin at Madison in
1942. From 1941 to 1945, he taught at the University of Maryland.
In 1945, he moved to Columbia University, where he remained until
the end of his life. Mills was married to three women: first in 1939 to
Dorothy (Freya) Helen Smith, whom he met when he was a student in
Austin and whom he remarried in 1941, after they had divorced; second
in 1947 to Ruth Harper, a statistical researcher whom he met while
gathering material for *White Collar;* and finally in 1959 to Yaroslava
Surmach, a Ukrainian-American artist whom he met while traveling in
Eastern Europe. Mills had one child with each wife: Pamela, Kathryn,
and Nikolas. In December 1960, Mills suffered a serious heart attack,
and he died from another attack in March 1962.[9]

Partly because of his Texas roots, scholars have portrayed Mills as
"peculiarly American."[10] The titles of the two most prominent books
about Mills reflect this tendency: Rick Tilman's *C. Wright Mills: A
Native Radical and His American Intellectual Roots* and Irving Louis
Horowitz's *C. Wright Mills: An American Utopian.*[11] Like others,
Tilman and Horowitz see Mills as a quintessentially American intellectual not only because of his background, but also because he drew from
American intellectual traditions, especially pragmatism, and because
his radicalism was untainted by European Marxist traditions. But
focusing on how "American" Mills's ideas and personality were brings
us no closer to understanding them. Was Mills really more "American"
than the contemporary New York intellectuals with whom he is often
contrasted, thinkers who, unlike Mills, were predominantly Jewish and
more grounded in Marxist traditions?[12] Rejecting the notion that Mills
was especially American, I nevertheless establish the vital significance
of *particular* American contexts for the development of his ideas. But
I also place Mills's intellectual and political development in an international framework. Mills took inspiration from German sociologists
such as Karl Mannheim and Max Weber as well as American thinkers such as John Dewey and Thorstein Veblen. Often Mills is credited
with bequeathing to the U.S. New Left a distinctly American radicalism, yet his New Left engagements reached well beyond the borders of
the United States. He was heavily influenced by and strongly oriented
toward developments in Europe and Latin America. His influential
1960 "Letter to the New Left" first appeared in the British *New Left
Review* and described the emergence of political opposition movements
across the globe.[13]

Scholars typically consider Mills a classic figure of the 1950s, one of the scattered "seeds of the sixties" whose influence aided the growth of radicalism during the following decade.[14] They often read the position Mills had adopted by the time of his death, that of an iconoclastic critic of American society and government, back into his earlier career. Yet Mills's cast of mind was forged during the 1940s. His conception of the role of the radical intellectual in society, for example, dates back to the early years of that decade, as do his first uses of the phrases *power elite* and *sociological imagination*. Accordingly, in the first half of this book I focus on the relatively unfamiliar early part of Mills's career, from the late 1930s into the 1940s, in order to trace the genesis of his distinctive themes and ideas. In the second half I demonstrate the continued significance of these early concepts in Mills's more influential later writings, while also assessing how his mature works marked a partial departure from his earlier approach. Exploring how developments in American social science and left-wing politics during the 1940s guided Mills's intellectual growth helps us better understand this important decade, which, sandwiched between the more easily recognizable themes of the 1930s and the 1950s, often does not receive the scholarly attention it deserves as a distinct period in American social thought.[15]

Radical Ambition traces some of the characteristic strengths and limitations of Mills's thought to his adoption of a maverick persona. But I leave the detailed study of Mills's personality to others in the hope that they recognize his rebellious personality as a carefully constructed persona rather than the full story of his life. Instead, I offer an account of the thought and times of one of the twentieth century's most important intellectuals. I use Mills to explore broader transformations in American politics and social thought. In particular, I relate Mills to two separate, though related, developments: the shifting contours of radical politics and the growing influence of sociological ideas within and outside the academy. By placing Mills's individual development in the context of these larger trends, I aim to fulfill Mills's own call in *The Sociological Imagination* for scholars to "grasp history and biography and the relations between the two in society."[16]

LONE RADICAL?

It is hardly controversial to argue that Mills's ideas were shaped through his interaction with the American left. However, no work has yet fully explored the precise nature of his sharply pessimistic and highly rationalistic radicalism, or the ways in which it developed over time. Mills never belonged to any political party, and there is no evidence that he ever participated in a political demonstration. Yet from his radicalization in the early 1940s until his death in the early 1960s, he viewed his writings as contributions to radical social change. Though always anti-Communist, Mills never identified himself with any particular left-wing intellectual tendency. Accordingly, his radicalism had a highly generic character, expressing the left's hostility to capitalism, social hierarchy, and militarism and its commitment to greater social equality, democracy, and the collective use of reason to create a better and more just social world. Though clearer about what it opposed than what it supported, Mill's radicalism obtained much of its appeal precisely from its nondogmatic and nonsectarian character.

Mills's career stretched from the death of the Old Left to the birth of the New Left. One of a very few intellectuals to retain a commitment to radical beliefs throughout this period, Mills provided continuity across the divide by transmitting left-wing ideas such as participatory democracy to 1960s-era protest movements. Yet his thought also marked an important transition between the two movements, particularly in his changing identification of agents for social change. Like most leftists of the 1930s and 1940s, Mills looked at first to the labor movement. In the years immediately following World War II, Mills's involvement with labor unions led to the 1948 publication of his first book, *The New Men of Power: America's Labor Leaders.*[17] By the late 1950s, however, Mills had rejected what he termed the "labor metaphysic," and he looked instead to an international New Left "young intelligentsia" that allied a middle-class cultural opposition in the West with non-Communist socialist revolutionaries in the third world, particularly those in Cuba.[18]

For most of his career, however, Mills's ideas were shaped not by the presence of left-wing movements but by their absence. The sharp decline of the left in McCarthy-era America decisively affected Mills's radicalism. Except for his postwar stint as a labor intellectual and his later discovery of the emerging New Left, Mills remained deeply disenchanted with the possibilities for left-wing transformation. Lacking a sense of countertendencies or dialectical contradictions that might lead to future progressive change, Mills offered a despairing analysis of the United States: a mass society dominated by repressive large-scale bureaucracies controlled by an "interlocking directorate" of corporate, military, and political leaders—the power elite.[19] As his friend the historian Richard Hofstadter once commented, "I personally find you most persuasive when you are being bleakly pessimistic. It sounds: a) more like Mills; b) more like reality."[20] In a well-known passage of *The Sociological Imagination,* Mills described his era as the "Fourth Epoch" or, in one of the earliest uses of the phrase, as the "post-modern period."[21] In the Fourth Epoch, Mills claimed, Enlightenment notions of freedom and reason could no longer be reconciled because the increasing rationalization of the world failed to provide the conditions for human freedom. "The underlying trends are well known," he argued, drawing on his dark interpretation of Weber. "Great and rational organization—in short bureaucracies—have . . . increased, but the substantive reason of the individual at large has not."[22] The result was the eclipse of democratic freedom defined as "the chance to formulate the available choices, to argue over them—and then, the opportunity to choose."[23]

Mills's pessimism was of a wholly different character than that expressed by postwar liberals such as Reinhold Niebuhr and Arthur Schlesinger Jr., who cautioned readers to adopt more chastened expectations of human nature.[24] It should also be distinguished from an existentialist strain of postwar American thought that perceived the human condition as an inherently tragic struggle with nothingness and absurdity.[25] Rather, an underlying faith in the potential of human reason underlay Mills's bleak depictions of contemporary society. Beneath his disillusionment was an optimistic faith in the power of social intelligence to reshape human destiny, a belief that had deep roots in American pragmatist and social reform traditions. The power of Mills's negative thinking rested in its ability to challenge the apathy of the masses by exposing the manipulations of the powerful and thus arousing the public to action. As a result, Mills seemed to live by the motto famously publicized by Antonio Gramsci, "pessimism of the intellect, optimism of the will." Yet because Mills saw little chance of his social critique being realized by any political force in society, his faith in the democratic use of reason often assumed a desperate character. His disillusioned radicalism focused on the intellectual's responsibility to criticize what seemingly could not be changed. "There is so God-damned much 'cant' and masking of everything," Mills once complained, "that we have to go back to the Muckraker era, which may be one measure of our defeat."[26]

The virtue of Mills's disillusioned radicalism was that it preserved left-wing ideals while offering a sharp critique of American politics and society when it was direly needed. Yet this stance had its limitations. At its worst, it threatened to reduce radicalism to the adoption of a romantic oppositional posture that urged intellectuals not to be "betrayed by what is false within them."[27] Exaggerating the undemocratic features of American society, Mills failed to identify forces or movements upon which the left could build. Too often Mills's portrayal of apathetic and alienated modern men became a caricature, as when he described white-collar workers as the "new little men" or even as "cheerful robots." Many of the limitations of Mills's thought emerged from the internal dynamics of his disillusioned radicalism. But the most significant flaw was his inattention to issues of gender and racial equality. Although Mills was committed to challenging oppression, he ignored institutionalized racism and patriarchy as crucial sources of hierarchical power in the modern world. Though it does not excuse him, Mills was no different in this regard from many (though certainly not all) white male radicals of his era. Indeed, Mills's first connections on the left were with anti-Stalinist New York intellectuals who for the most part never took issues of race or gender very seriously.

Mills's radicalism expressed his distinctive response to the left-wing politics of the day. However, similar sentiments were voiced by several other midcentury radicals whose traditional left-wing faith in human progress was sharply undermined by the traumas of fascism, Stalinism, and McCarthyism. In small but influential American left-wing journals, such as Dwight Macdonald's *politics* of the 1940s and Lewis Coser and Irving Howe's *Dissent* of the 1950s, intellectuals offered grim analyses of modern society even as they sought to keep radical ideals alive. Mills's disillusioned radicalism also shared important elements with Frankfurt School intellectuals, German émigré thinkers who had a decisive influence on him. For instance, in the 1964 book that brought Frankfurt School ideas to a mass American audience, Herbert Marcuse described American society in terms similar to those of Mills: a "one-dimensional society" that had effectively suppressed possible sources of political opposition.[28] The postwar historiographical trend of "consensus history" originated in the disillusioned radicalism of left-wing scholars Louis Hartz and Richard Hofstadter, both of whom projected onto the American past the lack of contemporary radical ideologies. In the 1948 text that inaugurated the consensus history tradition, *The American Political Tradition,* Hofstadter bemoaned the fact that "the range of vision embraced by the primary contestants in the major parties has always been bounded by the horizons of property and enterprise."[29] The same mood of disillusioned radicalism, despairing of contemporary society but envisioning little prospect of realizing alternative left-wing ideals, was also more widely evident in the culture of the period. It could be seen, for instance, in the 1949 dystopian novel *Nineteen Eighty-Four*, written by the British socialist George Orwell.[30] It also pervaded many films noir of the late 1940s—dark movies that exposed the "unreality of the American dream"—made by left-wing writers, directors, and actors who anticipated the Hollywood blacklist.[31]

Mills's social analysis resembled not only that of other disillusioned radicals, but also that of postwar liberals who discovered a broad consensus at the heart of American society. Indeed, his ideas often read as a curiously inverted version of the postwar liberals' optimistic notion of the "end of ideology," which praised the political, social, and intellectual accomplishments of the postwar period. Sociologist Seymour Martin Lipset, a leading exponent of the "end of ideology" thesis, declared, "The fundamental political problems of the industrial revolution have been solved: the workers have achieved industrial and political citizenship; the conservatives have accepted the welfare state; and the democratic left has recognized that an increase in over-all state power carries with it more dangers to freedom than solutions to economic problems."[32] Lipset concluded that serious ideological conflict in the West was obsolete: "The ideological issues dividing left and right have been reduced to a little more or a little less government ownership and economic planning."[33] Mills rejected the concept of an "end of ideology," viewing it as an excuse for political complacency. In *The Power Elite* he challenged the liberal assumption that the United States possessed a pluralist, democratic political structure, and in his "Letter to the New Left" he wrote, "Let the old women complain wisely about the 'end of ideology.' We [leftists] are on the move again."[34]

Although their evaluations of the postwar order differed, Mills and his liberal opponents shared more than either cared to acknowledge. Mills, too, saw postwar society as dominated by a kind of consensus, only he rejected it as a false one. Like postwar liberals, Mills suggested that ideological conflict was no longer central to American society. Moreover, both Mills and postwar liberals assumed that the central problems of modern society pertained to individual psychology rather than to material economic deprivation. Lipset, for instance, voiced concern about the "problem of conformity" in American society identified in such works as David Riesman's *The Lonely Crowd*. In *White Collar*, a book that shared many themes with *The Lonely Crowd*, Mills suggested that in the modern world, "exploitation becomes less material and more psychological."[35] Mills's faith in the ability of the postwar economy to produce general affluence was as solid as any liberal's; at one point he predicted a tripling of the material standard of living that would reduce the American workweek to twenty to thirty hours.[36] Accordingly, like postwar liberals, Mills ignored or minimized issues of poverty, racial oppression, and environmental sustainability. Entranced by notions of postwar consensus and conformity, Mills and postwar liberals alike saw American society as less dynamic and conflicted than it really was. When we take a longer view of the intellectual history of the postwar period, the wishful thinking of postwar liberals and the pessimistic radicalism of Mills and his compatriots appear not as polar opposites, but as two sides of the same coin.[37]

RENEGADE SOCIOLOGIST?

Mills's affinity with postwar liberal thought points to another unappreciated aspect of his intellectual development: his embeddedness in the discourse of midcentury social science.[38] One common version of the Mills-as-maverick story lauds him as a model "public intellectual" who shunned the ivory towers of academe.[39] To Stanley Aronowitz, for instance, Mills exemplified "a vanishing breed in American life: the public political intellectual," who refused to let "fear and careerism" cause him to be "safely tucked into the academy."[40] Certainly one of Mills's virtues was his ability to reach a large audience outside the academy through his compelling and relevant ideas and his clear and vivid prose. However, those who celebrate Mills as a public intellectual draw far too sharp a line between the allegedly cloistered world of university research and that of nonacademic public discourse. Like many others now praised as public intellectuals, Mills relied upon the knowledge produced in academic disciplines for much of his insight. Those who fail to understand Mills's firm grounding in sociological ideas miss a crucial source of his radical critique.

Mills is most accurately viewed as a public sociologist: one who conveyed distinctively sociological ideas and perspectives to both academic and nonacademic audiences. As he once remarked, his aim was "to develop an intelligible way of communicating modern social science to nonspecialized publics."[41] Mills hardly stood alone among social scientists of his era in seeking a wider audience. The unprecedented prestige of the social sciences in American culture in the post–World War II period, aided by the general expansion of liberal university education, provided new opportunities for social scientists who wished to address a broader public. *Commentary* magazine, started in 1945, included a regular column, "The Study of Man," which presented social scientific findings to an audience with a general education. Introducing the column, Nathan Glazer wrote, "The ivory towers now stand abandoned. . . . Almost every scholar of note in the fields of sociology, psychology, and anthropology concerns himself with how the studies devoted to the extension of man's knowledge of man may advance solutions to the problems of a free society."[42] Mills's discipline of sociology played a central role in post–World War II intellectual and political discourse, as reflected in the influence of works by Mills, Lipset, Riesman, and Daniel Bell, as well as those by sociologically inspired journalists such as Vance Packard, A. C. Spectorsky, and William H. Whyte.

Within the sociological profession today, Mills retains an image as "the great disestablishment guru."[43] Most sociologists remember Mills as a professional renegade who launched a devastating attack on academic social science in his 1959 work *The Sociological Imagination.* Mills is often assumed to be the sole notable exception to the paradigmatic dominance of a scientistic "mainstream sociology" based on the structural functionalist theory of Talcott Parsons, the survey research methods of Paul Lazarsfeld, and the middle-range theory of Robert Merton. However, this common depiction of post–World War II sociology overstates both the dominance and the coherence of "mainstream sociology."[44] It also fails to grasp Mills's indebtedness to key developments in midcentury social science. Although it is certainly true that Mills had key conflicts with disciplinary leaders, his marginality within the profession has frequently been exaggerated. In *The Coming Crisis of Western Sociology,* for instance, Alvin Gouldner falsely claimed that Mills's radical beliefs prevented him from becoming a full professor at Columbia, concluding that this fact should "remind us that the serious players are always those who have an ability to pay costs."[45] In fact, Mills had been promoted to full professor in 1956, achieving the position at an earlier age than his rival, Parsons.

Mills's case supports Michael Burawoy's recent claim that public sociology is always in creative tension with professional sociology oriented toward disciplinary experts.[46] Mills developed his ideas within the matrix of academic social science. While a student at Texas and Wisconsin, Mills encountered the philosophical and sociological ideas that decisively shaped his work throughout his career. His study of pragmatism and the sociology of knowledge led him to a contextualist and historicist approach to the study of social science. German sociology also proved a powerful influence on Mills. In the early 1940s, he worked with the émigré sociologist Hans Gerth, who introduced Mills to the ideas of Weber, which helped develop Mills's career-long concerns with social structure, social stratification, and political power. In 1945, Mills took a position at the Bureau of Applied Social Research (BASR) at Columbia University, a leading postwar center of sociology. He conducted much of the research for his first two books, *The New Men of Power* and *White Collar,* at the BASR.

Mills's commitments to radical politics and public sociology ultimately brought him into conflict with disciplinary leaders. After a protracted dispute with the bureau's director, Paul Lazarsfeld, Mills left the BASR. He taught for the rest of his career in Columbia's undergraduate wing, Columbia College, where he was removed from the training of graduate students, work that is essential to power in academic disciplines. Yet if Mills was no longer at the center of the discipline after the 1940s, neither was he altogether outside it. Even during the 1950s, he drew on common sociological currents. Mills may have portrayed himself as a lone critic of the discipline in *The Sociological Imagination*, yet several leading sociologists sympathized with his critique. Most important, in spite of his scathing attacks on the discipline, Mills never gave up belief in what he called the "promise" of social science.

Understanding Mills in this fashion asks us not only to reconsider his image, but also to broaden our understanding of midcentury social science. If Mills owed more to academic social science than has been recognized, leading sociologists of his era were more embedded in the social and political discourse of their time than has typically been acknowledged. Howard Brick has persuasively argued that Talcott Parsons's left-liberal political views formed a crucial component of his abstract social theory, and David Hollinger has recovered the antifascist political context of Robert Merton's early work. Rather than being ensconced within the ivory tower of academia, Parsons and Merton, like Mills, deeply engaged the public issues of their day.[47] Thus, I suggest not that we narrow our view of Mills as merely a social scientist, but that we widen our view of social science so that it includes Mills. To see Mills as a public sociologist is to recognize the complexity of his relationship to the professional discourse of his day. Mills drew on distinctively sociological insights even as he chastised many of his

fellow sociologists for the narrowness, abstruseness, and political complacency of their work.

The historian Charles Beard once called on thinkers to have "the
daring to be wrong in something important rather than right in some
meticulous banality."[48] One of the most striking aspects of Mills's work
was his intellectual ambition. He was fond of saying that he liked to
"take it big."[49] Mills's central concern was to employ sociologically
embedded reason to achieve a more just and rational society. His
engagements with both social science and the left were designed to
realize this momentous, Enlightenment-inspired goal. Because Mills
thought big, he became influential in his own day and remains relevant
in ours. He was in many ways an extraordinary thinker, but his ideas
were far more embedded in wider historical currents than the common
conception of him as a maverick intellectual acknowledges. His aspirations were not his alone, and the strengths and limitations of his
thought were of his time and place. Mills's career illuminates, as no
other does, the promise and the dilemmas of left-wing social thought
in mid-twentieth-century America.

CHAPTER 1

Student Ambitions

The Education of a Social Scientist

Today Mills is often celebrated as a public intellectual whose insights gained power because he ventured outside the ivory tower. Yet he developed his major themes, ideas, and approaches in an academic context. The origins of his thought lie not in an early involvement in literary, bohemian, political, or journalistic circles, but in a university education in the social sciences. Mills's student years at the University of Texas at Austin (1935–1939) and the University of Wisconsin at Madison (1939–1942) established the foundation upon which his later work would build. In order to understand Mills, it is necessary to grasp the concerns that drove his thinking in these years. His early works in sociological theory have been either dismissed by critics as "impenetrable" or pigeonholed into a framework derived from his later intellectual trajectory. To do either, however, prevents us from understanding both the methodological basis of Mills's later work and the ways in which his ideas developed over time.[1]

During his student years, Mills was already a singular personality, iconoclastic and remarkably self-confident. In this period, Mills described himself as an "impersonal egoist." He explained the expression later in life: "impersonal because of the craft I cultivate; egoist because my ambitions far outrun my capacities."[2] In the late 1930s and early 1940s, Mills dedicated his extraordinary ambition to social scientific education. He impressed his professors with his intelligence and drive and commanded the notice of prominent figures in the field.

By the age of twenty-five he had already had articles accepted by the two leading professional journals of American sociology. But Mills was no careerist; his passion was always for crafting means of understanding the world, not for mere professional advancement. He sought to make a name for himself as a scholar, but, more important, to construct his own sense of the proper aims and methods of social research. Mills never lost the faith he cultivated as a student in the liberating potential of what he would famously call "the sociological imagination," a phrase he first used in 1942.[3]

Mills's early thought was steeped in the discourse of cutting-edge social science, particularly the disciplinary matrix of American sociology. Through his work in the sociology of knowledge, Mills assigned himself the ambitious task of making sociological inquiry more fruitful by investigating the social basis of knowledge. In particular, he identified with a younger generation of sociologists attuned to European sociological traditions. Indeed, Mills's early essays had important elements in common with the works of two of the emerging disciplinary leaders of the period, Talcott Parsons and Robert Merton. Mills's early writing style reflected his embeddedness in an almost purely academic discourse. Though he would later ridicule the use of sociological jargon in a well-known passage of *The Sociological Imagination,* in which he translated passages of Parsons into plain English, Mills's early works were difficult, specialized, and often abstruse. A peer reviewer for his first published paper commented that Mills's first draft "was the 'lousiest style' he had ever seen."[4] In an autumn 1939 paper, reminiscing that he had once written a novel titled *The Lake of the Eyeballs,* Mills remarked, "Now it has been two years since anything but jargon and technicality has come out of me."[5]

Even though it emerged from within American social science, Mills's perspective was distinctive, largely because of the particular range of social scientific approaches he encountered at the University of Texas. There, Mills was exposed to intellectual traditions—pragmatism, Chicago School sociology, and institutional economics—that experienced declining influence in midcentury American social science, but which Mills helped keep alive over the course of his career. Drawing on these traditions, Mills formulated the deeply historicist and contextualist philosophy of social science that set him apart from most leading postwar figures in the human sciences, scholars who focused instead on developing a rigorous synchronic analysis of the social world.[6] In particular, Mills's study of pragmatism offered him a vantage point quite different from that of other sociologists. In the early 1940s, he became virtually the only American social scientist to defend Karl Mannheim's sociology of knowledge, doing so on pragmatist grounds. Mills's unusual approach to the study of society culminated in his attempt at disciplinary self-critique, applying the methods of the sociology of knowledge to investigate the discipline of sociology and uncovering the unrecognized presuppositions that underlay sociological research.

At this point in his life, Mills was primarily interested in discovering a method for understanding the world, not a means of changing it. In a 1936 letter to his parents, Mills referred to political agitation at the University of Texas, writing that he was not interested in participating, but he was fascinated by the campus as "a laboratory for sociologists."[7] Mills elucidated a methodological critique of American social science before he acquired an explicit commitment to radical politics. Yet as Alvin Gouldner once observed, "sociology may produce, not merely recruit, radicals. . . . it may generate, not merely tolerate, radicalization."[8] The abstract methodological and philosophical commitments that Mills developed as a student contained latent political potential, which influenced his left-wing turn in the early 1940s. In the one instance in which Mills combined a methodological critique with a political one and merged sociological theory with concrete research in the sociology of knowledge, he produced a classic essay, "The Professional Ideology of Social Pathologists," an important forerunner to the reflexive critiques of sociology later articulated by such prominent left-wing sociologists as Gouldner and Pierre Bourdieu.[9]

PRAGMATISM AND SOCIAL SCIENCE

Mills was born in Waco, Texas, on August 28, 1916. For most of his childhood, his father worked as an insurance agent and was often away on business trips. The family moved frequently within Texas while Mills was growing up. According to the wishes of his mother, Mills was baptized a Catholic, but as an adolescent he broke with the Church and insisted on attending public school, graduating from Dallas Technical High School in 1934. One of Mills's favorite books as a teenager was the autobiography of Clarence Darrow, the socialist lawyer best known for pleading the cause of evolutionary science in the Scopes trial of 1925. In what was probably his first published piece, an August 10, 1934, letter to the *Dallas Morning News*, Mills refuted a fundamentalist minister's attack on science. Mills expressed his preference for a science that "aims at truth" and is rooted in "observation and reason" over dogmatic religion that "begins with 'the truth.'"[10] Even in his youth, Mills saw the world in the classic terms of the Enlightenment.

At his father's insistence, Mills initially enrolled at a university that provided a particularly unwelcome environment for a young man of his intellectual predilection: Texas Agricultural and Mechanical College (A&M), at the time a military school. In two remarkable letters to the school newspaper coauthored with his roommate, Mills criticized A&M's hazing culture, excoriating the system of freshman obedience and deference to upperclassmen as a "society which has sprung up on a false basis and is sustained on false principles of human conduct justified only by ignorance and narrow thinking."[11] Declaring that the "highest form of patriotism is criticism," they called for the creation of a campus culture "free from sham, hypocrisy, and feudalistic customs."[12] Strikingly, in criticizing A&M culture, Mills drew upon his coursework in sociology: "If this [performing chores and errands for upperclassmen upon demand] is leadership then my sociology text is very wrong—because this sort of control is based on nothing save force. Any social control which rests on force is wrong."[13]

By the time Mills transferred from A&M after his freshman year, he had already developed a commitment to the ideals of reason and science, an intense dislike of traditional hierarchy, and a predisposition to studying social science. It was at the more cosmopolitan University of Texas, however, that Mills encountered the specific intellectual traditions that would shape his work. In 1939, Mills concurrently received his B.A. in sociology and his M.A. in philosophy. Mills's work in the Texas philosophy department proved most influential to the development of his thinking, particularly his critical engagement with pragmatism, an influential philosophical movement of the late nineteenth and early twentieth centuries whose most prominent exponents included John Dewey, William James, George Herbert Mead, and Charles Sanders Peirce. As Mills commented in the fall of 1938, after three years of coursework at Texas, "My intellectual godfathers were pragmatists; when I first awoke I discovered myself among them."[14]

Two young philosophers played crucial roles in introducing Mills to pragmatism. Both George Gentry and David Miller were products of the seedbed of pragmatism: the University of Chicago Department of Philosophy, where they had studied with Mead. Gentry received his Ph.D. in 1931, Miller in 1933. Miller helped edit a posthumous collection of Mead's papers, *The Philosophy of the Act*, which bolstered

18 Student Ambitions

Mead's influence. Indeed, Miller made a career out of defending Mead's legacy and extending his insights.[15] But Gentry, who published little, had the greater influence on Mills, directing his master's thesis. Mills would later write of Gentry, "Whatever else Texas can give a man . . . it can give him George Gentry on [pragmatist philosopher] C.S. Peirce. Get that. There is no better bases [sic] for any man in social science anywhere."[16]

Other scholars have noted Mills's debt to pragmatist philosophy. However, they have failed to grasp that during his student years Mills was interested in pragmatism for a very specific purpose: to aid the "methodologically confused social sciences."[17] In this respect, it is significant that Mills's professors were representatives of the Chicago pragmatist tradition. Though professional philosophers in the first decades of the twentieth century increasingly viewed philosophy as a specialized discipline with its own technical issues, Chicago pragmatists had a much broader conception. They saw philosophy and social science as engaged in a common endeavor and eschewed rigid disciplinary boundaries.[18] Thus, Gentry and Miller encouraged Mills's exploration of social scientific methodology in his philosophical work. The legacy of this Chicago pragmatist approach resonated throughout Mills's career. He never lost his strong sense that the human sciences were engaged in a common project, and he always opposed making sociology a specialized science sharply demarcated from other forms of social inquiry, a position that would distinguish him from such discipline-building sociologists as Parsons and Merton.

Mills adapted the pragmatists' conception of science as a dynamic, continuous, nondogmatic process of inquiry and their emphasis on the close relationship between ideas and action. Pragmatists viewed science not as the discovery of timeless truths, but as a method for understanding and changing the present world. The pragmatists' suspicion of deducing truths from abstract schema and their appeal to empirical inquiry as a means of verification made them part of a broader "revolt against formalism" in early twentieth-century American and European thought.[19] According to pragmatists, one gains knowledge not through the application of a formal system to a body of data, but by investigating a specific situation or problem. To Mills, the promise of pragmatism was its "drive toward empirical statement" in which "it would seem possible to define questions hitherfore considered in exclusively formal and epistemological terms in such a manner as to make them answerable by concrete research."[20] Thus, early on, Mills was suspicious of what he later termed "grand theory" in sociology, which applied universal laws to particular areas of research.[21] Pragmatism also provided Mills intellectual ammunition for rejecting the dogmatic models of truth that he encountered in the hated Catholic schools of his youth.[22]

In addition, pragmatism influenced Mills to recognize the significance of theory in sociological research. No naïve empiricists, pragmatists argued that facts make sense only when viewed from a particular conceptual framework. As a result, theory plays an invaluable role in practice. Applying this principle to social science, Mills contended that sociological inquiry could become more productive through consciousness of its methods of inquiry. As Mills awkwardly explained, "through methodologic self-awareness reflection that is precise and firm is made possible."[23] In his Texas years, Mills aimed to improve the practice of social science through philosophical reflection on its methods.

From the pragmatists, Mills also gained a deeply contextualist and historicist sense of the role of ideas. His interest in the sociology of knowledge grew out of the pragmatist quest to contextualize ideas by relating them to the broader social world. Pragmatists viewed inquiry as specific to a particular framework of problems in which ideas evolve through action. This may have been the first pragmatist principle that Mills grasped. In a paper written for a 1937 seminar on the philosophy of George Herbert Mead cotaught by Gentry and Miller, Mills followed Mead in arguing that "even the most abstract thought is definitely related to activity, not activity in some general way but to activity of a specific kind, and that it is further related to activity in specific situations, not the world in general but to specific aspects of the organism's social environment."[24]

Though Mills's student writings demonstrate his indebtedness to the pragmatists, many of his papers dealt with what he saw as the deficiencies of pragmatist philosophy. Even as he acknowledged the pragmatists as his "intellectual godfathers," Mills noted that he was developing criticisms of them from "what I have come to call a 'sociologistic' corner."[25] Mills's scrutiny of the pragmatists contributed to his development of a perspective ultimately more focused on understanding the concrete dynamics of society rather than on epistemological questions about the nature of knowledge. Despite his strong early theoretical bent, Mills's interests ran more to the sociological than the philosophical. While Mills found philosophical reflection to be an indispensable element of social scientific work, he ultimately perceived pragmatist philosophy as lacking the kind of empirical analysis of social structures that only sociological work could provide.

Mills's master's thesis, "Reflection, Behavior, and Culture," was a "sociologistic" critique of Dewey. Though he gave Dewey credit as one of the first thinkers to "give an empirical and comprehensive account of mind and reflection," Mills argued that Dewey's attempt to locate inquiry in society was "formalistic and distressingly vague."[26] According to Mills, pragmatist philosophers seemed unaware that their conception of the process of thought derived from their own particular social contexts and might not be applicable elsewhere. Moreover, in failing to go beyond the general statement that ideas reflected social reality, pragmatists were unable to provide guidelines for explaining how the thought of particular individuals arose in specific social structures. For Mills, such models needed to be culturally and historically grounded. He argued that the root of Dewey's problem was his attempt to generalize methods of inquiry drawn from the natural sciences and apply them to the social sciences. In particular, Mills objected to Dewey's use of biological terms such as *adaptation* to account for social behavior. While such metaphors might work in the case of an individual immigrant adjusting to society as a whole, they could not explain how human behavior was shaped by institutions and social structure.

For Mills, pragmatist principles remained too abstract until they were applied in concrete research that firmly located ideas in their social contexts. To a large extent, Mills's critique of pragmatism relied on pragmatist principles. He attacked pragmatists for failing to develop fully their own notions of empirical inquiry and of the deeply social nature of human activity. Mills's critique was also influenced by Chicago School sociology and Veblenian institutional economics. He encountered both of these intellectual traditions at Texas. While each reinforced the impact of pragmatist ideas on Mills, they also prompted him to criticize those elements of pragmatist philosophy that seemed inadequate for sociological inquiry.

The principal Texas sociologist to influence Mills was Warner Gettys. Gettys was chair of the Department of Sociology, which had been established as a separate department following his arrival at the university in 1927. Under Gettys's watch, faculty and students in the Department of Sociology maintained close relations with their counterparts in philosophy and economics, which encouraged Mills to pursue his interdisciplinary inclinations.[27] Mills's relationship with Gettys was particularly close during his early years at Texas. Gettys allowed

Mills to audit his advanced sociology classes during his first semester, nominated him to the sociological honor society, and drove him to at least one meeting of the Southwestern Social Science Association. When Gettys retired in 1958, Mills flew to Austin to speak in his honor.[28] Gettys's only book was a coauthored sociology textbook, yet he maintained an interest in sociological theory that no doubt influenced Mills. For example, Gettys was among the first to hail Talcott Parsons's *Structure of Social Action* as "an outstanding contribution to American sociological scholarship."[29] Perhaps it was also Gettys who exposed Mills to the notion that social science must develop its own methods separate from those of physical science. In his most important article, Gettys criticized certain elements of the ecological approach adopted by Chicago School sociologists such as Robert Park, claiming that they had failed to construct a coherent and persuasive theory of human ecology because they had uncritically imported hypotheses derived from biology.[30]

Though skeptical of ecological theory, Gettys nevertheless operated within the Chicago School tradition; he had worked as an instructor in the sociology department at the University of Chicago in the early 1920s. Although the Chicago School did not have a single unified approach, as is sometimes supposed, sociologists in this tradition did share many ideas and practices. Though they made use of statistics, Chicago School sociologists were primarily known for their use of qualitative sources such as personal documents, interviews, first-hand observation, life histories, ecological analysis, and social mapping. Such an approach lent itself to the study of a particular community, and, indeed, many sociologists in this tradition treated the city of Chicago as their sociological laboratory.[31] Mills's exposure to Chicago sociology likely reinforced the influence of pragmatism on his thinking. Like the Chicago pragmatists, with whom they were closely associated, Chicago School sociologists valued direct empirical investigation of society over more speculative and abstract approaches. As Andrew Abbott has argued, the fundamental insight of Chicago sociology was that "social facts are *located*," with the result that "one cannot understand social life without understanding the arrangements of particular social actors in particular times and places."[32] Though Mills was attracted to the philosophical depth of the pragmatists, he built on his familiarity with sociological research in the Chicago tradition for his "sociologistic" critique of Dewey. In his master's thesis, Mills contrasted Dewey's work with the best-known work of Chicago sociology, the multivolume *The Polish Peasant in Europe and America*. "The ninety-page 'Methodological Note' to the research job of Thomas and Znaniecki," Mills asserted, "is concretely and directively worth more to the sociologists than any thousand pages of Dewey's writing; for it arose out of a set of researches under way, and the formulations and canons it contains have gone back in advisory capacity, into a dozen further researches."[33]

Mills was also influenced by University of Texas economist Clarence Ayres. Although Mills did not enroll in a class with Ayres until his final year, he earlier had audited Ayres's classes and become close friends with Ayres's graduate students.[34] Another product of the University of Chicago Department of Philosophy, Ayres was a gifted teacher with extraordinarily wide-ranging interests who did not easily fit into conventional intellectual or political categories. Ayres's willingness to speak his mind created conflict with university administrations at successive institutions. An unconventional scholar, Ayres had previously served as associate editor at *New Republic* and as director of the consumer division in Franklin Roosevelt's Department of Labor.[35] It is not difficult to speculate that both as a social scientific generalist and an outspoken iconoclast, Ayres provided a role model for Mills. Through Ayres's influence, Mills first encountered the intellectual tradition of institutional economics. With its roots in the thought of Thorstein Veblen, institutional economics shared pragmatism's hostility to formalistic systems of thought, in this case neoclassical economics. Rather than constructing mathematically rigorous models, institutional economists sought access to the real world of economics, which they saw as inextricably linked to other aspects of society. Under the leadership of Wesley Mitchell, institutional economics became more quantitative and professionalized during the interwar years.[36] However, Ayres remained closer to Veblen's original vision, stressing historical study and critique of social institutions.

Though Ayres certainly believed that Veblenian economics was compatible with Deweyan pragmatism, institutional economics placed a greater emphasis on the role of institutions and social structure in shaping human behavior than did pragmatist philosophy. In particular, institutional economists were more concerned with the location of social power in American society. Though this issue did not occupy Mills's full attention until after he left Texas, the institutionalist influence led him to make one of his few criticisms of pragmatism during this period with a political flavor. In a paper written for Miller, Mills used the institutionalist perspective to criticize the pragmatists' tendency to relate ideas to society as whole, thereby ignoring the social divisions that shaped the development of knowledge. For example, Mills alleged that pragmatists naïvely claimed that scientific progress served society as a whole when in fact it benefited big business the most.[37] Neglecting such social divisions, Mills claimed, pragmatists failed to adequately locate ideas "within contemporaneous fields of socio-politico-economic values."[38] In this statement, Mills expressed a budding interest in the questions of power, social structure, social stratification, and elite dominance that would come to define his best-known work.

Mills's first published article, "Language, Logic, and Culture," accepted for publication in the spring of 1939 while he was still a student at Texas, revealed how his exposure to pragmatism and other American intellectual traditions shaped his early forays into the sociology of knowledge. Mills began by complaining that the argument that ideas reflect social reality was often made in too abstract and formalistic a manner. While Mills concurred with the general principle that ideas reflect social reality, he believed that most scholars failed to show exactly *how* they did so. According to Mills, not only the pragmatists, but also Marxists and even more sophisticated proponents of the sociology of knowledge such as Karl Mannheim, lacked "understanding and clear-cut formulations of the *terms* with which they would connect mind and other social factors."[39]

Mills offered two hypotheses to demonstrate how sociologists of knowledge could connect ideas to social factors. The first hypothesis drew upon Mead's social psychological concept of the "generalized other." Mead's pioneering argument about the "social self" viewed individuals as continuously involved in an internal dialogue with other members of society. According to Mills, Mead implied that social factors were not an extrinsic influence, but were instead intrinsic to all thought. However, Mills argued, Mead's formulation of the "generalized other" was too abstract, positing an "individual" shaped by a "society" but failing to provide a framework for grasping the specific historical and sociological context in which ideas arose. Thus, Mills suggested modifying Mead's concept to account for the concrete social forces at work in the formulation of particular ideas. Mills saw all thought as a form of conversation that took into account the specific values and interests of those to whom it was directed. Whether or not the thinker was conscious of it or not, his ideas responded to "'problems' defined by the activities and values of his audience."[40] Thus, Mills suggested that research could establish the social context of thought by examining a thinker's audience, thereby connecting larger social and historical forces with the individual's social psychology.

Mills's second hypothesis in "Language, Logic, and Culture" was that the sociologist of knowledge should investigate the meaning of the language that a thinker used. Here, Mills built on Peirce's insight that logical rules of reasoning rely upon the consent of those who employ them. Instead of assuming that language was a neutral tool for expressing ideas, Mills pointed to recent research that had described even scientific language as value-laden. "Socially built and maintained," Mills concluded, language "embodies implicit exhortations and social evaluations."[41] Language was thus one of the principal means by which social factors were embedded in thought. The sociologist of knowledge could proceed by investigating which words a thinker used, what they meant by them, and how their language related to that used by others. For Mills, the linguistic turn among pragmatists during the interwar years represented a promising approach to social scientific methodology. In that period, Kenneth Burke, Grace de Laguna, Charles Morris, and Edward Sapir built on pragmatist concepts to study language as a symbolic system.[42] Seeing language as inherently determined by culture, Mills found this linguistic turn in pragmatism promising, since it did not arbitrarily impose concepts drawn from the physical sciences to the study of social phenomena. When read closely, "Language, Logic, and Culture" also reveals an undercurrent of interest in how power relations in society shape the production of knowledge. Here, Mills drew on his critique of the pragmatists that owed much to his absorption of institutional economics; he specifically credited Ayers for suggesting to him how the changing meaning of the term *capital* reflected changing economic relations.[43] At one point Mills asserted the need to explore the "class bias" of ideas.[44] At another point, he argued that sociologists of knowledge should expose the "institutional and political coordinates" of ideas.[45] In time, this theme would come to the forefront of Mills's thought.

"Language, Logic, and Culture" was an impressive achievement for its young author. The article demonstrated Mills's growing mastery of the scholarly literature in the social sciences, conveying a familiarity with both American and European social theory. Though the article was a highly technical contribution to a specialized field and suggested "precise hypotheses" for future research, it also articulated a deeply contextualist and historicist approach to the study of ideas and laid out an ambitious research program for the sociology of knowledge. For Mills, the sociology of knowledge involved much more than the determination of how the conscious interests of thinkers affected their ideas, because at all levels, including those that thinkers and their audiences failed to recognize, knowledge was culturally determined. It was not merely that social considerations dictated the problems that thinkers addressed. The process of thought was social at its core.

THEORY FOR A DISCIPLINE IN DISARRAY

Given the promise he displayed as a student at Texas, it was natural that Mills applied to doctoral programs. Turning down an offer to study philosophy at the University of Chicago, he instead elected to study sociology at the University of Wisconsin.[46] Although Wisconsin's fellowship offer was undoubtedly a factor in his decision, sociology was also a good match for the young and ambitious Mills. Philosophy by this time had become a highly specialized discipline, but sociology remained a relatively open field of study in need of theoretical definition. The acceptance of "Language, Logic, and Culture" by one of the discipline's leading journals, the *American Sociological Review,* was a clear sign that sociology was a promising outlet for Mills's talents.

Sociology has always been the most general and the least defined of the social sciences, but the late 1930s was a period of particular disciplinary confusion. As Robert Bannister has noted, "Sociology remained imperfectly professionalized during the interwar period: uncertain of its boundaries, sensitive to attack, and a tempting target for any group that wanted to promote a new paradigm."[47] Though the Chicago School was hardly a hegemonic group in the profession, it was clearly the most recognizable, and the University of Chicago Department of Sociology housed both the American Sociological Society (ASS) and its journal, the *American Journal of Sociology,* until 1936. In the 1930s, an eclectic group of sociologists challenged the prominence of Chicago sociologists in the ASS. Leading the revolt were the objectivists, who, in contrast to the Chicago School, argued that the discipline could become scientific only by modeling itself on physical science, that is, by confining it to the predominantly quantitative study of observable human behavior and strictly insisting upon the ethical and political neutrality of the social scientist. In 1936, this revolt led to the establishment of another

journal, the *American Sociological Review,* and the severing of formal
ties between the ASS and the University of Chicago. Yet this attempt to
reorganize the discipline along objectivist lines failed, and professional
sociology remained divided at the time Mills entered graduate school
at Wisconsin.[48]

While many bemoaned the chaotic state of the discipline, the absence
of any overriding research paradigm was precisely what attracted Mills,
since it allowed for diverse views within the discipline and required
theoretical work to clarify research aims and methods. Regardless of
which disciplinary camp they adhered to, leading sociologists in the late
1930s agreed that the state of the discipline was a problem and argued
that sociologists required a more sophisticated theoretical understanding of their practices. Sociological theorists agreed that theory should
provide a clear sense of sociology's mission and develop more rigorous
methods for sociological research. As Talcott Parsons wrote in 1938,
"There is a widespread feeling that we must settle the deepest current
controversies before we can do *anything.*"[49] In addition to Parsons, a
number of important sociologists, including Herbert Blumer, George
Lundberg, Robert Lynd, and Robert Merton, addressed the problem of
disciplinary consensus in the late 1930s.

Though influenced by the Chicago School, Mills identified with a
younger generation of theorists who were reevaluating the discipline's
purpose and methods. One of these theorists was Howard P. Becker,
who played an instrumental role in the publication of "Language, Logic,
and Culture" and served as Mills's graduate advisor at Wisconsin.
Becker received his Ph.D. from Chicago, though he also participated
in the ASS rebellion of the mid-1930s. Becker quickly disappointed
objectivist friends by insisting that sociologists address theoretical
issues. Having studied in Germany during the 1920s, Becker played
a key role in importing German sociological thought to the United
States as book review editor of the *American Sociological Review.*[50]
Another member of the editorial board ascribed the journal's tendency
"to run anything and everything of German origin" to the influence
of "that nazi Becker."[51] In many respects, Becker was a poor choice as
advisor for Mills. Although they shared an interest in the sociology of
knowledge, Becker aligned himself with German sociologists such as
Leopold von Wiese, who were hostile to the Mannheimian program
that attracted Mills. Their differences later became apparent in conflicts over the scope of Mills's dissertation. According to one account,
the gulf between them became so great that at the end of Mills's dis-

sertation defense in 1942, Becker told Mills, "Go to hell," to which Mills replied, "After you, sir."[52]

Nevertheless, Mills shared with Becker a common sense of the requirements of sociological theory, as can be seen in their similar reactions to George Lundberg's objectivist tract *Foundations of Sociology*. Perhaps their reactions were so similar because Becker got his ideas from Mills. In April 1940, Mills mentioned to Robert Merton that an article on Lundberg coauthored by Becker and Mills was forthcoming. Yet at the December 1940 meeting of the ASS, Becker delivered a paper on Lundberg under his own name. One of Mills's friends wrote him that the plagiarism had made him "sick double sick." Mills confirmed that Becker had stolen his ideas.[53] Indeed Becker's published article on Lundberg, "The Limits of Sociological Positivism," shared almost all of its main points with an unpublished manuscript of Mills's.[54] No doubt this incident soured the relationship between Mills and Becker. However, Becker's willingness to put forth Mills's ideas as his own also indicates that their perspectives had much in common.

Lundberg was one of the few proponents of a straightforwardly positivist program for sociology. Though he attracted few adherents in the discipline, Lundberg's work was a convenient touchstone for other sociologists seeking to define their own programs for sociology. Lundberg argued that social science should explicitly model itself on physical science. To develop a universally valid set of verifiable propositions, social science would have to limit itself to those hypotheses it could "operationalize." In exchange for greater rigor, Lundberg was willing to reduce social science to the study of perceivable and quantifiable behavior. Values were not a proper subject for scientific study, and man could be understood just as any other object, subject to the same general laws.[55]

Rejecting Lundberg's positivism, Mills raised several key points that Becker echoed in his article. First, there was no adequate universal scientific method: "What all scientists think in common is only a dozen platitudes known to bright children who have teachers in the Deweyan tradition."[56] Mills argued that humans could not be adequately understood as objects like any other: "Nothing in its purely physical dimension interacts like persons." Social science should investigate how humans defined their own situations, accounting for the interests and values of its human subjects. Thus, sociologists needed to adopt methods appropriate to the study of social material, not apply an abstract model drawn from physical science. Moreover, sociological theory needed to arise out of concrete practice: "The rules for sociological method that are genuinely applicable to social materials arise from sociological inquiry."[57]

Mills's reaction to Lundberg exemplifies how his earlier immersion in pragmatist theories of science shaped his sociological theory. However, not only Becker, but also most other sociological theorists of the time, would have agreed with Mills's main criticisms of Lundberg. An adequate sociological theory would bear a close relationship with research; would develop its own methods adequate to dealing with the distinct realm of social phenomena, for which physical and biological categories alone would not suffice; and would account for the values and meanings of its human subjects. In adopting these principles of sociological research, Mills displayed his debt to Chicago sociology. Indeed, the leading spokesperson for Chicago sociology in the late 1930s, Herbert Blumer, then editor of the *American Journal of Sociology,* was a significant source of support and encouragement for Mills during his years as a graduate student. Blumer endorsed Mills's critique of Lundberg, writing, "You have made an illuminating and telling criticism on Mr. Lundberg's point of view and needless to say I distinctly share your ideas." Blumer also had high praise for "Language, Logic, and Culture": "I am glad to see you have carried your thinking much further than I have."[58] A leading critic of the post–World War II ascendancy of structural functionalism in American sociology, Blumer would remain an admirer of Mills's sociological work throughout Mills's career.

Even though Mills owed much to the Chicago tradition, he also hoped to introduce something new to American sociology. In particular, he saw himself as aligned with "a few of the younger men in American sociology [who] are becoming tired of the paste-pot eclecticism and text-book tolerance which have characterized much of their tradition."[59] In the late 1930s and 1940s, Mills's sociological work shared a great deal with the work of figures who would become his chief adversaries in the postwar period. In particular, his position had aspects in common with the most significant statement of sociological theory in the late 1930s, Talcott Parsons's *Structure of Social Action,* a work that Mills cited in both "Language, Logic, and Culture" and a later article, "Methodological Consequences of the Sociology of Knowledge."[60] Like Mills, but nearly two decades earlier, Parsons learned institutional economics from Clarence Ayres as an undergraduate, when he was at Amherst College. In the 1920s, Parsons studied in

Germany, and in 1930 he published a translation of Max Weber's *The Protestant Ethic and the Spirit of Capitalism*. The publication of *The Structure of Social Action* in 1937 established his reputation among sociological theorists.[61] In this work, Parsons made a number of arguments similar to those advanced by Mills. For instance, he asserted that theory was necessary as a program for research and as a conceptual frame of reference, without which facts were meaningless. Parsons was also motivated to find methods adequate to the study of social phenomena. Much of *Structure* was designed as a critique of positivist and behaviorist views. Parsons later described it as a volley in "the 'war of independence' of the social sciences *vis a vis* the biological."[62] His "voluntaristic theory of action" accounted for the elements of subjective meaning and volition in human life while maintaining that it was possible to study these matters scientifically. Both Parsons and Mills were involved in a long-term trend in twentieth-century social science toward developing a distinct approach to the understanding of society that stressed that humans could not be adequately understood solely in terms of biological categories such as heredity and environment, nor in terms of the rational actor theory drawn from economics.[63] Whatever differences Parsons and Mills had—and these would grow more apparent in future years—they always shared this basic sociological perspective.

Though Mills concurred with other sociologists that the study of society needed a theoretical coherence and rigor that it presently lacked, unlike his contemporaries, Mills did not prioritize the establishment of sociology as an autonomous discipline. Becker argued that sociology should be "regarded neither as the mistress nor the handmaiden of other sciences, but as their sister."[64] Parsons's attempt to provide a charter for the discipline that would establish it as "a special analytical science on the same level as economic theory" was the most influential.[65] In Parsons's formulation, sociology was one of three action sciences that study events in time. Parsons claimed that sociology, distinct from politics and economics, focused on the phenomenon of "common value integration," by which he meant the integration of those cultural values that enabled the social cohesion of freely choosing individual actors. Parsons's approach achieved a more concrete definition of the discipline at the expense of restricting sociology's subject matter. Limiting sociology to the study of events in time from the perspective of common value integration marginalized the study of political structure and class analysis and downplayed the significance of social conflict.[66]

Operating against the drive to carefully delineate an autonomous field of study as outlined by Parsons and others, Mills decried arbitrary distinctions of subject matter within the field of social science. In a 1939 unpublished paper, "A Note on the Classification of the Social-Psychological Sciences," Mills examined the frequent attempts of social psychologists to delineate a clearly bounded field of study. Mills believed that the drive to delimit an autonomous discipline was due to institutional considerations and was detrimental to developing the best methods for the study of society. He complained of the "confusion of the methodological and institutional dimensions of the issue in which, members of departments, apparently arguing over the domain of social-psychological sciences, in reality are contending for a section of students with attendant increased funds."[67] Mills recognized only one legitimate intellectual distinction: between the physiological perspective, which studied the human organism using biological techniques, and the social perspective. Mills thus offered a definition of the study of society that was considerably more expansive than Parsons's definition of the field of sociology. "We are explaining behaviors socially," Mills wrote, "when we utilize social, economic, [and] political structures and processes in constructing the allegedly necessary conditions of that behavior."[68] Throughout his career, Mills retained this belief that the social sciences and humanities were engaged in a common endeavor and could not be separated by clear boundaries. As Mills wrote to a friend in 1941, "Woe unto those who stand at junctures in science, at the academic fence . . . and wag their fingers. It is from such surprising, 'confusing' borders that our genuine problems and new constructions emerge."[69] Consequently, Mills was attracted to interdisciplinary fields of study that allowed him to integrate his wide range of philosophical and social scientific interests. One such field was the sociology of knowledge.

'IDEOLOGY AND UTOPIA' IN AMERICA

Mills's position in the debate over Karl Mannheim's *Ideology and Utopia* further distinguished him from Parsons and other leading sociologists. The reception of works from Germany played a key role in the theoretical discourse of American sociology during the late 1930s. Karl Mannheim's *Ideologie und Utopie* sparked a methodological controversy when it was published in Germany in 1929. The publication of the English-language *Ideology and Utopia* (a revised version of the

German work that included two additional chapters) in 1936 ignited a similar methodological debate among American social scientists.[70] The controversy centered around two interconnected issues: Mannheim's epistemological perspective and his expansive program for the sociology of knowledge.

Mannheim argued that the sociology of knowledge emerged from the concept of *total ideology*. He distinguished *total ideology* from the *particular conception of ideology*, which was used to discredit ideas by demonstrating how they arose from their thinker's specific social situation. According to the particular conception of ideology, it was possible to "refute lies and eradicate sources of error by referring to accepted criteria of objective validity."[71] In contrast, the total conception of ideology recognized that all ideas were inseparable from the overall worldview and social position of their advocates. Consequently, no truth was possible "independent of an historically and socially determined set of meanings."[72] All ideas were thus subject to an ideological analysis that revealed their connection to social factors; Mannheim considered not only the class position of thinkers, but also such factors as education, status, and generation. According to Mannheim, it was the task of the sociologist of knowledge to subject all perspectives— including his own—to such an ideological analysis. The sociology of knowledge, he argued, emerged as a distinctive form of inquiry in the modern world because of the proliferation of competing ideas and the loss of common social values. Mannheim claimed that the test of an idea was its appropriateness to its epoch and its ability to synthesize elements of different contemporary ideologies. Thinkers should thus strive to be "unceasingly sensitive to the dynamic nature of society and to its wholeness."[73] The group that Mannheim hoped would achieve this holistic understanding was the "free-floating intelligentsia," which lacked roots in any particular interest-bound social group.

Mannheim distinguished between two varieties of the sociology of knowledge, each of which he advocated. The nonevaluative conception of the sociology of knowledge entailed the scholarly study of the relationship of ideas to social factors without the imposition of value judgments by the scholar. Had Mannheim stopped here, he would have provoked no controversy, but he also advocated an evaluative conception of the sociology of knowledge that was considerably more expansive. Under the evaluative conception, the sociology of knowledge was an ambitious program for cultural change, central to the rehabilitation of the Enlightenment project of integrating reason and politics. Exactly how they were to be reconciled was never entirely clear, but Mannheim offered at least three suggestions. The sociology of knowledge could serve as a means for eliminating biased and partial viewpoints in social science, as an educational tool for political parties, and as a method for allowing people to recognize the unconscious determinants of their behavior and thus exert rational control over them.[74]

Mannheim's hope that scholars in the United States would prove receptive to his ideas was largely disappointed. German intellectuals played a key role in attacking Mannheim's ideas in the United States. Hans Speier, a refugee from Nazi Germany at the New School for Social Research, argued that Mannheim's sociology of knowledge was applicable to "promotive" thinkers intent on effecting social change, but not to "theoretical" thinkers who sought universal, timeless truths.[75] A different and more influential critique, however, came from the German sociologist Alexander von Schelting. Von Schelting's review of *Ideologie und Utopie*, solicited by Howard Becker, was published in 1936 in the *American Sociological Review*. Because the review appeared before the publication of the English translation, *Ideology and Utopia*, it set the terms of the American debate.

Von Schelting's critique of Mannheim rested on a neo-Kantian perspective, which he attributed to Max Weber. According to this position, values were relevant for determining what questions a social scientist would ask, but the validity of research results was wholly independent of value judgments. Von Schelting believed Mannheim had confused the motives of the social scientist with the results of his work: "The nonsense first begins when one believes that factual origin and social factors . . . affect the value of ideas and conceptions thus originated."[76] To von Schelting, the danger of Mannheim's relativism was that it treated social science like any other ideology and thus undermined the scientific status of sociological knowledge. Von Schelting's position was endorsed by leading American sociologists. In the same journal issue in which von Schelting's review was published, Parsons reviewed von Schelting's own *Max Webers Wissenschaftslehre*. Parsons agreed with von Schelting that the problem with Mannheim was his claim that "theories, especially those of social science, are relative to their social basis, not only on the genetic level, but also in their logical and methodological foundations."[77] Citing *Ideology and Utopia*'s "close relations to certain concepts of thought associated with pragmatism," Parsons worried that Mannheim's ideas might find a following in the United States and recommended von Schelting as the necessary antidote.[78]

The connection between pragmatism and Mannheim's ideas was noted by virtually all contributors to the American debate over *Ideology and Utopia*. Though Mannheim's epistemology was complicated and often contradictory, he did share with the pragmatists an active and dynamic conception of knowledge, a strong sense of the interrelatedness of social phenomena, and a desire to transcend the false dichotomies between subject and object, empiricism and idealism, and fact and value that had plagued earlier thinkers. In order to enhance his reception in the United States, Mannheim instructed his former student Hans Gerth to announce at a December 1937 meeting of the ASS that Mannheim accepted pragmatism's instrumentalist view of truth as his own.[79]

Parsons need not have worried that Mannheim's affinity with pragmatism would enhance his American reception. Virtually the only American social scientist to defend Mannheim from the pragmatist perspective was Mills, who argued, "Mannheim's view overlaps the program that Dewey has pursued since 1903, when he turned from traditional concerns and squabbles over the ubiquitous relation of thought in general to reality at large to a specific examination of the context, office, and outcome of a type of inquiry."[80] In "Language, Logic, and Culture," Mills criticized Mannheim's inadequate social psychology. Yet, as he later wrote to Robert Merton, Mills believed that despite Mannheim's flaws, "the guy has a very *suggestive* idea which . . . although blurred and loose and all becomes something really fine when one weds it to, interprets it not from the neo-Kantian view, but from the standpoint of American pragmatism."[81]

In "Language, Logic, and Culture," Mills had argued for the social nature of knowledge, describing it as rooted in a thinker's engagement with an internalized audience and his use of socially constructed rules of logic and language. In "The Methodological Consequences of the Sociology of Knowledge," published in the *American Journal of Sociology* in November 1940, Mills extended these arguments to challenge Mannheim's critics, who, he alleged, would "restrict the object matter and implications of the sociology of knowledge."[82] Contrary to Speier, Mills contended that it was not only thinkers consciously seeking to influence social outcomes whose thought was socially determined, but also those who believed they were uncovering timeless truths. Responding to von Schelting, Mills conceded that in a scientific system of verification, the genesis of an idea did not affect its validity. However, he claimed that it was foolish to assume that this settled the matter, for the genesis of ideas was deeply social and went beyond the simple matter of an individual's motivations for seeking answers to questions. A scientific system of verification was itself historically and culturally specific: Mannheim and others had shown how closely connected it was to its bourgeois and Protestant origins. Mills wrote, "There have been and are diverse canons and criteria of validity and truth, and these criteria, upon which determinations of the truthfulness of propositions at any time depend, are themselves, in their persistence and change, legitimately open to social-historical relativization."[83] Interestingly, on a few occasions, Mills referred to these "diverse canons of validity and truth" as "paradigms," more than two decades before the historian and philosopher of science Thomas Kuhn popularized the term in his *Structure of Scientific Revolutions*.[84]

Mills argued that the most important consequences of the sociology of knowledge were methodological; the examination of ideas in their social context could allow social scientists to reflect on the methods and aims of their research. Because it was empirical and not speculative, the sociology of knowledge offered a means of reflection that relied upon actual social inquiry and thus avoided imposing an abstract and formalistic schema on the study of social science. For instance, Mills suggested that sociologists of knowledge were well positioned to address the questions of when and how values entered social scientific research and to what degree social scientists should adopt methods similar to those used in the physical sciences. Mills concluded by calling for the "detailed self-location of social science," a task he later undertook in his article "The Professional Ideology of Social Pathologists." Nevertheless, though Mills's acceptance of Mannheim's historicist and contextualist epistemology distinguished him from other sociologists, he shared with many of his sociological peers his stated goal for the sociology of knowledge: "detection of errors in methods," "sounder paradigms for social research," and "precise definition of issues that are now vague."[85] As with Mannheim, Mills's more expansive program for the sociology of knowledge included a call for the improvement of social scientific research with which disciplinary specialists could agree.

The most interesting reaction to "Methodological Consequences" came from Robert Merton. A Harvard Ph.D. who had studied with Parsons and Pitirim Sorokin, Merton was one of the young scholars who had turned to sociological theory in the late 1930s. Merton played a crucial role in introducing the ideas of French sociologist

Émile Durkheim to an American audience. A rising star in the discipline, Merton became chair of the Department of Sociology at Tulane University before the age of thirty, and in 1941 he received an appointment at Columbia. At the time Mills first encountered him, Merton was connected to left-wing intellectual circles, having written for the Anglo-American Marxist journal *Science and Society*. Like Mills, a Texan and former Catholic, Merton had a background that was unusual for an American sociologists at the time. Born in 1910, Merton was of Jewish origin (he had changed his name from Meyer Schkolnik to the very Anglo-sounding Robert King Merton), and he had been a gang member while growing up in a working-class neighborhood of Philadelphia.[86]

Having written his first book on the development of science in seventeenth-century England—a path-breaking work in the sociology of science—Merton was keenly interested in the emerging field of the sociology of knowledge. Like Mills, he was invested in the reception of Karl Mannheim's work. Though Merton accepted von Schelting's critique, he believed that if Mannheim's followers abandoned philosophical pretenses, they could expand upon his valuable suggestions for substantive research in the sociology of knowledge.[87] Merton considered Mills's "Language, Logic, and Culture" a promising step in this direction, since Mills had recognized that "wissensoziologische analysis requires a formulated set of postulates, definitions, and theorems."[88] Merton was less enthusiastic about "Methodological Consequences." He objected that Mills's defense of Mannheim's epistemology failed to provide an adequate basis for scientific knowledge, since it implied that it was "simply a matter of taste as to which criteria we adopt."[89] Indeed, given the Nazi advance across Europe, Merton saw this relativism as containing "an irreducible element of . . . nihilism."[90] To Mills, however, Merton had simply misunderstood the issue: "What you and Speier and von Schelting and the rest of those with, after all, neo-Kantian orientation . . . do not see is the problem of the actual derivation and function of what I have called paradigms."[91]

At stake in this exchange was the issue of the limits of the sociology of knowledge. Merton articulated the general consensus among sociologists that Mannheim's epistemological relativism and expansive program for the sociology of knowledge blurred the lines between philosophy and sociology and undermined their project of bolstering the autonomous scientific status of their discipline. While Merton confined the sociology of knowledge to a clearly defined subdiscipline within sociology, Mills wanted it to be an interdisciplinary endeavor that drew from and had implications for philosophy, social psychology, economics, and political science. For Mills, the sociology of knowledge was a method of investigating and challenging the fundamental presuppositions of contemporary social science. Rather than seeing Mannheim's approach as a threat to social science, Mills believed it bolstered the significance of social science by stressing how deeply "social" the production of knowledge was. Here are the beginnings of an argument that Mills would carry on with the sociological profession in the 1950s, a debate in which leading sociologists, including Merton, sought to limit sociology's boundaries to ensure that its conclusions would be as rigorous as possible while Mills rejected such restrictions. However, the differences between Mills and Merton, especially during this period, should not be exaggerated. Despite Merton's claim that Mills had fallen into a nihilistic impasse in his epistemological outlook, Merton stressed their shared goal of promoting sound studies in the sociology of knowledge and suggested that their differences might be mostly semantic.[92] Merton respected Mills's work enough to play an instrumental role in getting Mills jobs at the University of Maryland and Columbia. Even if other sociologists did not always agree with Mills, they recognized his perspective as valuable and offered it a hearing. Mills's views were distinctive, but they were situated within, not outside, the discourse of academic social science.

Mills's exchange with Merton pointed to a tension within his own perspective. On the one hand, Mills sought for the sociology of knowledge an expansive role that called into question the basic foundations of sociological knowledge. To claim that social scientists should use the sociology of knowledge to better consider their own role and position in society was also to imply the possibility of a more public and political role for the social scientist. On the other hand, Mills still shared his colleagues' belief in the superior rigor of professional social science. For instance, he defended the virtues of a more sophisticated and systematic social science against the insights of public intellectuals who were not properly trained. In a generally positive review of *Ideas Are Weapons*, by the well-known left-wing writer Max Lerner, Mills sharply distinguished between the speculations of cultural criticism and the demands of sociological analysis. Mills contrasted Lerner's "political journalism" with the more sophisticated perspective of the sociology of knowledge. If Lerner had more exposure to European sociologists of knowledge, Mills argued, he would not have mistakenly assumed that the primary way that social factors influence ideas was through the conscious interests of the individual thinker. The title of Lerner's book asked readers to think about how ideas serve as weapons on behalf of particular social and political groups, an idea suggested in Mills's work that he would soon explore further. In this review, however, Mills, though recognizing the timely political purpose of Lerner's essays, chided him that ideas "may also be weapons in the research quest for analytic discrimination and in the discovery of subtle relations."[93]

REFLEXIVE SOCIOLOGY

What was most distinctive about Mills's sociology of knowledge was the way he subjected social scientific knowledge to critical reflection. As the debate over *Ideology and Utopia* revealed, Mills was far more willing than his contemporaries to relativize the truth claims of social science in terms of social and historical context. Moreover, rather than focusing on establishing fixed theoretical principles for research, Mills's perspective entailed the notion that the methodology of the social sciences was always an open question, subject to constant revision. Indeed, much of the appeal of sociological theory to the young Mills was its ability to stimulate the sociological imagination. As he wrote to a friend in 1941, "All new things are 'up in the air.' If you stay too close to 'earth,' you can never fly over new regions. Theory is an airplane, not a pair of heavy boots; it is of the division of reconnaissance and spying."[94]

Initially, Mills hoped that his dissertation would be a pioneering methodological work. His original outline divided his project into three interrelated parts: a critical examination of pragmatism as a theory of the sociology of knowledge, a methodological statement of the sociology of knowledge, and a detailed empirical account of pragmatism using the tools elaborated in the methodological section.[95] Yet Mills's attempt to combine empirical sociological inquiry with philosophical reflection and methodological prescription did not easily fit disciplinary norms. His advisor, Becker, objected to Mills's attempt to address theoretical issues through empirical study. Becker advanced the increasingly widespread notion that sociological theory and practice, while interrelated, needed to remain separate areas of study. Moreover, Becker worried that Mills's plan "intruded into a domain traditionally reserved for philosophers" and suggested his dissertation needed to be a strictly empirical study if it were to remain unambiguously within the bounds of sociology.[96] Becker's opposition was not the only obstacle to Mills's ambition. He had to finish his dissertation hastily in 1942 in order to retain his new post as associate professor of sociology at the University of Maryland. The final dissertation contained no introduction, no conclusion, and an appendix of self-criticism. One of his self-criticisms was that his substantive work in the sociology of knowledge was not "accompanied by *explicit* self-awareness both of detailed procedure and of larger epistemological concerns," an omission he attributed to "intellectually irrelevant considerations."[97]

The dissertation, "A Sociological Account of Some Aspects of Pragmatism," interpreted the careers of three pragmatists: Peirce, James, and Dewey (a planned chapter on Mead was dropped due to time constraints). Mills had already developed many of the dissertation's arguments in his earlier work at Texas. The most significant new argument of the dissertation was Mills's critique of Dewey's liberalism, which owed more to his newfound political commitments than to his work in the sociology of knowledge. Mills examined the social backgrounds of each pragmatist to explicate their ideas. Peirce's work, for example, was understood in the context of his scientific experience and his status as an academic outsider. Mills was clearly attempting to tie the pragmatists' ideas to the broad social changes of their lifetimes—the rise of research universities, the emergence of the modern scientific outlook, and industrialization. Yet, as Mills acknowledged in his appendix, he failed to specify in a consistent and systematic way the connective terms in which pragmatism reflected social structural change. He attributed his omission of a "more concise *phraseology and developmental statement* of the course of the movement as a whole as it lies within a changing social structure" to his own limited knowledge of American history.[98]

If, by his own judgment, Mills's dissertation failed to live up to its original promise, his 1943 article "The Professional Ideology of Social Pathologists" successfully fulfilled Mills's earlier call for the "detailed self-location of social science."[99] To Mills, the best way to reconsider sociological methodology was through empirical research in the sociology of knowledge that ensured an interpenetration of sociological theory and practice. Because he advocated a sociology of sociology that used social scientific tools for disciplinary self-criticism, Mills may be seen as an early proponent of the "reflexive sociology" later advanced by such figures as Alvin Gouldner and Pierre Bourdieu. In Gouldner's words, reflexive sociology offers a "distinctive awareness of the ideological implications and political resonance of sociological work."[100]

In "Language, Logic, and Culture," Mills suggested that the sociologist of knowledge should closely analyze the concepts and methods used by a group of thinkers. In "The Professional Ideology of Social Pathologists," Mills examined the sociology textbooks that defined the field. In focusing on "social pathology," Mills targeted sociologists' preoccupation with crime and deviance. Mills found that the key concept of social pathologists was "adjustment." In methodological terms, social pathology was characterized by its low level of abstraction. Rather than considering matters of total social structure, social pathology textbooks examined everyday problems on an individual, atomistic level. A paradigmatic case studied by social pathologists was that of the individual immigrant adjusting to American society. Mills's article examined the underlying social factors that accounted for these characteristic aspects of social pathology. He contended that the attempt to provide systematic explanations in textbooks geared for undergraduate audiences led to "a taxonomic gathering of facts and a systematization of them under concepts that have already been logically defined."[101] However, he pinpointed the homogenous social background of the social pathologists. Mills's data on authors of social pathology textbooks painted a clear picture of men with rural or small-town origins who followed similar career paths into the professional middle class during a time of economic growth and industrialization and who shared mildly reformist political sentiments and affiliations.

For Mills, the rural and small-town backgrounds of the textbooks' authors explained how they classified individuals as "pathological." Mills argued that social pathologists used the concept of "adjustment" not in a statistical or a structural sense, but in a normative one. Social pathologists classed large groups, especially in urban areas, as "maladjusted." The social background of the authors led them to define social norms in terms of primary groups of small, homogeneous communities characterized by face-to-face interaction. Any behavior that failed to correspond to this ideal was then termed "pathological." The concept of "adjustment," according to Mills, was thus little more than "propaganda for conformity to those norms and traits ideally associated with small-town middle-class milieu."[102] At the same time that social pathologists' backgrounds led them to adopt a backward-looking concept of adjustment, Mills argued, their own professional success in an industrializing American economy caused them to remain optimistic that social problems could be solved without serious structural change. He tied the low level of abstraction in social pathology textbooks to the authors' reformist faith that social problems could be solved on an individual level, criticizing them for their "failure to consider total social structures."[103] Social pathologists did not question whether individual adjustment was in certain cases impossible without significant change in the social structure. Their low level of abstraction "did not rise to permit examination of . . . normative structures themselves, or of their political implications."[104] The mild reformism of social pathologists inhibited them from contemplating extensive social transformation. The sociological concepts exhibited in the professional discourse of social pathologists were thus not "usable in collective action which proceeds against, rather than well within, more or less tolerated channels."[105]

"Professional Ideology," written after Mills's leftward turn of the early 1940s, hinted at a radical critique of the discipline. Nevertheless, it can hardly be interpreted as an attempt by Mills to disassociate himself from the field of sociology as a whole, and not only because Mills awkwardly tried to fit the article into the prevailing mode of value-neutral social scientific discourse with a disingenuous abstract that claimed that the article did not "explicitly evaluate the worth of these [social pathological] concepts."[106] Many of the sociological theorists that Mills was in dialogue with would have agreed that much of inter-war sociological work was deficient, even if they would have avoided criticizing that work on explicitly political grounds. By indicating that earlier methods of American sociology were inadequate and needed to be revised by a theoretically informed viewpoint, Mills found himself in agreement with several of the discipline's emerging leaders, such as Parsons and Merton. Merton, for instance, argued that behavior considered deviant by sociologists was often functional for the group in question and not pathological.[107]

As an analysis of earlier sociological work, "Professional Ideology" is a classic critique, still cited by sociologists today, yet it should not be read as a wholly accurate account of early twentieth-century American sociology. Mills neglected to include in his study key works of Chicago School sociologists, scholars to whom it would have been difficult to assign a rural or small-town bias and whose concepts were considerably more sophisticated than those of other sociologists he described.[108] Nor did he draw any clear distinction between social pathology and sociology as a whole, thus leaving it unclear how far his critique of the discipline extended. Yet "Professional Ideology" was significant less for its specific arguments than for the commitment it displayed to reflexive sociology. Unfortunately, the article left readers confused about the precise nature of the position Mills advocated. This murkiness resulted from the journal's decision to cut Mills's original article because of space considerations. The unpublished second part of the article, "Methodological Consequences: Three Problems for Pathologists," reveals that Mills's intention was that the article embody his vision of methodological reflection proceeding alongside empirical study of sociological inquiry, representing a close interpenetration of theory and practice.[109] In this unpublished section, Mills argued that his study of social pathology textbooks had important implications for the place of values in social science. According to Mills, it was misguided to ask whether values should be a part of social scientific inquiry. As the social derivation of the social pathologists' normative vision of adjustment showed, values would inevitably shape social science. Instead of attempting a "Great Repression of Value Judgments," social scientists should promote a greater consciousness of how values shape social inquiry and scrutinize how their own values shaped their work. All perspectives, especially the social scientist's own, needed to be subjected to ideological analysis. Mills argued that social scientists could gain rational control over their own concepts through ideological self-analysis: "Now what is required is that the epithets, concepts, and unintegrated facts which are used to *define* social problems be *themselves* made objects of scrutiny."[110]

From this, Mills drew two somewhat different conclusions. On the one hand, he suggested that the purpose of critical self-reflection was to take as many social scientific perspectives into account as possible and to correct for their biases. Social scientific objectivity, he suggested, lay "at the intersection of fully articulated perspectives."[111] Here Mills echoed Mannheim's call for an ideological analysis of all positions that sought to preserve what was valuable in each of them. Behind this notion was the suggestion that the self-critical social scientist, as part of Mannheim's "free-floating intelligentsia," could transcend particularistic viewpoints and achieve comprehensive knowledge of society. On the other hand, Mills indicated that his purpose was more explicitly political, designed to expose the interests behind dominant ideas. After all, his critique of social pathologists was not simply that they failed to make their value judgments explicit; it was an attack on the social pathologists' value judgments themselves. Ideological analysis without a complementary examination of social structure was inadequate, Mills argued, because "ideologies are not merely beliefs, wide-spread throughout a milieu, they are legitimations of social structure." Thus, Mills concluded, "You cannot escape the realities of politics even though academic sociologists in America have done their courageous best." Social scientists needed, therefore, to "squarely face the problems of power."[112] Mills did not call on social scientists to be agents of political change. Rather, he argued, any thorough self-reflection would reveal that social scientists lacked the power to solve political problems by themselves. What they could do was examine social problems and state the political implications and assumptions of their own work.

His first published sociological work reflecting a commitment to leftist politics, "Professional Ideology" suggested a latent political potential in Mills's early work. Even though Mills lacked a developed political consciousness prior to 1941, the particular social scientific traditions that he absorbed while pursuing the rather abstract philosophical and theoretical questions of epistemology and methodology helped make him a radical. Pragmatism, for instance, offered Mills an inherent suspicion of received doctrine that clearly pointed in the direction of political reform. As James Kloppenberg has argued, the "radical theory of truth" put forth by American pragmatists and their European counterparts found a political complement in progressive and social-democratic movements promoting social welfare and greater democratic participation.[113] Similarly, Robert Westbrook has demonstrated that Dewey's pragmatist philosophy went hand in hand with a commitment to radical democratic politics.[114] Even though Mills saw his own politics as more radical than Deweyan progressivism, he drew strength from the pragmatist notion that the social world was uncertain and contingent, and hence available to be remade by collective democratic action that could transcend past social arrangements. Indeed, for the first class that he taught at the University of Maryland, Mills selected the following Dewey quote to place at the beginning of his syllabus in order to emphasize the subversive nature of pragmatist epistemology: "Let us admit the case of the conservative: if we once start thinking no one can guarantee where we shall come out, except that many objects, ends, and institutions are doomed. Every thinker puts some portion of an apparently stable world in peril."[115]

Perhaps most important, pragmatist philosophers presumed a significant public role for social science. In *The Public and Its Problems*, John Dewey suggested the need for social scientific knowledge to create democratic publics. In complex, modern societies, individuals needed knowledge of society as a whole in order to participate in decision making. Accordingly, Dewey argued that "a genuine social science would manifest its reality in the daily press, while learned books and articles supply and polish the tools of inquiry."[116] As Hans Joas has noted, "On the one hand, pragmatism's social philosophy thus provided a complex of fundamental concepts for social scientific research and theory construction. On the other hand, it ascribed to these very social sciences an enormous moral and political importance. For they were supposed to . . . make a decisive contribution to promoting the solidarity of a universal human community that collectively recognizes, discusses, and solves the problems of humanity."[117] Thus, Mills's pragmatist education suggested to him the key public and political role that the social scientist could play, even if his early work was more oriented toward polishing the tools of inquiry than reaching a larger audience in the daily press.

In large part through his detailed work in the sociology of knowledge, Mills became attuned to how power relations shape the production and distribution of ideas. This theme, an undercurrent of Mills's work in the sociology of knowledge from the start, culminated in the full-blown expression of reflexive sociology in "Professional Ideology." Indeed, it was in "Three Problems" that Mills first used the term "power elite," writing that sociologists of knowledge needed to be aware that ideas were often "the social weapons of the power elites."[118] Yet a more subtle but perhaps more fundamental element of Mills's early work that portended his future radical turn was his methodological call for the detailed self-location of social science. What most distinguished the early Mills from his sociological contemporaries was his willingness to subject the basic presuppositions of social scientific inquiry to critique. Even before he became a political radical, Mills was a radical in the classical sense: his analysis went to the root of the matter. To Mills, part of the attraction of a radical political perspective must have been similar to the appeal of an expansive conception of the sociology of knowledge. Each allowed him to get outside the object studied and bring into question its fundamental values.

Whatever the latent political potential of his earlier methodological work, Mills's recognition of the political element of sociological work made "Professional Ideology" a classic essay, one even more perceptive when read alongside its never-published methodological epilogue. The insights that Mills gained through his work in the sociology of knowledge were crucial to his later intellectual development. The meth-

odological implications he drew for social scientific inquiry remained
a fundamental aspect of his sociological perspective, and his engagement with the sociology of knowledge left him with the problem that
remained at the center of his attention for the remainder of his career:
the connection between ideas and social structure, or, to put it another
way, the relationship between intellect and power. Thus, in a sense,
Mills remained a sociologist of knowledge for his entire life. Following
"Professional Ideology," however, Mills moved away from the methodological work with which he had introduced himself to the social
scientific world. This shift is evident in Mills's decision not to revise
his dissertation for publication as a book, perhaps along the lines suggested in his original outline, a remarkable choice given Mills's dogged
persistence in seeking publication for many of his graduate papers. In
"Three Problems," Mills argued that sociologists should address questions of power and social structure. In the early 1940s, Mills came to
believe that such issues needed to be tackled directly, not just through
the attempt to explain the social derivation of ideas. He thus turned his
attention away from the methodological consequences of the sociology
of knowledge. Instead, he focused the formidable sociological ambition
he had displayed as a student on the more explicitly political question
of what was happening in the world.

CHAPTER 2

What Is Happening in the World Today

Weberian Sociology and Radical Political Analysis

In February of 1942, Mills sent a letter to prominent left-wing New York intellectual Dwight Macdonald. Mills closed his letter with the request that Macdonald "from time to time let me know what is going on in the world."[1] Throughout his life, Mills frequently ended his correspondence with this phrase. It is significant that he began to use it in the early 1940s, when he first developed a left-wing interpretation of world events and began to seek a new audience for his ideas. Still, Mills remained embedded in social scientific discourse. His interest in current political events went hand in hand with a sociological interest he did not fully develop until the early 1940s and which fit with disciplinary trends. The influence of Max Weber, filtered through Mills's interactions with the German émigré sociologist Hans Gerth, encouraged him to ask big questions about large-scale social trends. Using Weberian forms of analysis, Mills explored both class divisions in American society and the repressive and alienating effects of concentrated political power and large-scale bureaucratic institutions.

Mills's newfound engagement with political analysis was influenced by the change in his physical location. His acceptance of a position at the University of Maryland in the fall of 1941 brought Mills close to the nation's political capital, and frequent trips to New York City placed him in touch with left-wing currents in the nation's intellectual and cultural capital. But world events themselves exerted the most important influence on Mills. He later recalled that World War II

45

"meant a greatly increased interest in politics. . . . Following it closely and thinking about it made a radical of me."[2] Mills worried less about the fight against fascism abroad than he did about wartime trends in American society: the militarization of the American state, the growing concentration of political power, and the increasingly cozy relationship between government and business elites. Influenced by left-wing thinkers such as Macdonald, Daniel Bell, and Franz Neumann, Mills forged a dystopian analysis of an emerging American totalitarianism constructed by a corporate state that integrated economic and political elites, suppressed left-wing alternatives, and undermined the basis for meaningful critical thought. Marked by a pessimistic analysis of the chances for social change, and lacking identification with any particular social movement or political party, the political perspective that Mills developed in the early 1940s was a disillusioned radicalism. Many of the characteristic strengths and limitations of the left-wing critique Mills would voice more influentially in his later works were already evident in his wartime writings.

Though it failed to live up to its promise as a pioneering work in the sociology of knowledge, Mills's dissertation registered the crucial elements of his nascent radicalism: a rejection of liberalism on the grounds that it provided an inadequate basis for action in the modern world, a call for the realistic recognition of the concentration of power in American society, and a sense of hopelessness regarding future alternatives to the established order. The crucial section of the dissertation was Mills's discussion of John Dewey's liberalism. Mills affirmed important Deweyan values, particularly the value of rational action in transforming the social world. He also rejected the contention of some leftists that pragmatism was an apology for the "crude commercialization of American life."[3] To Mills, Dewey was "fighting the drift into corporate forms of organization, fighting what formal rationality does to his liberal individual thinking man."[4]

Mills criticized Dewey not for the political values he professed, but for his failure to see that radical measures would be necessary to realize them. According to Mills, Dewey maintained an unrealistic desire to return to the face-to-face democracy characteristic of the early American republic. Dewey's liberalism, Mills contended, assumed the existence of "a relatively homogenous community which does not harbor any chasms of structure and power not thoroughly harmonized by discussion."[5] Mills shared Dewey's vision of a deliberative democracy. However, he suggested that conditions of "classic democracy" lay in the country's Jeffersonian past, not its "corporate" present. To Mills, the main flaw of Deweyan liberalism was its failure to "face squarely the political and legal problem of the present distribution of power as it exists within the social order."[6] Without adequately recognizing the powerful interests arrayed against his own values in the modern world, Dewey displayed an unwarranted "optimism" about the "progress of man" and the ability of "intelligence to 'win out.'"[7] According to Mills, Dewey mistakenly believed that liberal progress was embedded in scientific technique, and that all problems ultimately could be solved through the application of social intelligence. In contrast, Mills presented his own social analysis as free from illusions, a demystifying approach unafraid to confront the unpleasant realities of political power. In the work of Weber, whom Gerth and Mills would describe as a "disillusioned liberal," Mills believed he found the sociological tools necessary to construct such a tough-minded analysis of the location of social power in American society.

Mills also criticized Dewey because the latter's concept of "action" was "*not* linked with a sizeable organization, a movement, a party with a chance at power," consigning the pragmatist to be "a kind of perennial mugwump confronted with rationalized social structures."[8] However, during the early 1940s, Mills himself was unable to identify an agent for social change. His call for a "collectivist" or "socialist" alternative to contemporary U.S. social structure was vague and abstract. Mills substituted for Dewey's unwarranted optimism a desperate pessimism. Partly because he remained unconnected to any movement for social change, Mills's disillusioned radicalism placed the social role of intellectuals at the heart of its agenda. In his focus on intellectuals, Mills drew upon his earlier work in the sociology of knowledge, which had suggested the need for intellectuals to be reflexively self-conscious of their place in society. Increasingly, Mills moved in an explicitly moralistic direction, stressing the proper, oppositional role of the intellectual in society and condemning those intellectuals who upheld the established order or retreated from the pressing issues of the day. Mills's critique of Dewey in "A Sociological Account" was the first time he articulated this theme, which received its fullest consideration in Mills's most significant essay of this period, "The Powerless People." Espousing a disillusioned radicalism that claimed to pierce liberal illusions to uncover an emerging American corporate state, Mills offered a politics centered on the responsibilities of radical intellectuals—not a politics of movements and parties, but a politics of truth.

MILLS AND GERTH: SOCIAL STRUCTURE AND POWER

Mills's new engagement with issues of social structure and political power in the early 1940s owed a great deal to Hans Gerth, the German émigré sociologist whom Mills met during his final year in Wisconsin. Gerth was steeped in the German sociological tradition. Originally a student of Karl Mannheim, he studied with Theodor Adorno, Max Horkheimer, Emil Lederer, Paul Tillich, and Alfred Weber. Gerth's student associates included Hannah Arendt, Norbert Elias, and Hans Speier. Born in 1908, Gerth wanted to study with Max Weber at Heidelberg. According to his own account, however, when he arrived at Heidelberg as an undergraduate in 1927, he discovered that Weber had been dead for seven years. As a result, Gerth worked instead with Mannheim, who once described Gerth as the "most gifted of all my former students."[9] Gerth assisted Mannheim in the preparation of *Ideologie und Utopie* and then followed him to the University of Frankfurt to begin work on a doctorate in sociology. In 1933, Gerth finished his dissertation, an analysis of early German bourgeois liberalism employing Mannheimian methods in the sociology of knowledge. By 1933, Mannheim, along with Gerth's other Jewish advisors, had fled the country following Hitler's seizure of power. Though a committed left-wing opponent of National Socialism, Gerth chose to remain in Germany, landing a job with the newspaper *Berliner Tageblatt*, for which he wrote propaganda pieces that he sought to infuse with covert criticism. In 1938, Gerth fled Germany for London, and he traveled to the United States shortly thereafter. Because he left Germany at a rather late date and was compromised by some of his newspaper articles, many German émigré intellectuals in the United States remained suspicious of Gerth. After holding a few temporary academic positions, Gerth landed a permanent post at the University of Wisconsin in the fall of 1940.[10]

Gerth represented the Weberian tradition of seeking to understand social structures by the careful use of analytic distinctions, or "ideal types," and the historical use of the comparative method. A lifelong socialist, Gerth developed a neo-Marxist interpretation of Weber's work that combined Marx's materialist interpretation of history, shorn of dialectical hopes for an immanent historical goal, with Weber's respect for the complexity of social structure and appreciation for the significance of noneconomic social spheres. Gerth's pessimistic critique of modern society derived from the notion that totalitarianism was a feature of democratic as well as fascist societies. His analysis shared much with that of another set of German émigré intellectuals, those of the Frankfurt School, who also influenced Mills's radicalism.[11]

Lewis Coser, another German émigré sociologist whom Mills later befriended, once observed that the impact of émigré scholars in the United States was greatest not because of their institutional affiliations or publications, but rather because of "who listened to them, who adopted their message, and for what reason."[12] This was certainly true in Gerth's case. Many of Gerth's students later recounted that his brilliance was most evident in his lectures and in personal conversations. Gerth never really adapted to the American intellectual environment: he published little, was best known as a translator of Weber, and would likely have published far less had he not found American collaborators such as Mills. Mills spent less than a full year with Gerth at Wisconsin and never took a class with him, yet the two quickly became friends and collaborators. Gerth's influence exceeded that of any other individual Mills encountered in his career. However, it is important not to exaggerate Gerth's impact on Mills. Guy Oakes and Arthur Vidich have erroneously argued that Mills was little more than a popularizer of Gerth's ideas who failed to give adequate credit to his mentor.[13] Yet Mills had developed a thoroughly contextualist and historicist view of social science before meeting Gerth. He already had encountered the German social scientific tradition in his work on Mannheim's sociology of knowledge, independently reaching conclusions similar to those of Gerth. Precisely for this reason, the more experienced Gerth recognized the young Mills as a worthy collaborator. Though Gerth considered himself Mills's mentor, Mills cannot be considered Gerth's protégé.

Gerth introduced Mills to the political and historical sociology of Weber and, to a lesser degree, Marx. The German sociological tradition was so important for Mills's intellectual development that by 1944, he claimed that he had "never had occasion to take very seriously much of American sociology as such" and that his "main impulse has been taken from German developments, especially the traditions stemming from Max Weber and, to a lesser degree, Karl Mannheim."[14] Gerth shaped Mills's sociological outlook in three important respects: he introduced him to a set of Weberian analytic categories with which to understand social stratification; he encouraged Mills to take a more structural and macroscopic approach to the study of society; and he helped focus Mills's attention on the issue of political power.

Gerth's influence was apparent in what Mills referred to as his

"Weber[ian] critique" of *The Social Life of a Modern Community*, the first in the well-known "Yankee City" series of community studies directed by W. Lloyd Warner.[15] In this lengthy review, Mills utilized his pragmatist sense of science to criticize Warner's naïve empiricism, which viewed science as "observation, then classification, then generalization" and resulted in the absurd claim that the study had "discovered" social class. As Mills noted, all sociological studies were informed by theoretical concepts such as "class" from the outset. Mills's critique thus emphasized themes familiar from his earlier writings. Yet Mills also argued that Warner's difficulty stemmed from his inadequate knowledge of "post-Marxist discussions in European sociological literature . . . especially Max Weber."[16] To Mills, Warner's definition of "class" conflated three meanings of social stratification that Weber's more sophisticated categories allowed the social scientist to keep analytically distinct. Following Weber, Mills suggested that "class" should refer solely to economic position, that "status" should refer to the cultural distribution of prestige, and that "power" should mean "who can be expected to obey whom in what situations."[17] Not only did Warner conflate the objective meaning of class (purely economic) with the subjective one (status), he also confused the economic meaning of *class* with the psychological and political one of *class consciousness*. Only when the sociologist employed the careful analytic distinctions provided by Weber, Mills argued, could social researchers actually ask meaningful questions: for instance, how was economic position related to social status in American society?

Gerth's influence on Mills was also apparent in their collaborative work. By the summer of 1941 they had planned to write a social psychology textbook together. Although it was not published until 1953, Gerth and Mills did significant work on *Character and Social Structure* in the early 1940s. Much of their correspondence from this period involved exchanging drafts of chapters for the book and planning how they could spend time together to work on it, a task made difficult since during the war Gerth was classified as an enemy alien and was thus unable to travel from Madison. A genuine social psychology, the authors argued in an August 1941 book outline, would move beyond the problems inherent in the orthodox Freudian approach, which made unwarranted "supra-historical" assumptions regarding human nature. More important, it would challenge the "behavioralist" approach dominant in the American human sciences, which, despite its valuable empirical orientation and "readiness to observe changeability of man," was "rather sterile and limited to small field analyses, with the fields not connected." Gerth and Mills argued that American social psychologists lacked a tradition of "*structural* sociology." All American sociology had thus been a "milieu sociology" that ignored the significance of large-scale institutions and the connections between different aspects of the social structure. Mills and Gerth proposed a comparative and historical approach for their book that would employ the Weberian method of "ideal types" to provide a general yet flexible framework to analyze "specific roles in their structural setting" without losing sight of the psychology of the individual human actor. In proposing to draw upon the best of both the American empirical tradition and the German theoretical tradition, the collaborators self-consciously sought to heed Karl Mannheim's 1932 suggestion in the *American Journal of Sociology* that "there were hardly ever two different styles of study as fit to supplement each others' shortcomings as are the German and American types of sociology."[18]

In a draft introduction to the book, Gerth and Mills made clear that their approach to social psychology was part of a larger critique of the "narrowing of attention" in social science that had led to "the loss of any larger focus upon the structural and historical features of societies." In terms that recalled Mills's debt to pragmatist notions of science, they criticized the "idea that 'science' is so narrow that its minimum ideals of disinterested naturalism must be sacrificed in order to deal with the big problems of man and society." However, Gerth and Mills did not describe their work as an isolated effort, but as part of a new trend in American social science. They believed that two factors had contributed to the newfound attention to total social structures among American social scientists. The first was a "theoretical renaissance . . . in American sociology during the last ten years . . . fertilized by a renewal of contact with German sociology and economics of the 19th and early 20th centuries." The second was a desire to understand the "rise of totalitarian social structures" that had led to World War II.[19]

Though Gerth and Mills did not name any sociologists whom they saw leading this new trend toward broader social studies, Talcott Parsons clearly represented both the theoretical renaissance and the attempt to understand totalitarian social structures. A leading advocate of European theory in the United States throughout the 1930s, Parsons became a towering figure in American social science in the 1940s. During World War II, in an attempt to understand the rise of fascism, Parsons's analysis shifted toward an investigation of specific national social structures. Parsons's changing use of Weber illustrated this shift. In *The Structure of Social Action*, Parsons treated Weber primarily as a sociological theorist. In the early 1940s, however, he applied Weber's theories to understand the "contemporary political crisis." In a series of essays on Nazi Germany, Parsons analyzed fascism as an antimodernist charismatic movement that emerged from the structural dynamics of modernization. In contrast to his later, more optimistic rendering of modernity, Parsons here depicted modern society, which he considered to be based on rational-legal authority and impersonal, universalistic norms, as a fragile one whose process of rationalization threatened to create psychological disorders that could result in fascist-type movements.[20]

Attempting to understand modern social structures through the lens of social psychology was characteristic of not only Parsons's work, but also that of many American social scientists of the World War II era who sought to explain the rise of totalitarianism.[21] Thus, Mills's turn to a more structural and macroscopic approach to social science did not simply develop from Gerth's influence, but it participated in a major trend in American social science during this period. The structural approach associated with the increasing prominence of functionalism in 1940s social science transcended the same atomistic analysis as did Mills and Gerth. "Social structure" became one of the buzzwords of 1940s American sociology, as in Robert Merton's influential 1949 collection of essays, *Social Theory and Social Structure*.[22] Whereas earlier American sociologists had generally taken the community as the subject of investigation, this newer, macroscopic approach took the nation and even modernity itself as its subject, marking a notable departure from earlier disciplinary traditions of both the ethnographic "milieu" sociology associated with the Chicago School and the quantitative approach of the objectivists.

However, to a greater degree than his sociological contemporaries, Mills insisted that the study of social structure needed to be informed by history. This was partly due to the Weberian tradition imparted to him by Gerth, which stressed that the comparative method relied not just on comparisons between different contemporary social structures, but also on comparisons between contemporary structures and those of the past. Indeed, Mills's later sociological work would rely more on comparisons between the contemporary United States and previous periods in American history than it would on comparisons between the modern United States and other modern societies. In making his approach more historical, Mills was also influenced by a notable set of young American historians whom he befriended at the University of Maryland, a group that included Frank Friedel, Richard Hofstadter, and Kenneth Stampp. Mills praised historians as a profession, writing, "I think that it is undoubtedly true that they possess and use a much higher degree of scholarship than any other one social science, certainly more than sociologists as a group. There are about a dozen monographs by [A]merican historians which no man trying to understand his world can fail to read with absorbed interest."[23] During the war, Mills enhanced his own knowledge of American history by teaching a course on the subject for army recruits at Maryland.

From his engagement with Weberian social science, Mills learned that different aspects of society were autonomous and yet interrelated. One notable feature of *Character and Social Structure* was that it viewed the social world in terms of five orders: political, economic, military, kinship, and religious. Like Weber, Mills resisted any type of determinism (economic or otherwise) and sought to draw connections between these different social realms. However, as for Weber, it was the significance of power relations in the political realm that struck Mills as most important. Politics, for Mills, could not be reduced to economics or ideology, though it was certainly connected to both. Indeed, for Mills, politics ultimately derived from the power of coercion. Mills offered a Weberian definition of "power" as the capability to "influence the conduct of others even against their will."[24] Following Weber, Mills viewed political power in institutional terms; in the modern world, he looked especially at bureaucratic organizations and the people who controlled them.

That Mills absorbed this Weberian approach to political power in part from Gerth is evident in "A Marx for the Managers," an essay they coauthored. In this piece, published in early 1942, Gerth and Mills reviewed James Burnham's widely discussed *The Managerial Society* (1941). A philosophy professor at New York University, Burnham had helped found the Trotskyist Workers Party in 1940. His analysis of the triumph of managerialism drew heavily on Trotskyist ideas about the bureaucratization of the Soviet revolution under Stalin's leadership. By the time he published *The Managerial Society*, however, Burnham had renounced Marxism. Consequently, his book was stripped of political and moral critique as Burnham claimed merely to identify in tough-minded terms the inevitable historical developments that would shape the future. (Only after World War II did Burnham prominently identify himself with the conservative movement.) In *The Managerial Society,* Burnham argued that capitalism was giving way not to socialism but to managerialism, which was beginning to take hold in apparently diverse countries such as the United States, the USSR, and Germany. Burnham argued that a new class of managers, technically indispensable to the functioning of modern industrial economies, were seizing power throughout the world and using interventionist states to plan the economy according to their own interests. *The Managerial Society* was schematic and oversimplified as a work of social analysis, but it garnered interest by boldly promising to explain (as its subtitle put it) "what is happening in the world today," the very question that Mills was beginning to ask himself. *Fortune* magazine declared it the "most debated book all this year," and Mills's eagerness to review the book suggested his new interest in entering into a broader public discourse about sociological and political issues.[25]

According to Gerth and Mills, Burnham correctly recognized the "centralization of industrial and administrative organization" in the modern world. Yet he went astray when he explained historical developments by looking merely at forms of organization while failing to consider who controlled these organizations and to what ends. Burnham conflated different social spheres and neglected the importance of political power. He mistakenly assumed "too automatic an agreement between the social-economic order and political movements" and confused "the technical indispensability of certain functions" in the modern social structure with "political power."[26] Rather than proving that the modern world as a whole was drifting toward the same form of managerial society, the reviewers suggested, the case of Germany demonstrated that the crucial question was how newly developing bureaucratic structures were used by those possessing political power. Gerth and Mills wrote about Germany, "The question is: Where is the power? And the answer is: It is the structure of domination, which is the state with its monopoly of physical force, and fused within it the industrialists and their agrarian colleagues."[27] As technically indispensable as they might be, the managers were not in control in Germany or anywhere else.

Gerth and Mills's critique of Burnham also indicated their debt to a Marxist analysis of political economy, which stressed issues of property and class. Burnham's exclusive focus on the bureaucratic form of organization led him to overlook basic matters of political economy that sharply distinguished the social structure of Germany from that of the USSR, such as the inheritance of property. Burnham's focus on managerial control, moreover, confused the regulatory power of the state with the ownership of capital: for Gerth and Mills, the New Deal and Nazism represented different attempts at preserving capitalism in the modern world, not stages beyond capitalism. As they had written in their 1941 outline for *Character and Social Structure*, Gerth and Mills believed that the age of capitalism was not yet complete: "We live in a historically unique epoch; capitalism is an epochal, cultural formation affecting all human activity."[28] If Burnham offered "too much Marx" in his functional determinism, his lack of a Marxist analysis of social structure prevented him from understanding the contemporary world. "The task of understanding what is happening in the world today," argued Gerth and Mills, "involves a comprehension of such basic issues as the retention or abolition of private property, the structure of classes, possible political and social movements, and war."[29]

As "A Marx for the Managers" indicates, Mills learned from Weber what many other left-wing thinkers took from Marx. In particular, Mills expressed interest in an analysis of various classes in society and their "chances for power." The key questions to ask about bureaucratic organizations were "the ends for which these structures will be used, who will be at their tops, how they might be overthrown, and what movements will grow up in such structures."[30] Such questions would preoccupy Mills for the rest of his career, appearing consistently in *The New Men of Power, White Collar, The Power Elite*, and "Letter to the New Left." "A Marx for the Managers" also suggested two contrasting methods of approaching such questions that would prove characteristic of Mills's thought. On the one hand, Mills criticized Burnham for his "cultural pessimism," portraying him as an overly deterministic thinker resigned to "the Draconian inevitability of iron necessity."[31] In contrast, Mills advocated a more open and flexible method of analyzing historical change such as that exemplified in Weber's work. Mills embraced a pragmatist sense of historical contingency and a suspicion of grand philosophies of history. Here was a Mills who would be on the lookout for new developments in class and power structures and new openings for left-wing politics. On the other hand, Mills's own wartime social and political analyses were nearly as bleak as Burnham's. Mills's commitment to radical politics went along with a profound belief that sources of radical political opposition were blocked. While Mills always rejected the notion that managers were the new class in power, he did perceive a frightening and irreversible expansion of centralized bureaucratic organizations that seemed to spell doom for democratic social movements. Thus, Mills's analysis of what was happening in the world was more similar to Burnham's than he would have cared to admit.

'TO THE LEFT OF DEWEY': BECOMING A RADICAL

That "A Marx for the Managers" was a collaborative effort suggests the close connections between Mills's attraction to the macroscopic study of social structure under Gerth's influence and his interest in developing a left-wing interpretation of world events. Yet "A Marx for the Managers" held a significance for Mills that it did not for Gerth. Even though the review was published in a professional journal, it helped Mills establish himself as a political thinker capable of analyzing what was happening in the world for a broader educated audience. Mills took the unusual step of purchasing offprints of the review so that he could send copies to several established left-wing intellectuals whom he admired. The strategy succeeded. Dwight Macdonald, one of the editors of the influential left-wing journal *Partisan Review,* wrote Mills that his review was "extremely interesting," a "thoroughly documented critique" that Macdonald wished he could have published along with his own critical review of *The Managerial Revolution.*[32] A graduate of Exeter, Yale, and Macy's management training school, and a former writer for Henry Luce's *Fortune* magazine, Macdonald was one of the leading members of a distinct set of left-wing anti-Stalinist New York intellectuals.[33]

From 1942 to 1944, Mills contributed a dizzying array of pieces for magazines of the intellectual left, including *Partisan Review, New Leader, New Republic,* and *Politics.* Mills's proximity to the New York intellectual scene while at the University of Maryland helped him become part of its conversation years prior to his move to New York City in 1945. Mills's turn toward political analysis went hand in hand with his desire to write for a different public than he was able to reach in professional journals of social science. In left-wing magazines Mills saw the opportunity to broaden his audience. In 1942, Mills wrote Daniel Bell, then an editor at the *New Leader,* "I'm going to write a lot of such 'popular' (i.e. non-technical or professional) stuff this year in order to learn how to write more smoothly, and I don't expect it all to be printed. I'm just practising frankly."[34] Mills was pleased to write a review for the *New Republic,* not only because it paid well, but also because he saw the magazine as "a sort of style manual for expository writing. . . . I am naturally anxious to do a slick piece of prose."[35] Given that Mills had earlier written in a technical sociological and philosophical language, adapting his prose for a broader audience was no easy task. Indeed, Richard Hofstadter reported after having met Mills in the fall of 1942 that his new friend was still "sadly addicted to sociological jargon."[36]

Mills's attempts to write for a wider audience alarmed his social scientific collaborator, Gerth, who worried that Mills was moving in too "journalistic" a direction and admonished Mills to "sit down and do scholarly work rather than publishing for the day."[37] However, neither Mills's turn to contemporary political concerns nor his attempt to write for a wider audience should be interpreted as marking a break with social science. Rather, Mills's writings for left-wing magazines are better seen as public sociology, making the methods and insights of contemporary social science available outside the academy. In 1944, Mills wrote that his pieces for "journals of opinion and various 'little magazines'" had been an attempt "to rid myself of a crippling academic prose and to develop an intelligible way of communicating modern social science to nonspecialized publics."[38] In fact, Daniel Bell, who had done graduate work in sociology at Columbia, recruited Mills as a writer for *New Leader* on the basis of Mills's articles in professional journals of sociology.[39] Instead of expressing concern about Mills's attempts to write for a nonprofessional left-wing audience, some leading social scientists applauded Mills's efforts. Robert Merton thought that Mills's *New Leader* article "Collectivism and the Mixed-Up Economy" was a "brilliant performance."[40] Robert Lynd reported that the article "brought me to my feet cheering" and used his contacts to set Mills up as a reviewer for *New Republic*.[41] Mills also tried (with limited success) to lure figures that he met through his political engagements into the world of academic social science. For instance, he invited Macdonald to speak at a panel on social class at the American Sociological Society, and he tried to persuade radical community organizer Saul Alinsky to coedit a book, never published, titled "Studies in the Sociology of Knowledge and Communications."[42]

Mills combined his sociological interest in issues of social structure and power with his political concerns in one of his earliest and most significant reviews from this period. In "Locating the Enemy," Mills praised Franz Neumann's *Behemoth* as "at once a definitive analysis of the German Reich and a basic contribution to the social sciences."[43] Neumann was a German émigré political scientist closely associated with the Frankfurt School. After his emigration from Germany ended a promising career as a socialist lawyer, Neumann completed his doctorate at the London School of Economics under the supervision of the socialist political scientist Harold Laski. As a result, Neumann was more open to adopting the empirical bent of Anglo-American social science than were many of his more philosophically inclined Marxist associates in the Frankfurt School. Like Gerth and Mills, Neumann hoped to combine the best elements of empirical (i.e., American) and theoretical (i.e., German) social science, and he admired Weber as a model social scientist.[44] For Mills, Neumann highlighted the continued relevance of Marxist interpretations of class and power: "Marx may be a nineteenth-century theorist in some matters . . . but, as Neumann again makes clear by a fresh intellectual act, the technique, the elements, and the drive of his thinking is more than ever relevant."[45]

Behemoth was a sophisticated analysis of the Nazi regime. Neumann's interpretation of German fascism as "totalitarian monopolistic capitalism" differed from other leading theories on the left: the "state capitalist" theory of the dominance of the German state over the economy, presented in the work of Friedrich Pollock and accepted by the majority of the Frankfurt School; the more orthodox Marxist theory of "monopoly capitalism," which saw the Nazi regime as merely a front for big industry; and theories of "bureaucratic collectivism" or a managerial revolution (such as Burnham's), which assumed that the managerial bureaucracy truly directed the Nazi regime. Rather, Neumann argued that German fascism resulted from the confluence of interests among four interconnected yet distinct power blocs: the state bureaucracy, the Nazi party, the military, and big industry. Although these groups did not share identical interests, they collaborated in establishing a totalitarian government and maintaining a policy of imperialist expansion. Neumann described the Nazi regime as a collaboration of powerful blocs rather than an autonomous state, which could at least predictably ensure certain minimal individual rights, characterizing it as a frightening "non-state" defined by "a rule of lawlessness and anarchy, which has 'swallowed the rights and dignity of man, and is out to transform the world into a chaos by the supremacy of gigantic land masses.'"[46]

Behemoth offered Mills a model of how to conduct an empirical study of a total social structure that emphasized the interrelations of several spheres while recognizing their autonomy. Neumann offered a materialist analysis of political power and political economy as well as a thorough dissection of Nazi political ideology. To Mills, Neumann's analysis showed that the "way to political reality is *through* ideological analysis," reinforcing Mills's continued emphasis on the sociology of knowledge as a pathway to questions of political power.[47] Neumann, Mills claimed, "has that knack of generalized description that describes more than its immediate object," allowing him to reveal "in sensitive outline many features of all modern social structure."[48] Mills also seized upon Neumann's definition of "capitalism." Recognizing that it was misguided to associate capitalism with laissez-faire competition at a time when markets were dominated by monopolies that manipulated market conditions, Mills adopted Neumann's suggestion that the crucial feature of a capitalist social structure was the existence of private property. Yet Mills agreed with Neumann that the form of capitalism in Nazi Germany was a new, highly politicized variant, in which competition occurred not among a series of small producers, but among large cartels that competed for state favors and used state power to crush labor unions. Perhaps most significantly, Mills concurred with Neumann's division of the Nazi power structure into four separate parts, a scheme that served as an important influence on Mills's later tripartite analysis of a "power elite" consisting of interlocking economic, military, and political leaders.

Mills's review of *Behemoth* appeared in *Partisan Review,* the main forum for the New York intellectuals, a set of Jewish and WASP thinkers who rose to prominence in American intellectual life during the 1930s and 1940s. Their cosmopolitan worldview, centered on introducing European modernist ideas into American discourse, appealed to Mills. More important, their passionate belief in the significance of ideas, their vigorous mode of political and cultural debate (aimed at a highbrow yet nonacademic audience), and their promotion of the adversarial role of the critical intellectual served as an inspiration for Mills. The anti-Stalinist leftism that New York intellectuals developed during the late 1930s was the most significant political influence on Mills during this period, though by the early 1940s many New York intellectuals had already begun to move away from their radical pasts.[49] However, many features of Mills's politicization set him apart from this group. Most New York intellectuals were attracted to left-wing ideas

during the 1930s, when the dramatic organization of American unions
and the conflict between Communists and anti-Stalinists dominated
left-wing discourse. But Mills's politicization was a distinct product of
the 1940s. As Mills later wrote, "I did not personally experience 'the
thirties.' At the time I just didn't get its mood."[50] For Mills, the euphoric
feeling of participating in a social movement did not come until his brief
but intense involvement with the labor movement after World War II.
Most New York intellectuals had an early experience with a political
party—whether it was the Communist Party, Socialist Party, American
Workers Party, Socialist Workers Party, or Workers Party—or with a
social cause or movement such as labor or antifascism. In contrast,
Mills's politicization was an almost entirely intellectual affair. He did
not commit to the left by joining a political party, by attending a rally
for Spanish antifascists, by backing a labor-organizing drive, or by
signing a petition criticizing the Moscow Trials. Rather, Mills became
a radical by contributing book reviews to left-wing magazines. Like the
New York intellectuals, Mills was an anti-Stalinist committed to building a non-Communist left. Yet Mills's politics were refreshingly free of
the sectarianism that often characterized the New York intellectuals,
and in particular the single-minded anti-Communism that was a vital
factor in their deradicalization during the 1940s.[51]

The various features of Mills's politics were evident by the early
1940s in his description of himself as a "radical."[52] Calling himself a
"radical" allowed Mills to identify himself as a committed proponent
of the left without having to specify allegiance to any particular group
or cause. Mills defined what it meant to be "radical" in intellectual
rather than strictly political terms. Writing to Saul Alinsky, Mills
quoted Marx: "To be radical is to grasp a thing by the root."[53] And, as
he wrote to Macdonald, "Radicalism comes out in detailed compelling
analaysis not in names and sloguns."[54] The other crucial feature of the
word "radical" is its clear demarcation from liberalism. Though Mills
might not be able to state where exactly on the left his politics were,
he insisted that they were somewhere "to the left of Dewey."[55] Though
unwilling to embrace revolutionary socialism or otherwise specify
what radical change might look like, Mills scoffed at reforms that left
the basic capitalist social order intact. At times, this led Mills into
radical posturing, drawing too sharp a distinction between those who
supported the status quo and those who challenged it. Mills defined
his politics by a strong opposition to capitalist exploitation, authori-
tarianism, and militarism, and a passionate support for democracy and

socialism, but he was vague about the positive political program he supported and what means could be used to obtain these political ends. This vagueness remained throughout Mills's career, but it was particularly evident in the early 1940s, when Mills's political analysis had a tentative and experimental character. Virtually all of the pieces he wrote from 1942 to 1944 were book reviews. As a new entrant to left-wing discourse, Mills remained more comfortable analyzing others' political views than stating his own.

Mills's intense skepticism that anything good could come of World War II was the single issue that dominated his early political consciousness. Mills expressed antiwar sentiments as early as 1940, urging his parents to vote for the socialist Norman Thomas, the only antiwar candidate in the presidential race. Mills also criticized the war in regular meetings with his left-leaning historian friends at Maryland.[56] Nothing that happened during the war changed Mills's mind: in 1945, he wrote his parents, "Like I told you 3 years ago, I'll sit this one out. It's a goddamned bloodbath to no end save misery and *mutual* death to *all* civilized values."[57] Mills's skepticism about the war effort derived in large part from his acute personal fear of being drafted, and a visceral negative reaction to militarism developed during his unhappy freshman year at Texas A&M. Mills's antiwar politics placed him in a similar position as Macdonald. Macdonald initially opposed the war from the position of the Trotskyist Workers Party, which argued that the war was a struggle of rival imperialisms, and that a socialist "third camp" needed to be established before fascists should be engaged on the battlefield. In 1943, Macdonald broke with *Partisan Review* editors over the issue of the war. Macdonald felt that by avoiding a forthright discussion of the war in the journal's pages, the magazine's other editors, William Phillips and Philip Rahv, had abdicated the responsibility of political analysis.[58] Unlike Macdonald, Mills never publicly expressed opposition to the war, nor did his antiwar stance dissuade him for writing for pro-war publications such as *New Republic* and *New Leader*. Mills even applied for government jobs, such as one at the Office of Strategic Services Research Division, in order to avoid the draft. Nevertheless, Mills's antiwar stance was fundamental to his politics during this period.

Mills's opposition to the war represented a major error in judgment. It revealed some of the principal limitations of Mills's radicalism at this time, such as his lack of an international perspective, which led him to seriously underestimate the fascist threat. In addition, turning a blind eye to issues of race (as he did throughout his career), Mills failed to appreciate that the war generated considerable momentum for racial equality, since its supporters could portray their cause as part of an antifascist struggle at home and abroad. Mills's analysis of an American "fascism" accordingly neglected the issue of race, which was vital to left antifascist supporters of the war effort.[59] Nevertheless, Mills's skepticism about the war inoculated him from certain illusions about the war effort maintained by its left-liberal supporters. As Frank Warren has argued, such progressives believed in a number of "noble abstractions" that submerged their domestic agenda and criticisms of American society beneath their support of the war against fascism.[60] By remaining aloof, Mills was able to perceive the powerfully conservative forces unleashed by the war, and to recognize the truth of Randolph Bourne's famous observation, referring to World War I, that "war is the health of the state."[61]

Mills's opposition to the war attuned him to the development of key trends that would mark American society during and following World War II: the concentration of political power in the executive branch, the increasing growth of partnerships between large corporations and the federal government, and the militarization of the American state.[62] Even though he exaggerated such developments, Mills was one of the few intellectuals of his time to grasp their significance. He was deeply concerned about the war's effects on American society. Thus, although he was not particularly persuaded by the geopolitical arguments made by left-wing opponents that the war was merely a clash of rival imperialisms, he was swayed by their argument that the war would result in fascist-like trends in American society. At the end of his review of *Behemoth*, Mills drew an ominous comparison between Nazi and American social structures: "The analysis of Behemoth casts light upon capitalism in democracies. . . . If you read [Neumann's] book thoroughly, you see the harsh outlines of possible futures close around you. With leftwing thought confused and split and dribbling trivialities, he locates the enemy with a 500 watt glare. And Nazi is only one of his names."[63]

Mills's suggestion that structural trends in the American political economy were analogous to those in Nazi Germany paralleled the analysis of the American "monopoly state" developed by *New Leader* editor Daniel Bell. Though Bell was one year younger than Mills, he had far more experience on the left, having joined the Young People's Socialist League at the age of thirteen. Bell's thought was steeped in a Marxist tradition of evolutionary socialism for which Mills had no analogue. Nevertheless, the two held much in common during the war years. Bell initially supported the war, arguing that wartime imperatives would bring about greater social democracy through government planning. By 1942, however, Bell began to contend that American big business was using state planning to further its own ends, bringing about a frightening corporate-dominated "monopoly state." As Howard Brick has written, Bell, also influenced by Neumann's *Behemoth*, realized that "war-induced social transformation tended not in the direction of social democracy but toward a new repressive order of consolidated monopoly control."[64] Bell advanced his analysis in an unpublished book manuscript as well as in a series of muckraking reports for *New Leader* on the increasing corporate dominance of government war-planning agencies that Mills eagerly read. "I'd like to see all of NL *[New Leader]* modeled after your diligent stuff on monopoly," Mills wrote Bell.

Bell likely solicited Mills's December 1942 piece for *New Leader,* "Collectivism and the Mixed-Up Economy." This article exemplified many characteristic features of Mills's emerging political perspective: deep anxiety about wartime trends in American social structure, critique of liberalism as outdated and naïve, attention to questions of power and social structure, and passionate if vague support of a democratic socialist alternative. It also built on the skills of ideological dissection that Mills had honed in his work on the sociology of knowledge. "Collectivism and the Mixed-Up Economy" responded to the views put forth by New Deal liberals John Chamberlain and A. P. Lerner in *New Leader.* Chamberlain and Lerner each argued for a continued "mixed economy," a combination of economic freedom for private enterprise and state intervention to ensure the social security of the American population. Such liberal ideas, Mills argued, were archaic and abstract. Mills skewered Chamberlain's notion that economic freedom for private enterprise helped secure a democratic political system. This premise might hold true, Mills argued, under conditions of "classic democracy," in which a majority of the population were independent entrepreneurs, but it could not hold for the modern industrial world, in which the means of production were centralized in a monopolistic economy and the majority were dependent workers. "No nostalgic wish nor reference to Jefferson," Mills wrote, "will ever make shopkeepers out of employees."[65]

Echoing his dissertation's critique of Dewey, Mills argued that liberal ideas were dangerously abstract and overly formalistic because they ignored the distribution of economic and political power. Lacking insight into "political economy," Chamberlain was unable to see that the "functional outcome" of his calls for economic freedom "would most likely be the further rule of bureaucratically managed corporations."[66] Moreover, Lerner's claim that Keynesian ideas offered a blueprint for a mixed economy was misguided since "It is less a question of *the diffusion of knowledge* than of power relations and economic stakes."[67] In the modern economy, Mills contended, to call for "economic freedom" was to misunderstand contemporary trends and ultimately to justify the aims of large corporations. The economy had already become deeply politicized, and corporations had infiltrated the agencies meant to regulate them. Pointing to the existence of "dollar-a-year" men, employees who staffed government agencies during the war but were still paid salaries by their corporate employers, Mills argued, "Economic power may be in Washington to stay, but Washington is full of businessmen who also aim to stay."[68] Rather than seeking an abstract "freedom" from government, Mills contended, big business increasingly sought to dominate government in order to subsidize its own activities, using "economic freedom" as an obfuscatory rhetoric to legitimize its political engagements. Liberals naïvely failed to recognize that "'business' and 'government' are more and more becoming one . . . their 'conflict' has been institutionalized within 'government' and . . . increasingly goes on without the benefit of Congress."[69] Mills did not go so far as to label this emerging American "corporate-business State" as fascist, but he clearly had in mind the interlocking system of elites that Neumann had described in *Behemoth*. Thus Mills's "power elite" thesis was rooted in his wartime analysis.[70]

Mills called "Collectivism and the Mixed-Up Economy" "one of the strongest things I've written for socialism."[71] Clearly, the article contained an impassioned critique of a class society based on the concentration of the means of production and political power in the hands of elites, and it suggested that a program far stronger than New Deal liberalism was needed to challenge their power. Mills offered a socialist alternative, "the democratically planned utilization of the means of production," as the necessary means to update democratic ideals to a modern economy.[72] Nevertheless, Mills failed to specify exactly what a collectivist economic system might look like, or which political actors might bring it about.

Bell had bolstered his vision of the growing concentration of wealth and power in large corporations with a series of muckraking investigations for *New Leader,* and Mills was presented with a similar opportunity in early 1945. The Smaller War Plants Corporation (SWPC), established by Congress during the war, commissioned Mills to conduct a study of several American cities to compare the influences of big businesses and small businesses on community life. The purpose of the study was to convince Congress to establish a national agency to aid small businesses. Mills jumped at the opportunity to conduct the study, seeing it as a chance to do "a kind of super journalism" that would enable him to investigate the effects of a "national trend . . . toward industrial concentration, absentee ownership, [and] the dominance of giant corporations."[73] Mills secured leave from the University of Maryland and conducted the study at breakneck speed over a short period of weeks. Collating census information and conducting firsthand interviews with a variety of citizens in each location, Mills analyzed data on three cities in which small businesses predominated and three in which large corporations did. After Mills completed the fieldwork, the report, "Small Business and Civic Welfare," was written by an economist working at the SWPC, Melville Ulmer, though Mills had substantial input on the final draft.

The report concluded that "big business tends to depress while small business tends to raise the level of civic welfare."[74] Mills and Ulmer presented statistical data to demonstrate that cities dominated by small business held advantages in terms of stability, consumer choice, income gaps, health, housing, education, cultural facilities, recreation, and various other criteria. The most interesting part of the report, however, was the authors' speculative assessment of why big businesses tended to depress civic spirit. The emergence of absentee-owned corporations in a city, the report argued, decimated the "independent middle class," which had traditionally been the chief participant in civic enterprises. Members of the independent middle class had certain incentives to work in civic organizations, including both business networking opportunities and the ability to earn prestige. The corporate managers of the new middle class, however, were oriented toward pleasing their out-of-town corporate superiors, and less inclined toward civic improvement.

"Small Business and Civic Welfare" also served Mills's newfound goal: locating the sources of power in American society. In the section "Real and Apparent Power," the report described how in cities dominated by big business, small businessmen were often used as fronts for corporate power. Because they dominated the local economy, cor-

porations controlled many local political decisions: they could always
threaten the city with relocating their offices, which would devastate the
local economy. However, citing several examples gained from Mills's
interviews, the report found that corporations generally preferred to
operate not with public threats but instead more surreptitiously, behind
the scenes of local economic and political organizations. Thus willing small businessmen functioned "as the camouflaged shock troops
of the corporate officials."[75] Ultimately, the report suggested that as
the American economy became increasingly concentrated, both civic
welfare and democratic local control would suffer. "Small Business and
Civil Welfare" offered a tale of democratic decline as the independent
middle class was transformed into the dependent new middle class,
a narrative that would later constitute an important part of *White
Collar.*

THE POWERLESS PEOPLE: THE SOCIAL ROLE
OF THE INTELLECTUAL

Political conversions are generally accompanied by a rise in political
hopes; few are willing to be converted to the service of a lost cause.
Mills was an exception. If he saw himself as without illusions in terms
of recognizing the powerful interests that ran the country, he also had
little expectation of seeing his political vision realized. Mills offered
few alternatives to the trends he identified in "Collectivism and the
Mixed-Up Economy," despite his passing suggestion that labor unions
might replace the independent middle class as bastions of civic welfare. Nor were the small businesses he focused on in "Civic Welfare
and Small Business" an adequate solution for a self-styled radical who
attacked liberalism for its out-of-date solutions. Unable to locate an
agent of social change, Mills viewed the politics of truth—the critical voice of the intellectual—as a necessary yet desperate moral stand
against a world whose main drift implied his political defeat.

   Though Mills, as a new convert to the left, had little sense of personal political disappointment, it is remarkable to note how many of
his close associates during the early 1940s did have such an experience.
Hans Gerth and Franz Neumann were German socialists who had
seen a revolutionary change in German society result in the triumph
not of socialism, but of fascism. Dwight Macdonald had broken with
the two institutions that had earlier sustained his political hopes, the
Workers Party and *Partisan Review.* Daniel Bell, an early supporter

of World War II, became convinced that the war was likely to result in a monopoly state in the United States. And Mills's closest friend at Maryland, Richard Hofstadter, who had a deep commitment to left-wing causes in the 1930s (and was briefly a member of the Communist Party), found himself with "no place to go" following the Nazi-Soviet Pact, alienated from both American capitalism and any oppositional political movement.[76]

Even though Mills was a recent convert to the left, he was poised to express what Howard Brick has perceptively described as "post-progressive radicalism." The political defeats experienced by leftists beginning in the late 1930s led them to question one of the key assumptions of liberal and left-wing thought: that historical change would necessarily result in social progress. As if the rise of Stalinism in the USSR and Nazism in Germany were not enough to discourage them, American left-wing intellectuals of the 1940s detected totalitarian trends within American society as well. Unable to identify agents for social change, intellectuals on the left became introspective, questioned the proper role of the intellectual, and were ultimately able to propose their alternative only in moral, not political, terms. As Brick writes, "Unable to find a sanction of success in history . . . post-progressive radicalism felt itself trapped by a reality that appeared intractable and stagnant. . . . Its characteristic expression was intellectual estrangement—radicalism conceived as a transcendent critique rather than as 'immanent force.'"[77]

Such radicals were preoccupied with the responsibilities of the radical intellectual, an issue at the forefront of Mills's mind given his background in the sociology of knowledge and the highly intellectual nature of his political conversion. In his most important political essay of the war years, "The Powerless People," Mills envisioned the intellectual's proper role in society. Here Mills moved beyond criticizing the works of others to concentrate on elaborating his own perspective. "The Powerless People" appeared in the April 1944 issue of *politics*, a new magazine founded by Dwight Macdonald. Mills was closely involved with establishing the magazine, promoting it to his friends and gathering contributions from academics.[78] In its early issues, *politics* closely approximated Mills's stance. Its title, which Mills in fact suggested to Macdonald, embodied Mills's predilection for a hard-hitting radical analysis of the realities of political power that brooked few illusions. Several of its first articles, such as Bell's "The Coming Tragedy of Postwar Labor" and Walter Oakes's "The Permanent War Economy," confirmed Mills's sense of the dangerous wartime trends that were transforming American society. The magazine also frankly addressed the problems of the left-wing intellectual who was still interested in political analysis and social change but found himself politically homeless—the dilemma that Mills considered in "The Powerless People." In this essay, he articulated many of the arguments that would make up the core of his postwar social analysis.

In "The Powerless People," Mills issued a forthright statement of the responsibilities of intellectuals. Mills defended public engagement against those who sought "simply to understand" the world. Ideas were meant to be socially relevant: "Knowledge that is not communicated has a way of turning the mind sour, of being obscured, and finally of being forgotten."[79] Though Mills's analysis of modern social trends was sharply pessimistic, he strongly rejected the tragic sensibility, increasingly popular in intellectual circles during the 1940s, that stressed the inevitable limits of human nature.[80] "Many who not long ago read John Dewey with apparent satisfaction," Mills remarked, "have become vitally interested in such analysts of personal tragedy as Soren Kierkegaard."[81] In contrast to this newly resurgent tragic sensibility, Mills defended "the power of man's intelligence to control his destiny" in classic Enlightenment and pragmatist terms.[82]

Yet, Mills's analysis suggested that it was increasingly difficult, if not impossible, for intellectuals to play a publicly relevant role. In "Locating the Enemy" and "Collectivism and the Mixed-Up Economy," Mills described a disturbing drift toward a society dominated by a handful of powerful institutions. In "The Powerless People," he analyzed the consequences for intellectuals of such "deep-lying trends of modern social organization."[83] In one sense, the intellectual's dilemma was common to that of other modern individuals, who were all faced with a world in which they did not possess political control over their own fates. Intellectuals were simply a special category of modern men who did not "have effective control over what they are dependent upon."[84] Mills attributed the powerlessness of modern individuals to the rise of large and remote organizations controlled by elites without substantial democratic input. Yet power becoming an "impersonal monster" presented a particular difficulty for intellectuals. In a "responsible" society, intellectuals could clarify issues for public debate. In the modern world, however, intellectuals found it difficult to reach a broad public with their ideas: their connection to an audience was mediated by the corporate conglomerates that controlled the mass media. Their predicament was exemplified by the "Hollywood writer" whose "work is bent to the ends of a mass appeal to a mass market." Thus, Mills concluded, "The means of effective communication are being expropriated from the intellectual worker."[85]

To Mills, intellectuals faced a precarious catch-22. If they accepted positions of power within the governing system, they would lose their critical independence and hence their access to truth—in other words, that which made them authentic intellectuals. However, if they retained their commitment to truth, they would lose access to power and hence the ability to turn their ideas into reality. Either way, intellectuals were a "powerless people" forced to choose between dependency or irrelevance. "In the world of today," Mills gloomily observed, "the more [the intellectual's] knowledge of affairs grows, the less effective the impact of his thinking seems to become." Such a dilemma created "a personal malady . . . in the intellectual who has labored under the illusion that his thinking makes a difference," leading him to feel "politically irrelevant."[86]

Even so, Mills suggested that intellectuals were one of the few social types capable of resisting modern trends. Their resistance would have to take the form of a "politics of truth" that would debunk commonly held notions that served the interests of those in power. "Fresh perception," Mills claimed, "now involves the capacity to unmask and to smash the stereotypes of vision and intellect with which modern communications swamp us." "Social scientists," for instance, could challenge the "many illusions which uphold authority" that much of contemporary social science perpetrated.[87] According to Mills, the radical intellectual's very marginality offered him unique insight into contemporary social problems. Thus, Mills argued, "We must constantly shuttle between the understanding which is made possible by detachment and the longing and working for a politics of truth in a society that is responsible."[88] Yet, failing to provide a basis for how intellect could be responsibly brought to bear on questions of power, Mills was left with a romanticized sense of intellectual authenticity. The only person to whom the intellectual could really be true was himself: Mills concluded his essay by urging intellectuals not to be "betrayed by what is false within them."[89]

Many find "The Powerless People" a time-tested defense of the critical role of the intellectual.[90] Indeed, the essay stands as a powerful statement of the public responsibilities of those whose primary social contribution lies in formulating ideas. Yet the essay also reveals some

of the characteristic limitations of Mills's thought as an expression of
the disillusioned radicalism of the period. The sociology of knowledge
clearly shaped Mills's desire to understand "the social position" of
intellectuals.[91] Yet Mills's arguments—and in particular his unsub-
stantiated claim that the means of intellectual production had been
"expropriated" from intellectuals—lacked a sociological basis. Other
than a brief reference to the pamphleteering of Thomas Paine, Mills did
not offer any evidence that intellectuals had ever enjoyed a golden age
of unmediated influence over a receptive public. In his effort to define a
clearly radical position, Mills also drew too sharp a distinction between
intellectuals who challenge the social order and those who are co-opted
by it, as if there were not many shades of gray in between. In stressing
his great confidence in authentic intellectuals to uncover truths hidden
by the mass media, Mills failed to reconcile this moral imperative with
the deeply historicist and contextualist analysis of the social origins of
knowledge that he had developed in his early work of reflexive sociology and continued to profess. Mills began with the notion of the social
basis of ideas, but he ended with an individual imperative not to "sell
out." If Mills suggested a heroic role for the critical intellectual, it was
clearly a heroism born of desperation. Ultimately, in "The Powerless
People" Mills failed to locate himself—the radical intellectual—within
society. Adopting a position as a marginal radical allowed Mills to see
and critique society as a whole, but it also prevented him from identifying those elements of social life that had produced this critique and
could suggest possible sources of political opposition.

"The Powerless People" demonstrated a trap that Mills would continually set for himself. Having pushed his disillusioned analysis of
the realities of contemporary power relations so far as to preclude any
significant conflicts or contradictions in the social order that might
potentially result in possibilities for progressive social change, he committed intellectuals to a seemingly unachievable task. By suggesting
that at best intellectuals could avoid selling out, Mills indicated that
the politics of truth was both necessary and impossible. The disillusioned radical position offered some promise as a stance of social
analysis: even as it encouraged an exaggerated sense of the hegemony
of contemporary power relations, its deeply skeptical and critical view
of established ideas allowed it to pierce key illusions of mainstream
political rhetoric and social analysis. Yet such a stance made it impossible to fulfill Mills's demanding requirements for the proper role of the
intellectual in society.

'FROM MAX WEBER'

As previously discussed, Mills's important sociological and political shifts of the early 1940s owed a great deal to the influence of Max Weber. Mills's structural, macroscopic approach to social science and his disillusioned radicalism were both on display in *From Max Weber*, a volume that Gerth and Mills coedited. Because of its excellent selection of key essays and the stylistic grace of its translation, *From Max Weber* probably did more than any other book to introduce Americans to Weber's work. The text is still commonly assigned in undergraduate classes today. Aware that Gerth was translating Weber into English during the war, Mills suggested to Macdonald in 1944 that *politics* print a translation of Weber's "Class, Status, Party," from his unfinished *Economy and Society*.[92] Building on that success, Mills convinced Oxford University Press to publish a book of Weber translations. Though Mills played a key role in securing a publisher, Gerth was the primary intellectual force behind the volume. Gerth did the initial translations, and Mills rewrote Gerth's awkward English prose. If Mills was responsible for the graceful prose, Gerth deserves credit for translating the meaning of the original texts and selecting which writings to include. In addition, Gerth was primarily responsible for the interpretation of Weber put forth in the book's lengthy introduction and wholly responsible for the biographical section. The introduction, however, stressed themes that were distinctly Millsian. To some extent, this fact reinforces the significance of Gerth's influence on Mills. Yet a careful reading of the correspondence between Gerth and Mills suggests that Mills also made significant contributions to the introduction's key sections on Weber's political and intellectual orientations.[93]

Mills was more aware than Gerth of the contemporary sociological and political significance of their interpretation of Weber. In particular, Mills believed their translations demonstrated theoretical and political differences with the leading American translator and scholar of Weber, Talcott Parsons. Mills persuaded Gerth that their arrangement of Weber's pieces in *From Max Weber* should stress Weber's "multi-perspectivism . . . as against Parsons etc with their formalized SYS-TEMS of every goddamned thing anybody tried to do anything with."[94] Though Mills and Parsons were both part of a disciplinary trend toward the macroscopic study of total social structures, Mills, unlike Parsons, emphasized the significance of specific social and historical contexts for social action, a particularizing, historicist approach that he had developed in his earlier methodological works and continued to balance against his ambition to tackle the big questions. If Parsons valued Weber for his incomplete attempt to develop a systematic theoretical framework, Mills praised Weber for his substantive historical and comparative investigations. Mills thus resisted the postwar trend exemplified in Parsons' work toward constructing universal theoretical frameworks applicable to all societies.[95]

Mills bragged to Dwight Macdonald, "The son of a bitch [Parsons] has translated it [Weber] so as to take all the guts, the radical guts, out, whereas our translation doesn't do that."[96] In the postwar period, social thinkers like Parsons often looked to Weber to provide an alternative to Marxist social theory. In contrast to his earlier essays on fascism, Parsons in 1947 offered a relatively optimistic rendering of Weberian modernity that stressed that a society governed by impersonal, universalistic standards of rational-legal authority and bureaucratic organization was free of "rigidly fixed traditionalism" and allowed for more efficient organization, as well as equality of opportunity and equality before the law.[97] Against Parsons's idealist interpretation of Weber that emphasized Durkheimian themes and concentrated on the significance of shared values, Gerth and Mills put forth a materialist interpretation that stressed that Weber's work could "be seen as an attempt to 'round out' Marx's economic materialism by a political and military materialism."[98]

According to Gerth and Mills, Weber challenged certain of Marx's ideas while extending others. For instance, Weber undermined Marx's monocausal emphasis on economic factors. And, although he recognized the crucial importance of social class and the compulsive character of large-scale economic institutions, Weber did not see class struggle as the principal theme of modern history. As Gerth and Mills observed, for Weber, capitalism was not an irrational structure destined to be overcome by socialism, but the height of bureaucratic rationality. The future would be marked not by a transition to socialism, but by "mechanism, depersonalization, and oppressive routine."[99] Yet, like Marx, Weber took up "the question of capitalism as an epochal structure."[100] Weber expanded upon Marx's analysis of "the wage worker as being 'separated from the means of production,'" revealing this alienation to be a condition of not just proletarians, but nearly all modern men.[101] Indeed, in stressing the similarities between Marx and Weber, Gerth and Mills emphasized the significance of "alienation" over "exploitation" as a Marxist theme.

The Weber depicted in the introduction to *From Max Weber* was much like Mills during the war period: striving for a sociological understanding of total social structures while offering a despairing analysis of modern social trends. Gerth and Mills's analysis of Weber as a "political intellectual" reveals how deeply Mills identified with Weber. According to Gerth and Mills, Weber sought sociological knowledge in order to "snatch from comparative inquiries a set of rules which would serve him in his search for political orientation in the contemporary world."[102] Such sociological knowledge was "of a kind that the complexity of modern civilization requires of one who would take intelligent stands on public issues."[103] Even though Weber was the most brilliant practitioner of this sort of sociological analysis, he faced an insurmountable challenge in making his social scientific insights politically relevant. Weber was intensely interested in politics, but he "had no power and no position from which his word could tip the balance of power."[104] Weber may have been a "nostalgic liberal" rather than a disillusioned radical, but he faced the same dilemma as Mills's powerless intellectual. Weber, like Mills, refused to relinquish the conviction that "knowledge is somehow power." Yet, like Mills, he failed to offer any compelling reason for how this was so.[105] Like Mills, Weber desperately wanted to merge an "ethics of absolute ends" with an "ethics of responsibility," which would allow the intellectual to balance a moral commitment with efforts to make a political difference; yet Weber's bleak analysis of the modern world, like that of Mills, left him unable to provide a sociological basis for showing how this task could be anything other than impossibly heroic.[106]

Like "The Powerless People," the introduction to *From Max Weber* implied that intellectuals would be "powerless" if no other social groups were willing or able to incorporate their insights into a political program. But Mills's turn toward Weberian pessimism and radical disillusionment in the first half of the 1940s was premature. Mills himself seems to have realized that he overstated his case in "The Powerless People." He wrote to Robert Lynd that he had cut a final section on "third parties" that had given the piece a more "positive and affirmative note."[107] Though Mills believed that the intellectual's dilemma resulted from long-term structural trends and not simply the recent decline of the left, his analysis was very much the product of a specific historical moment of left-wing defeat. In fact, Mills soon began an involvement with the labor movement that offered him a basis for his hope that the power of intellect could be harnessed in the quest for radical social reconstruction.

CHAPTER 3

The Union of the Power and the Intellect

The Labor Movement and Bureau-Driven Social Research

In 1945 Mills moved to New York City to take a position as a research associate at Columbia University's Bureau of Applied Social Research (BASR). Eager to learn the new methods of social research pioneered by the bureau, Mills felt confident that he could make them serve his own sociological and political ends. Once in New York, Mills also began a brief but intense romance with the American labor movement, which for a short period following the war seemed to offer great promise as an agent for left-wing social change. After his bleak pessimism of the war years, the four-year period from 1945 to 1948 was one of tremendous hope and enthusiasm for Mills. As a young intellectual rapidly ascending the heights of professional sociology, he remained enthralled by the possibilities of social science. As a leftist looking for an agent of social change, he found in labor a political movement with the potential to realize his radical vision.

This period was not without its conflicts and dilemmas, and Mills did not entirely set aside his disillusioned radicalism. Still, Mills's commitment to bureau research and to the labor movement offered him a model of intellectual engagement less fraught with the impossible antinomies that he had suggested in "The Powerless People" constituted the authentic intellectual's inevitable conundrum. His position at the BASR introduced Mills to social scientific innovations he believed could broaden and extend his insights into American society. His spell as a labor intellectual led him to believe that radicals did not need to be permanently estranged from society: they could actively work for social change. At his most optimistic, Mills believed that an alliance of left-wing intellectuals and workers—a "union of the power and the intellect"—could reverse the alarming trend toward a corporate society and usher in a new age of modern American democracy.

Mills's dual commitments of this period remained important for his future intellectual development, because they offered him a model of what an engaged social scientific intellectual might accomplish if given the right professional and political opportunities. His first book, *The New Men of Power: America's Labor Leaders* (1948), based on research he conducted as head of the BASR's Labor Research Division, was motivated by his participation in the Inter-Union Institute for Labor and Democracy, an organization of left-labor intellectuals. Yet by the time he finished *The New Men of Power*, Mills was already becoming disenchanted with both bureau-driven social science and American unions. In 1947, Mills clashed with the BASR's director, Paul Lazarsfeld, over the project Mills had been hired to conduct. At roughly the same time, Mills grew concerned that labor leaders would be unable or unwilling to mobilize against an increasingly sophisti-cated corporate capitalism. *The New Men of Power* was thus marked by a deep ambivalence: though Mills drew heavily upon a statistical survey of labor leaders, he advanced a more sweeping analysis of con-temporary social change; though he continued to hold out hope for a union of power and intellect, he was doubtful that labor would prove a willing partner.

MILLS AT THE BUREAU OF APPLIED SOCIAL RESEARCH

By the end of the war, Mills had become dissatisfied with his position at the University of Maryland. The university's president and former football coach, H. C. "Curley" Byrd, had recently lowered academic standards and increased faculty workloads. Along with his historian friends Hofstadter, Friedel, and Stampp, Mills opposed Byrd's policies. As Byrd secured military contracts, the military presence on campus became stronger. Mills could hardly have been comfortable at a campus where ROTC kept a twenty-four-hour patrol outside the administration building.[1] Mills described Maryland as a "sinking ship" in a 1944 letter he wrote to Robert Merton asking for help in finding another job.[2] It did not take long for Merton to deliver. In the fall of 1944, Columbia University offered Mills a summer visiting assistant professorship in sociology that had the potential to lead to a more permanent position. To Mills, the offer was "a hell of a big break for a kid 28 years old."[3] In early 1945, Mills received another offer from Columbia: to direct a large-scale study in personal influence as a research associate at the Bureau of Applied Social Research. He hoped that accepting the BASR position might lead to a permanent position on the Columbia faculty. Mills took a leave of absence from Maryland and never returned. In early 1946, he was appointed assistant professor at Columbia College, in the undergraduate wing of the sociology department (as opposed to the department proper, located in the Graduate Faculty of Political Science). "Well, I made it," Mills wrote his parents, "as you know that['s] what Ive been working for."[4]

Columbia's Department of Sociology was one of the nation's elite. Established in 1895, the department was dominated in its first decades by Franklin Giddings, whose emphasis on statistical methods made Columbia the leading challenger to Chicago. When Giddings retired in 1928, he was replaced by Robert MacIver, a social theorist who believed that many sociological problems could not be adequately handled by quantitative methods. In 1941, the department began to take the shape that it would maintain throughout Mills's seventeen-year tenure. In a compromise over whether to hire an empirical researcher or a social theorist, the department hired one of each. Rather than continue factional struggles, however, the new hires, Paul Lazarsfeld and Robert Merton, became close collaborators. Together they remade the department in the coming decades, achieving a tighter coherence, stronger institutional basis, and greater national prominence for the Columbia sociology department than had their predecessors. In the process, they helped reshape American social science.[5]

Mills's move to Columbia initially offered great promise both for him and for Columbia sociology. For Mills, it meant a remarkably fast rise in the ranks of academe. He had achieved the sort of prominence that few reach before the age of thirty, if at all. The resources and status that such a position offered promised to support his continued work. Indeed, Mills was so excited after Lazarsfeld and Merton offered him the BASR position over dinner that he "wandered into another restaurant and ate another huge meal!"[6] For Columbia, landing a brilliant young sociologist promised to help it reach its goal of becoming the preeminent institutional center of postwar sociology. When Mills came to Columbia in 1945, sociology department head Robert Lynd wrote the university's president with an ambitious proposal to enable the department to "surpass all others." Mills was part of that plan. "We like the man," Lynd wrote in an addendum to his proposal, "and regard him as not only outstanding but sure to develop into one of the leading sociologists in the country."[7] Robert Merton's high opinion of Mills's work clearly had a great deal to do with his hiring. Merton saw Mills as part of a younger generation of sociologists who could transform the discipline in the coming years. In 1944, Merton wrote the social psychologist Kingsley Davis, "Perhaps . . . we can work out plans for a small time-bomb to be manufactured by the three of us [Merton, Mills, and Davis], and to be set under the complacent, chair-sitting rear ends of our more traditional colleagues in the field of sociology."[8] When the New School for Social Research considered Mills for a position in 1946, Merton described him as "the outstanding sociologist of his age in the country" and indicated, "I, for one, shall recommend to Columbia that it do whatever it can to keep him within our Department."[9]

Columbia would make its impact on postwar sociology primarily through the Bureau of Applied Social Research. Although the BASR had no official institutional connection to the sociology department, it functioned as its semiautonomous wing. Virtually all of the BASR directors were sociologists, and it trained many sociology graduate students in research techniques (those students in turn provided part of the labor force for research). The bureau's leaders—Lazarsfeld and Merton—were the principal figures in the sociology department by the end of the 1940s. In fact, the BASR was to a large extent Lazarsfeld's personal creation: since emigrating from Austria in 1933, he had tried to create a lasting research bureau, which he accomplished only when Columbia established a permanent institutional affiliation with the BASR in 1945.

The BASR helped establish Columbia sociology as a leading force in American social science, primarily by pioneering techniques of large-scale survey research. Other prominent research bureaus established in the 1940s included the National Opinion Research Center (at the University of Chicago) and the Survey Research Center (at the University of Michigan). Nationally, the disciplinary trend toward survey research was evident in the devotion of wartime resources to sociological studies such as the massive and widely hailed survey of American troops, overseen by Samuel Stouffer, that was published in 1949 as *The American Soldier.* Whereas social scientists had previously relied on information gathered by others, survey research allowed them to generate their own data by importing methods used in market research. The great emphasis placed on the new techniques of social research redefined the sociological discipline. It was reflected in the discipline's adoption of Lazarsfeld as one of its leaders, for Lazarsfeld had been trained as an applied psychologist and mathematician and did not identify himself as a sociologist until several years after his emigration.[10] In contrast to academic departments, research bureaus required a hierarchical structure. Bureaus employed a large number of skilled researchers who operated outside the standard university system of tenure and collegiality.[11] Research bureau hierarchies were also highly gendered. Though the BASR's top leaders were men, the majority of its staff members were women, a number of whom provided important assistance to Mills in his research. In particular, Helen Schneider did much of the statistical work for *The New Men of Power,* and Ruth Harper, whom Mills married in 1947, assisted him with both the research and writing of *White Collar* and *The Power Elite.*

The BASR was a general-purpose research bureau driven by methodological and theoretical concerns rather than by any substantive area of research. Led by Lazarsfeld, its researchers pioneered several methods of survey research, including both the panel survey, which involved reinterviewing individuals over time in order to gauge how they made decisions, and sociometric surveys, which linked individuals studied to their social networks. Although Lazarsfeld himself was often noted for his obsessive interest in research methods alone, the bureau did more than simply advance better techniques of social research. The BASR also tested theoretical insights, creating models that could be generalized and applied to several areas of research. This theoretical emphasis was partly due to the influence of Merton, who famously argued that sociologists should develop empirically verifiable "theories of the middle range" as opposed to the more abstract and sweeping theories developed by classical sociologists (and by Talcott Parsons, his former teacher).[12] Examples of such middle-range theories developed at the BASR include the self-selection of radio audiences and the two-step flow of influence.[13]

Before Mills joined the bureau, most of his sociological work had been theoretical in nature.[14] Now, he was excited to learn the new techniques of social research. He had earlier emphasized the importance of empirical inquiry to science, and now he had the opportunity to learn from bureau research. Initially, Mills felt confident that bureau techniques could be integrated into his macroscopic concern for the understanding of total social structure, yet he was forced to confront the politics of bureau research prior to taking the position. By formalizing its relationship with Columbia, the BASR received space on campus, and the university subsidized 10 percent of its operating expenses. This funding, far less than Columbia's sociologists had requested, left the bureau dependent on outside sources of income. According to one of the bureau's former directors, the university's refusal to provide a greater subsidy for the BASR meant that its formalized relationship with Columbia amounted to little more than "a license to hunt for outside support of projects." During Mills's tenure, the BASR received most of its funding from business contracts, though it also received significant funding from government entities, foundations, and other nonprofit organizations.[15]

The prospect of fulfilling research contracts for the big businesses that Mills believed were leading the United States toward an undemocratic corporate state presented an ethical dilemma, yet he may not have confronted this issue directly had it not been for Robert Lynd, who expressed to Mills serious reservations about the political direction of the BASR. A former advertising executive, seminarian, editor, and foundation official, Lynd had made his name with a trenchant community study, *Middletown*, written with his wife, Helen Merrill Lynd. Columbia hired him in 1931 on the basis of this study, despite his lack of formal sociological training. A powerful presence at Columbia and in the discipline yet always something of an outsider, Lynd offered an unusual perspective. He strongly supported empirical and statistical research and often criticized abstract sociological theory, but he was also a political radical who believed that social scientists had a moral obligation to ensure that their research served progressive social ends, a position that he expounded in his 1939 classic, *Knowledge for What?*[16] Mills met Lynd during World War II through their shared left-wing politics and growing fears about the dominance of big business in American politics. Lynd greatly admired Mills's early political writings. "There are too damned few people with your slant on things," Lynd wrote him in 1943, adding, "I want to know you."[17] Lynd had offered critical support to Lazarsfeld during his early years in the country, and he continued to believe in the promise of the newer research techniques. However, he was seriously concerned about the BASR's increasing reliance on commercial funding. Lynd wrote Mills a five-page letter that offered his blessing to accept the position, but also voiced recriminations against Lazarsfeld, Merton, and the BASR for "selling out" and intimated that Mills's efforts might be better served by continuing to direct his efforts against "business fascism."[18] Lynd's letter offered Mills some insight into the bitter departmental conflicts over the bureau's increasing dominance of Columbia sociology in the years to come. Even as the BASR helped Columbia achieve growing prominence in the sociological profession, it alienated many sociologists in the department who were not identified with the new research techniques.[19] In less than three years, Mills himself would be involved in one such major dispute.

In 1945, however, Mills saw no insurmountable conflict between bureau research and radical politics. He took the job, though he was wary of disputes among Columbia sociologists. "I'm very eager for the research experience," he wrote Gerth, "but I dont want to get balled up in academic politics."[20] Mills was unconcerned that a position at the bureau might compromise his radical politics. He simply believed that because he was "constitutionally unable to sell out by being a big busin[ess] flunkey," he would maintain his radical stance even while doing commercial research. Moreover, he felt that he could mediate between the bureau and the department, since he expected to maintain close relations with Merton, Lazarsfeld, and Lynd.[21] He reassured himself that Merton and Lazarsfeld knew what they were doing by hiring him: "They know two things about me: one, that I have a reputation for being absolutely honest in radical opinions, that nobody thinks I would ever 'sell out.' Two: they know that Lynd has that attitude towards me very much and that furthermore Lynd [sic] likes me a lot. By getting me . . . they bring the office [i.e., BASR] and the department of sociology closer together. . . . It thus seems one of those rare human occas[ions] where everybody working for his own self and organizational interests coincides with one individual's (mine) self interest."[22] For his first several months at the bureau, Mills got along well with Merton and Lazarsfeld. As Mills reported to Gerth, "[Merton] and I are quite friendly and have worked out a nice adjustment. . . . We have worked out a sorta balanced deference system that is working very well! Paul L is in part responsible for it, for he is really quite a guy and we both are fond of him, and learn much from him."[23]

No doubt there was a strong element of rationalization in Mills's statements, which allowed him to satisfy any doubts about taking such a prestigious position. Nevertheless, Mills genuinely believed in the value of the newer social research techniques when put to proper ends. He was irritated by left-wing social scientists who believed that such empirical techniques held an inherently conservative bias. As he wrote in a reader's report for Oxford University Press of Frankfurt School theorist Max Horkheimer's *Twilight of Reason*, "For God's sake get the author to cut out these adolescent barbs at 'statistics,' 'questionnaires,' and 'polls.' . . . In trying to understand the world, we may use any method we can lay our hands on."[24] Since Mills believed that the newer techniques of social research contained no inherent value bias, he believed he could use them to criticize—not uphold—the prevailing American social order. As Mills explained to his radical friends, he hoped that a post as research associate at the bureau would allow him the resources and training to pursue his planned investigations of social class and status in the United States. Mills informed Dwight Macdonald that the position "gives me the means of big research staff with assistants etc., also from what I understand a good deal of autonomy in what I'll research on and how I'll do it."[25] As he wrote Daniel Bell, he could not "see how in the hell any such study as they have in mind can possible be properly designed without finding out a great deal about class and status solidarity." He concluded that there were "legitimate points of coincidence between commercial and radical research."[26]

Indeed, the BASR's commercial work, in its concern for market segmentation, did reveal insights into social stratification. For instance, Lazarsfeld's pioneering study in radio research concluded that audiences for radio programs self-selected largely on the basis of class.[27] Interestingly enough, Mills's interests were similar to those that Lazarsfeld held in his earlier days in Austria. A socialist who had been raised in the household of the prominent Marxist theorist Rudolf Hilferding, Lazarsfeld initially wanted to study voting behavior. He was unable to pursue that research in Austria for political reasons, so he turned instead to commercial research, believing in the "methodological equivalence of socialist voting and the buying of soap."[28] By the 1940s, Lazarsfeld was no longer interested in integrating Marxism into his research. Thus, although Mills would soon discover sharp differences with Lazarsfeld, in a sense he was merely attempting to complete the task Lazarsfeld began: applying techniques perfected in conducting commercial research to construct a left-wing understanding of society.

THE LABOR LEADER AND THE RESEARCH INTELLECTUAL

Mills applied bureau resources and methods to left-wing ends most successfully when he established the Labor Research Division (LRD) of the BASR in early 1946. Mills convinced Lazarsfeld to create the

division by persuading him that it could bring in more outside contracts, and perhaps by playing on Lazarsfeld's lingering prolabor
sympathies.[29] In a 1946 article, "The Politics of Skill," Mills, without
specifically mentioning the LRD, explained his rationale for creating
the division. Research techniques such as those developed at the BASR,
he wrote, were being "monopolized" by "a handful of businessmen."
Yet, he claimed, many of "the new research people" were "disaffected
and morally unhappy" about having to "sell their minds to people they
don't like for purposes they don't feel at one with." The solution was
to put these "new skills and visions" to use for the labor movement.
Bureau research did not need to remain commercial. It just needed to
serve different clients.[30]

Mills's identification of labor unions as institutions worthy of
support was a response to the reinvigoration of the labor movement
immediately following World War II. Mills had suggested in his wartime writings that marginalized intellectuals were one of the only possible forces of opposition to the emerging postwar order dominated
by economic, political, and military elites. Labor was another. "The
chief social power upon which a genuine democracy can rest today
is labor," he concluded in 1943.[31] During the war, Mills defended the
right of the United Mine Workers under John L. Lewis to strike, even
though the strike outraged many by threatening the war effort.[32] While
Mills accepted the left-wing orthodoxy that only a broadly based labor
movement able to form its own political organization could challenge
the increasing power of big business, he had little hope that labor could
play such a role. Even as Mills accepted the necessity of a labor party,
he predicted that "it won't come into being at all in the foreseeable
future."[33]

Mills's pessimism about labor as an agency of social change reflected
the fact that unions had suppressed their militancy during the war.
The heady organizing drives of the upstart Congress of Industrial
Organizations (CIO) during the 1930s gave way to a stifling wartime
no-strike pledge. In contrast, the years immediately following World
War II offered great promise for those leftists who hoped for labor-
based social change. Never before and never since have a greater percentage of American workers belonged to unions. Throughout the war,
labor's rank and file demonstrated its militancy in a series of wildcat
strikes. When the CIO put an end to its no-strike pledge after the war's
conclusion, many labor leaders were quick to exploit that militancy.
The postwar strike wave of 1945–1946 constituted the most massive

work stoppage in American history. In the immediate postwar period, many labor leaders and their labor-liberal supporters were drawn to social-democratic ideas. Prominent figures within labor's orbit pondered the prospect of a labor party, speculating that the CIO's Political Action Committee would either transform the Democratic Party into a labor party or provide the nucleus for a third party. The CIO's Operation Dixie organizing campaign in the South attempted to break the region's reactionary hold over national politics. Given the broad social-democratic agenda of ambitious union leaders and signs of militancy in the rank and file, labor's progressive supporters had good reason to expect that unions would play a pivotal role in shaping the postwar political order.[34] The ability of labor to attract intellectuals like Mills to its cause was one indication of its postwar potential as a social movement. Although unions have always employed the services of a number of staff intellectuals, other intellectuals have been drawn to labor only when it has promised a wider political transformation that could utilize and advance their social critique. For a brief period, Mills became a veritable labor intellectual, heavily engaged with labor's cause and deeply drawn to labor's promise. Indeed, in 1946 and 1947, Mills's concern with labor took priority over other projects he had already undertaken.[35]

Mills's newfound commitment to labor was sustained through his involvement with the Inter-Union Institute for Labor and Democracy (IUI). The institute's leader was the venerable labor journalist J. B. S. Hardman, whom Mills described as "a wonderful old man; Russian socialist about 64. I've learned a lot by association with him. He's a type I've not known too well before."[36] Born in St. Petersburg in 1882, Hardman was exiled from Russia for his involvement in the 1905 Russian Revolution. Prior to establishing the IUI, from 1925 to 1944, Hardman edited *The Advance,* the official organ of the Amalgamated Clothing Workers of America. Though Hardman played a pivotal role in shaping Mills's thinking on labor, his politics were more moderate than those of the anti-Stalinist intellectual circles that Mills had recently entered. Hardman had a radical past, but by the 1940s his position was closer to the social-democratic thinking that flourished in labor and liberal circles just after World War II. Hardman believed that a politicized labor movement had a real opportunity to push the United States in the direction that European nations were headed. He advocated a left-Keynesian stance that included centralized economic planning to ensure full employment, and he supported corporatist institutions like the wartime War Labor Board and Office of Price Administration, whose tripartite structures solicited input on economic planning from business, labor, and the public.[37] Though Mills advanced a more radical program for labor, he and Hardman agreed on the need for a labor movement more intellectually aware of its direction and more willing to play a determining role in American politics. Mills would dedicate *The New Men of Power* to Hardman, writing, "He will not be in agreement with many of the conclusions, but without his aid I should not have reached them."[38]

Hardman's institute was a product of intellectuals' new enthusiasm for labor in the postwar environment. In August 1945 the IUI began publishing *Labor and Nation,* a magazine that put intellectual analysis in the service of the labor movement. Mills began attending IUI meetings in late 1945 and became a contributing editor to the magazine in April 1946. One of the main goals of *Labor and Nation* was bringing labor leaders and intellectuals together to create a more educated and nationally aware labor leadership. The magazine's editors also hoped to foster a group of dedicated intellectuals "in the service of labor," as the title of an IUI-planned collection of essays put it. The IUI was an inclusive forum where men of different shades of the left (Communists excluded) could discuss the state of the labor movement. *Labor and Nation* aimed to "air differences" and "clarify thinking."[39]

Because the magazine solicited many perspectives, its contributors were an eclectic group. Labor leaders and politicians such as David Dubinsky, William Green, William Leiserson, Philip Murray, Walter Reuther, and Henry Wallace contributed pieces in 1946. The heart of *Labor and Nation,* however, was a group of staff intellectuals who typically served in their respective union's education, research, or economics department, and who were represented on the editorial board by such men as Solomon Barkin and Broadus Mitchell. The group of contributors was rounded out by a number of left-wing New York City academics and intellectuals, including Henry David, Waldo Frank, Eli Ginzburg, Nathan Glazer, Robert Lynd, and Ben Seligman. Less interested in the nuts and bolts of daily union politics, the independent intellectuals of the IUI tended to offer a broader and more militant perspective. Often more radical than other contributors, they exhorted labor leaders to play a more active role in leftist politics, as did Robert Lynd, the chair of the *Labor and Nation* editorial advisory board, in an early issue of the magazine.[40]

Mills was on the radical side of the IUI milieu and not entirely comfortable with the more moderate labor-liberal politics of some of its members. However, the IUI offered him a stance other than the estrangement and marginality he had suggested was the intellectual's fate in "The Powerless People." Mills viewed the IUI as a "Fabian-like" organization in which union officials and thinkers could work together "for the benefit of working people." He predicted that an alliance with labor would give social scientific intellectuals like himself a new sense of purpose: "What some of them really want is to connect their skill and intelligence to a movement in which they can believe; they are ready to give a lot of energy to an organization that would harness these skills in the service of the left. And the left, to most of them, means labor."[41] For Mills, the point was not just to serve labor but to influence its direction. In assuming that the presence of intellectuals in the labor movement would move it in a more politically radical direction, Mills borrowed on a strong tradition of thought about labor. Influential University of Wisconsin labor economist Selig Perlman, for example, with whom Mills had taken classes while a graduate student, attributed the existence of labor radicalism to the influence of intellectuals. Perlman famously attacked the "onrush of overpowering social mysticism" that leftist intellectuals felt when imagining labor's potential in society.[42] Reacting against the job-conscious unionism supported by Perlman, Mills and others at the IUI thought the influence of intellectuals essential in helping labor play a broad political role.

How, exactly, were intellectuals to influence the course of the labor movement? Mills grappled with this question at the 1946 IUI roundtable, "The Professional Intellectual in the Labor Movement," and published a revised version of his contribution as "What Research Can Do for Labor" in the June–July 1946 issue of *Labor and Nation*. Mills argued that the independent intellectual played a critical role in uniting a collection of labor unions into a progressive labor movement: "The free-lance intellectual is often the political gadfly of the trade union leader. He generalizes the economic fight between workman and employer in a given trade or industry into a larger and broader battle, and he explicitly takes up the political aspect that this purely economic struggle sooner or later always comes to have."[43] However, Mills had trouble explaining why labor leaders would listen to intellectuals. Because he felt that the practical experience of individual unions could no longer be the basis for a long-term strategy, Mills argued that the labor leader would eventually have to "lean on the intellectual" if he wanted to "be in the know about the big scene."[44]

But, as Mills was acutely aware, the intellectual could not expect to influence labor leaders through the "sheer magic of his speech."[45] Unlike Leninist third-party organizers, the freelance intellectual had no power base from which to influence the decisions of labor leaders. Thus, Mills indicated some concrete goals that the freelance intellectual could help the labor leader achieve in the areas of interunion unity, public relations, and organizing. Mills argued that research could contribute to labor unity by trying "to orient each to what other labor unions are doing at any particular time."[46] In addition, research could help labor's public image. Since so much of the public's information was biased against labor, objective research could disprove commonly held misconceptions about unions. Research, for instance, could dispel the notion that most labor leaders were foreign-born, as Mills had demonstrated in his "The Trade Union Leader: A Collective Portrait." Finally, intellectuals could help with labor organizing by using market research techniques to survey the potential "market" for union membership, which could help organizers develop effective strategies for the massive organizing drive in the South, Operation Dixie, and for organizing white-collar workers.[47]

Mills offered convincing reasons why labor leaders should draw on the work of research intellectuals who had mastered the "newer social science techniques."[48] Yet how would such a researcher become a "political gadfly" for the labor movement? The business historian William Miller wondered why his friend Mills did not use the term "technician" rather than "intellectual." "Why not," Miller asked, "say the unions need quantitative and statistical sociologists and tell them what they can do, without confusing the problem by using old-fashioned words like 'intellectual'?"[49] But Mills insisted that only an intellectual who had not only mastered specific research techniques but also thought in terms of major goals could truly aid labor leaders in their "political and economic fight."[50] Mills's hoped that by winning the confidence of labor leaders through performing concrete tasks, the intellectual could later advise them on "over-all plans and very big strategy." Even so, "What Research Can Do for Labor" implied a role for the intellectual that was necessarily subordinate to that of the trade union leader. As Mills wrote in the first draft of the essay, the intellectual "ought to recognize that the *kind* of thing I've talked about here is about all he *can* do. . . . And if he is truly dissatisfied doing that, then he ought either to forget about the whole labor thing, or he ought to give up the advantages of being unattached."[51] The research

goals that Mills laid out were modest for one who had turned to labor
to counteract the emergence of an undemocratic corporate-dominated
society. Nevertheless, Mills's willingness to commit himself to these
relatively mundane tasks in the service of labor showed how much he
now identified his own goals with those of the labor movement.

In 1946, Mills set out to demonstrate what research could do for
labor. In the spring of that year, he was appointed head of the BASR's
newly created Labor Research Division. The LRD was only a partial
success. Mills failed to obtain from labor unions the financial commitment required to establish the division as a permanent arm of the
BASR. He also failed to secure the funds needed to complete a planned
comprehensive survey of the left, which would have determined "the
socialist or radical potential in the United States" by surveying unions
and other left-wing organizations.[52] Yet Mills did rely on the LRD to
support his own extensive work on labor over a period of approximately two years. In 1944, while still at Maryland, Mills conducted
a survey of labor leaders. The resources of the BASR allowed him to
complete a far more extensive survey. In May of 1946, Mills and a team
of researchers sent out the first questionnaires to a number of AFL and
CIO leaders. This survey would provide the quantitative data for *The
New Men of Power.*

Mills's work with the LRD was closely tied to his involvement with
the IUI. As early as November 1945, Hardman and Mills discussed
conducting a series of polls on various labor issues, and the IUI sup-
plied a sizable portion of the funding for the BASR survey of labor
leaders. Beginning with the November–December 1946 issue of *Labor
and Nation,* Mills and his research associates at the BASR wrote a
regular column, "What the People Think," designed to analyze the
accuracy and significance of labor polls and to present some of the
survey's findings.[53] Research tasks that the LRD performed were
fairly minor in impact, yet Mills found his work in the service of labor
exhilarating: when a friend asked when he might drop by the bureau
for a visit, Mills replied that it was best to send him a note in advance
because "sometimes at night or day I'm out with the proletariat."[54]
Performing concrete tasks for a movement dedicated to social change
proved an antidote to the corrosive pessimism evident in Mills's wartime writings. Still, Mills had not entirely abandoned his disillusioned
radicalism from the war years, sometimes portraying his identification
with labor as an individual existential choice rather than a contribution to a social movement with a chance for power. At one point he

ruminated, "Well, I am one of those who have decided to throw in with the-little-groups-that-cannot-win. If you think about it, the big groups never win either. . . . It is only a question of where one decides to keep placing one's weight."[55]

Though Mills's newfound embrace of labor after the war offered him new allies and new hope, it also led him to an important break with Dwight Macdonald and *politics*. One of the reasons that Macdonald founded *politics* in 1944 was that he saw a new potential in labor, but his expectation was quickly disappointed. The former Trotskyist dismissed the postwar strike wave as exciting only to those "Old Believers in the class struggle doctrine."[56] In his seminal "The Root Is Man," part of the *politics* "New Roads" series, Macdonald concluded that the "modern labor union" was just another "bureaucratized mass-organization which simply extends the conventional patterns of society into the working class."[57] Macdonald's rejection of the traditional agency of the left was part of his larger reconceptualization of radical politics. He placed increased emphasis on individual freedom, decentralization, and moral protest, and sought to "reduce political action to a modest, unpretentious, personal level."[58] Thus, *politics* articulated a new radicalism taking hold among certain American and European intellectuals, one that embraced pacifist and anarchist ideas and envisioned, in the words of historian Gregory Sumner, "a decentered, pluralistic order founded on the dignity and moral autonomy of individuals."[59]

Mills remained a peripheral part of the *politics* circle, even after Macdonald renounced organized labor. Yet Mills challenged Macdonald's notion that individual moral protest could serve as an adequate substitute for traditional political action. To Mills, politics remained above all an institutional struggle for economic and political power. While Mills called "The Root Is Man" a "splendid piece," he wrote Macdonald that it faltered "when you come to political action. Out of this mountain there comes not a mouse but a squeak of a mouse."[60] In promoting labor as the necessary agent of radical political change, Mills found himself in agreement with Marxist critics of Macdonald's "New Roads" series, such as Lewis Coser and Irving Howe.[61] Mills felt that by displaying a lack of interest in labor struggles, *politics* was abandoning its original mission. As he wrote Macdonald, "Listen, I'm getting a lot of kicks from a lot of people about *politics*[:] all this weird philosophic nonsense instead of hard hitting political analysis . . . why not more analysis of US labor business squabbles they are getting interesting as hell just now."[62] Moreover, Mills dismissed

Macdonald's arguments about the inherent amorality of science. To Gerth, Mills expressed disgust with the direction Macdonald and *politics* were taking: "You are right about Macdonald: he now seriously considers in conversation whether to be 'against science.' He goes sorta 'humanist' and very moral and hence more 'cult like' all the time. Hell, in the end we'll have to start up another magazine!"[63]

THE DECATUR STUDY

One of the ways Macdonald disappointed Mills was by failing to recognize the essential contributions of social science to the modern world. In the coming years, Mills told him, social science would become "central to more general and more moral reflection."[64] Though Mills undoubtedly referred here to the sort of theoretical understanding of the modern world made possible by the macroscopic study of total societies, he also meant the detailed empirical work characteristic of large-scale bureau-driven research. Mills was hired by the BASR to conduct a massive study of the effects of personal influence on individual decision making in Decatur, Illinois, in the summer of 1945. The Decatur study initially appealed to Mills because it provided an opportunity to learn the newer research techniques and gather information useful in his understanding of American social stratification. However, it ultimately led to a protracted dispute with BASR director Paul Lazarsfeld and the Columbia Department of Sociology. This conflict initiated the long process by which Mills's path diverged from that of professional sociology. The book based on the study, *Personal Influence* (1955), was a foundational text for postwar media studies, but by the time it was published, Mills had long since been taken off the project. Lazarsfeld had found in Elihu Katz another coauthor for a text that Todd Gitlin has argued "can be read as the founding document of an entire field of inquiry."[65]

The Decatur study was designed to test the theory of the "two-step flow of communication," which had been developed in *The People's Choice,* an earlier BASR study based on voting in the 1940 election. The two-step theory held that influence resulted from the flow of ideas from the mass media to "opinion leaders" who persuaded others in their primary groups. *The People's Choice* concluded that other people significantly influenced an individual's voting intentions and hence suggested that previous scholarship had overestimated the direct influence of the mass media.[66] For the Decatur study, Mills and a team of researchers selected fourteen representative tracts in the city and attempted to interview the woman in every seventh house about her recent decisions in the areas of fashion, household consumer purchases, movie attendance, and current events. This pool of women was interviewed twice—once in June and again in August—to determine if they had made any important changes to their decisions during that time. Meanwhile, Mills and his team employed a new method of "snowball sampling" to more precisely study the interpersonal flow of influence by interviewing all those whom the initial respondents listed as having influenced their decision making. The study could thus trace the flow of personal influence between individuals and offer data on which characteristics were typical of the opinion leader and the opinion follower. In total, nearly three thousand interviews were conducted for the project.[67]

Gathering the data required painstaking efforts by Mills and his team, yet Mills was energized by the work, particularly when he examined the path of political influence. "The swift pace of events[:] atomic bomb, Russia coming in, surrender of japan etc have caught me beautifully," he wrote in August, "since I am running repeat interviews. . . . I can catch the impact of these events in the flow of changing opinion."[68] Early on, however, Mills felt that the drive to collect such a large amount of quantifiable data sacrificed a more qualitative understanding of the social phenomena he was interested in, such as class stratification. As he explained to Gerth, he would prefer to do "100 really intensive, five hour interviews, of a careful sample, rather than 3000 30 minute interviews."[69] He wrote his publisher that he hoped to conduct fifty intensive interviews in order to "build up a series of *images* of stratification held on the diff. levels of the city" and "tie in the mass statistics . . . with a qualitative understanding of how people make up their minds."[70] In fact, Mills did conduct forty-five "open-ended" interviews in Decatur.[71]

Though Mills probably acted on his own authority in supplementing the study's original design with more qualitative fieldwork, it was not until the data was gathered and tabulated that problems arose. The first challenge that Mills faced was presented by the study's sponsor, Macfadden Publications. As the publisher of *True Story,* a magazine aimed at a working-class audience, Macfadden was attracted to the two-step model of influence because it suggested that "opinion leaders" could be found among all social and economic categories, not only among the wealthiest and most highly educated. Macfadden thus sought a theory—verified by social scientific experts—that could persuade companies to advertise in their publication. A slide show created by Macfadden drew on the scientific authority of the bureau (suggested by numerous pictures of "Dr. Mills" talking to his staff) to argue that "Mrs. Wageworker" could be just as influential in convincing community members what to wear, buy, or watch as "Mrs. Tophat."[72] Though Mills knew the study would have commercial applications, he was troubled by the ideological valence of the slide show, which concluded, "Today, mass production and mass consumption loom as the salvation of the American Way. . . . We must sell things—but also ideas—American ideas; and get those ideas spread faster and more effectively than before! If this report makes any more effective selling, and idea spreading, however small, it will have fulfilled the aims of its sponsor."[73] Mills wrote to Herbert Drake of Macfadden to object diplomatically to the implicit association of this political opinion with the Bureau of Applied Social Research.[74]

Mills found Lazarsfeld's demands for a discussion draft of the Decatur study more difficult to meet. In his report, Mills first sought to integrate a leftist consideration for the distribution of political power with a commercially funded project designed to help sell magazine advertisements. Second, he tried to develop his interest in hierarchical social stratification while advancing the bureau's "two-step theory of communication," which emphasized horizontal interpersonal influence. Third, Mills attempted to reconcile his macroscopic concern with social structure with a theory of individual decision making. Finally, he aimed to combine his qualitative understanding of the nature of American society with the bureau's rigorous quantitative techniques. Mills's attempt to integrate his own intellectual concerns with the methodological and practical requirements of Lazarsfeldian bureau research was highly ambitious, and probably doomed to fail. Yet it is important to understand that Mills did not reject bureau techniques outright, but instead sought to build upon them. In doing so, he reimagined what large-scale, quantitatively based bureau research could yield.

In a 1946 talk, Mills laid out a method of interpreting the Decatur data that promised to combine "macroscopic" and "microscopic" approaches. Mills's idiosyncratic definition of "macroscopic" referred not so much to a concern with large-scale units, but to a basic concern with locating hierarchies of power: the "macroscopic" approach determined a "chain of leaders" in order to "grasp the power and influence structure." Mills's model of macroscopic research was Robert and

Helen Lynd's *Middletown* studies. In *Middletown* and *Middletown in Transition,* the Lynds employed an ethnographic approach to investigate the power structure of Muncie, Indiana. They determined that the town was sharply divided between a working class and a business class, and they eventually concluded that a single family controlled the town.[75] Mills suggested that incorporating a concern with hierarchies of social power could improve upon the methods previously developed at the BASR. Mills noted that one drawback of the Decatur study's precursor, *The People's Choice,* was that "the study is so little structural that there is no mention, either in the design or in the interpretation, of the system of power in this community, or the organization of political parties." Mills found the Decatur study promising because its technique of snowball sampling could build "a bridge between macroscopic and microscopic conceptions of research." By tracing the flow of influence from one individual to another, researchers could learn not only about the process of influence, but also about hierarchies of power, since opinion leader and opinion follower "stand typically in the relation of leader and led."[76]

Mills's integration of empirical and theoretical concerns was a goal shared by the bureau's other researcher with a theoretical background, Robert Merton. However, Mills's desire to determine the structure of power, his belief in the decisive power of large-scale institutions, and his emphasis on the hierarchical nature of political influence required significant revisions to the standard BASR approach. Sometime in early 1947, a serious conflict between Mills and Lazarsfeld arose over the Decatur study.[77] The dispute centered around three basic issues—intellectual autonomy, social scientific methodology, and political ideology—all of which were central to the subsequent development of Mills and of American social science.[78]

When Mills accepted the position at the BASR, he assumed that he would be an autonomous researcher; indeed, he thought he would be a near equal with Lazarsfeld, writing Gerth when he took the job that he, Lazarsfeld, and Merton were "supposed to be the logicians and theoreticians: the idea people."[79] Mills did, in fact, have a significant degree of freedom to pursue his own interests in those projects he instigated, such as the LRD. In the Decatur study, however, Mills's autonomy was restricted by his assignment to develop Lazarsfeld's pet theory, the two-step flow of influence, which had been developed in earlier studies and which the bureau continued to refine in later years. Mills's attempt to integrate his own concerns with the original aims of the study irritated

Lazarsfeld. In Lazarsfeld's view, the study's true author was the BASR itself as a corporate research entity, with Lazarsfeld as its head and Mills as its employee. Mills, however, perceived himself as the ultimate author of the Decatur study and felt it should express his individual perspective. He expected to publish the report under his own name with a commercial publisher.[80]

This conflict was particularly intense because Mills conceived of intellectual independence as a liberating force in a repressive social world in need of radical change. As we have seen in previous chapters, there was little that Mills cherished so much as his own autonomy. He was never able to become the "institution man" or "managerial scholar" that Lazarsfeld described himself as being.[81] It was perhaps inevitable that Mills would rebel against the hierarchical and bureaucratic nature of the modern research bureau, in which all work was subject to the supervision of the bureau's director. Yet Mills's conflict with Lazarsfeld over the control of his own work, while particularly intense, was hardly unique. Even Lazarsfeld's students complained that instead of allowing them to develop their own ideas, Lazarsfeld manipulated them to work as "extensions of himself."[82] Indeed, Lazarsfeld asked no less than five sociologists (including Mills) to write the Decatur report and found them all wanting, until he was finally satisfied with the performance of Elihu Katz.[83]

Mills's conflict with Lazarsfeld also involved contrasting social scientific methodologies. It would be misleading, however, to describe their conflict as one between macroscopic and microscopic approaches to social science. Mills was interested in using microscopic techniques such as those utilized in the Decatur study to answer large-scale theoretical questions about the nature of modern society, and Lazarsfeld's approach was *not* microscopic in the sense that community studies such as those conducted by the Chicago School had been. Because Lazarsfeld's theory of decision making focused on the individual rather than the community, his approach was psychological rather than sociological, or, as Mills would later assert in *The Sociological Imagination,* that of an abstracted empiricist. As we have seen, Mills took a considerable interest in bureau methods and attempted to incorporate them into his own approach. Nevertheless, Lazarsfeld did not share Mills's quest for a theory with which to understand large-scale societies and modern social trends, believing instead that such theories could not be empirically proved, at least not until after decades of further research. Mills sought the best possible answers to big questions of pressing social importance, whereas Lazarsfeld pursued only those questions that could be adequately answered with what he considered the most rigorous techniques available. At times, Lazarsfeld seemed more interested in the refinement of social scientific techniques than in the content, relevance, or impact of social scientific work. One of Lazarsfeld's associates recalled, "Paul was more delighted in having a clever methodological table come out of the Holerith machine . . . and whether it had major substantive importance was second to that."[84]

Fundamentally, what was at stake in the conflict between Lazarsfeld and Mills was the question of the limits of social science. Influenced by pragmatism and classic German sociologists such as Mannheim and Weber, Mills had been trained to believe firmly in the ability of social science to enlighten public discussion and to help one understand the modern social world. If social science were unable to do these things, then it was a trivial pursuit at best. Mills clashed with Lazarsfeld not because Mills was more of a social critic than a social scientist, but rather because Mills had a far more ambitious sense of the purpose of social science than did Lazarsfeld. Mills later remembered Lazarsfeld in these terms: "I have never known a more dogmatic man. I suppose because he wasn't dogmatic about any set of beliefs but about the limits of reason itself."[85]

Finally, the Decatur study conflict involved politics. In part, the question revolved around the proper political role of the social scientist. Mills believed that political values were unavoidably implicated in social science and that they should be stated explicitly. Though Lazarsfeld maintained some sympathy for left-wing causes, he professed the value neutrality of social scientific work and insisted upon a strict separation of the intellectual's scholarly and political roles. Yet the differing interpretations of the Decatur data offered by Mills and Lazarsfeld had clear political ramifications. By interpreting the Decatur data—and synthesizing his belief that the United States was in part an elite-dominated mass society with the insights into interpersonal influence suggested by Lazarsfeld's research—Mills developed a more nuanced portrait of American society than he had in his early 1940s political analysis. Mills's work on the Decatur report helped temper his tendency—evident both in the early 1940s and later—to overemphasize the hegemonic power of repressive large-scale institutions in American society. In contrast to his stark depiction of politically apathetic Americans in *White Collar*, Mills's interpretation of the Decatur data suggested a more open and vibrant American public sphere: "a

complex, informal net-work of persons and small groups interchang-
ing, on all occupational and class levels, opinions and information,
and variously exposed to the different types of mass media and their
varying content."[86] Mills even applied the notion of interpersonal
influence by opinion leaders to suggest possible sources of opposition
within American society by indicating that Americans had the capacity
to challenge the messages they received from the mass media. Opinion
leaders, he concluded, "can and do *reject* what the mass media contain;
they can and do *refract* it, as well as *pass it on.*"[87]

While Mills adopted elements of Lazarsfeld's two-step model of
influence, he continued to stress the significant influence of elites who
controlled the mass media and the disproportionate influence that
upper-class opinion leaders exerted in the political realm. A committed radical, Mills could not accept the unstated ideological content of
Lazarsfeld's two-step model of influence. By emphasizing the importance of horizontal personal influence, Lazarsfeld's middle-range
theory suggested that the United States was not a repressive hierarchy,
but a relatively democratic society operating with the consent of its
population. By equating political decisions with marketing decisions,
Lazarsfeld implicitly advanced a consumerist version of democracy
(explicitly espoused by the study's sponsor) that was at odds with the
participatory democracy that Mills advocated in *The New Men of
Power* and later works. Limited to the study of personal interaction,
Personal Influence avoided asking questions about institutional structures of concentrated economic power (as in the corporate-controlled
mass media)—the very sorts of questions that Mills believed were most
important.

Because Mills failed to complete the report to Lazarsfeld's satisfaction, the sociology department delayed his promotion to associate
professor. In 1947, the department wrote him a letter explaining that,
although its members maintained a faith in Mills's potential, they were
disappointed by his failure to fulfill his research responsibilities. The
dispute strained Mills's relationship with Robert Merton.[88] It took several years for this controversy to reach a final resolution, and hence
Mills's disassociation from professional sociology was a slow process.
In 1947, Mills and Lazarsfeld arranged a compromise: Lazarsfeld took
responsibility for writing the initial Decatur draft while Mills completed a new report, *The Puerto Rican Journey,* in order to earn money
for the BASR.[89] Nevertheless, Mills was quickly becoming disenchanted
with the methods of bureau research.

The Decatur conflict initiated Mills's marginalization from Columbia sociology, and indeed from the discipline as a whole. The resulting rift reflected a narrowing of concerns and perspectives within the sociological profession. Although bureau-driven research alone would never have offered answers to the ambitious questions Mills asked, his rejection of bureau research had some unfortunate results, as his depiction of American society became more strident and less empirical. Mills had never been a mainstream sociologist, but he had developed many of his distinctive insights in creative tension with disciplinary work. In the wake of Decatur dispute, Mills increasingly came to see professional sociology as confining and arbitrary—something not to be built upon, but to be abandoned altogether. He began to see his own work as an alternative sociology that lived up to the promise of social science upon which most academic social scientists had defaulted.

THE NEW MEN OF POWER

Despite his conflict with Lazarsfeld, Mills continued to hope that his other BASR research activities would aid the cause of labor. In the summer of 1947, Mills wrote Macdonald that he had finished a "pretty good draft" of a book on labor leaders that he completed in late 1947 and early 1948.[90] *The New Men of Power: America's Labor Leaders* alternated between the presentation of empirical data based on the BASR survey of labor leaders and broad political analysis of labor's position in American society. Marked by ambivalence, Mills's first book offered both a despairing analysis of American labor leaders and a radical program resting on a union of labor power and left-wing intellect. In *The New Men of Power*, as the postwar confrontation between business and labor came to a head, Mills posed a stark alternative for labor and American democracy: either unions would follow the "main drift" planned by sophisticated conservatives or they would serve as the vanguard for a democratic socialist alternative.

Mills's dissatisfaction with bureau-driven social science increased as the conflict over the Decatur study brewed. A 1947 installment of Mills's *Labor and Nation* column indicated his shift away from using bureau techniques toward asking labor's big questions of urgent political significance. In a column designed to evaluate statistics on labor, "What the People Think," Mills offered a qualitative assessment of "Five Publics the Polls Don't Catch." Mills defined a "public" as a group of politically active people, as differentiated from the passive mass of Americans. In the column he enumerated five publics: the far left, the independent left, the liberal center, the practical conservatives, and the sophisticated conservatives. Making intellectual coherence a more important criterion for a public's importance than the number of its members, Mills discounted the liberal center, which he admitted had the largest number of adherents, because of its muddled thinking. Instead, Mills identified sophisticated conservatives and far leftists as the two crucial American publics.

Mills's analysis of the "sophisticated conservative" bloc built on his political writings of the early 1940s and foreshadowed his "power elite" thesis. Unlike the practical conservative, the sophisticated conservative was no union buster. Rather, he wanted to use unions for conservative ends. Sophisticated conservatives believed that "unions are a stabilizing force against radicalism and should be encouraged and aided as a counter-force to radical movements and changes." They planned to enlist labor leaders as "junior lieutenants of the captains of industry," securing their cooperation in order to suppress the radicalism of the rank and file. Here, Mills pointed to the example of United Steelworkers Union staff intellectuals Clinton Golden and Harold Ruttenberg, who in *The Dynamics of Industrial Democracy* urged labor unions to discipline their own radicals. Mills saw sophisticated conservatism as the chief danger to the labor movement: "Labor may, in fear of the practical right, and in order to hold their organizations together, be ever so grateful to accept the lure set forth by cooperative big business with its liberal front that is abuilding."[91] In fact, recent events seemed to point Mills toward his conclusions. The Taft-Hartley Act of 1947 reflected the logic of sophisticated conservatism. Although the law recognized the legal right of unions to exist, it circumscribed the role that unions could play and gave more responsibility to union leaders to quash discontent among its membership.[92]

Mills downplayed the political power of the Communist Party, relegating it to a faction of the liberal center. To Mills, the far left consisted of a small number of Trotskyist sects with a clear and consistent program of "capitalism smashed and socialism with 'worker's control' triumphant." Unlike liberals, who saw unions primarily as economic interest groups, far leftists grasped labor's radical political potential. Unlike the independent left of anti-Stalinist intellectuals, who wanted to believe in the radicalism of the rank and file but lacked the "labor metaphysic that is required," the far left saw unions as potentially radical. Consequently, they judged labor leaders according to the extent to which they brought about a "real left-wing movement"; those who failed to do so were "really mis-leaders of the laboring class," a bureaucratic caste that suppressed grassroots radicalism. Though Mills criticized far leftists as "somewhat inflexible," he appreciated their radical program for labor and their desire to create an independent socialist "third camp" independent of any existing state power.[93]

Mills's inclusion of the far left among his political publics reflected his increasing connections with Trotskyists in the Workers Party (WP), a small organization led by Max Shachtman that had a disproportionate impact on American political and intellectual life. The WP was formed in 1940 after splitting from James Cannon's Socialist Workers Party over the question of the class nature of the Soviet Union. While the Cannonites, along with Trotsky himself, maintained that the USSR was a degenerated workers' state, the Shachtmanites argued that Stalinism represented a new form of "bureaucratic collectivism." A similar critique of bureaucratic entrenchment marked the party's position on labor, as Shachtmanites sharply challenged union leaders for retarding militant action at the point of production.[94] Several of Mills's friends, including Macdonald and the writer Harvey Swados, had at one time or another belonged to the WP. In 1947, Mills gravitated toward the Shachtmanites' "workers' control" position on labor, which advocated direct control over production by workers themselves. Mills addressed the party in January of 1947, delivering a speech titled "The Defeat of Socialism 1920–47 and the Need for Reorientation." By 1947 Mills had read and clipped articles from the party's newspaper, *Labor Action*, and acquired a number of party pamphlets.

Mills incorporated "Five 'Publics' the Polls 'Don't Catch'" into the first chapter of *The New Men of Power*. This book traded heavily on the inevitability of a showdown between sophisticated conservatives and far leftists over the allegiance of American labor leaders. *The New Men of Power* blended survey data and political analysis to construct a collective portrait of American labor leaders, combining "the statistical and the qualitative."[95] Until now, Mills had written in the mode of either the sociological article or the left-wing essay. *The New Men of Power* combined these two genres, as would *White Collar* and *The Power Elite*. In this case the result was an uneven mixture of empirical social science and radical political analysis. Mills's data offered important information on such matters as labor leaders' social backgrounds, their opinions about a possible AFL-CIO merger, and their political party ties. But Mills aimed to offer more than a careful and accurate portrayal of American labor leaders: he wanted his book to be "politically relevant."[96] To that end, he focused on American labor leaders as "strategic actors . . . lead[ing] the only organizations capable of stopping the main drift toward war and slump."[97] Mills's analysis revealed an increasing disenchantment with the labor movement's potential, even as he proposed a radical program for labor-backed social change.

Mills's sociological analysis led him to conclude that the labor leadership as presently constituted was far more likely to follow the main drift than to challenge it. At the end of the book he tallied an admittedly crude "militancy score" to determine the likelihood that labor leaders were capable of filling the vanguard role Mills hoped they would. The "militant" leader, Mills claimed, possessed a "realistic image of business," recognizing its "immense power and influence"; acknowledged the intent of business to break or shackle unions; perceived the two-party system as a trap for labor; and favored the formation of a labor party over the next decade. Only 8 percent of CIO leaders (4 percent of AFL) received the grade "A" for militancy, while only 19 percent of CIO leaders (9 percent of AFL) received a "B" grade.[98] Most labor leaders, Mills concluded, were timid fence-sitters. They either failed to recognize the magnitude of the threat they faced or lacked the willpower to fight it. Anachronistically pursuing a strategy of business unionism, labor acted as an interest group, winning economic benefits for union members but failing to give political voice to American workers in an increasingly politicized economy. Mills found most labor leaders to be politically shortsighted and opportunistic rather than programmatic and visionary. His survey revealed that only 17 percent of AFL leaders and 45 percent of CIO leaders thought labor needed a broad political program. Mills predicted that this political myopia would have "long-run political consequences which may be ignored only at the risk of destruction."[99] Labor leaders, the "last representatives of economic man," seemed willing to settle for a role as "essentially a minority affair, which must balance its power against others, rather than as a potential majority movement with which to reorganize modern society."[100] Labor leaders were therefore "poor bets as far as political action is concerned," incapable of serving as the vanguard force Mills hoped for.[101]

Mills supplemented his empirical analysis of the BASR labor leader survey with political speculation on what labor leaders' timidity might mean for the future of American politics. According to Mills, most labor leaders had swallowed the "liberal rhetoric" that posited a natural harmony of interests between business and labor. Without a long-range strategy, they seemed likely to fall for sophisticated conservatives' trap of recruiting labor as a junior partner in the emerging corporate state. In one of the book's most famous insights, Mills envisioned the labor leader becoming a "manager of discontent," cooperating with management in the suppression of rank-and-file radicalism in return for union recognition and concessions on narrow economic issues. Indeed, during the postwar period, labor leaders signed collective bargaining agreements that made unions responsible for the loss of business due to unauthorized work stoppages. As a manager of discontent, the labor leader not only failed to act as a radical, but he also exerted a powerful force on the side of conservatism: "In disciplining radicals and extremists, the labor leader is upholding the liberal goals of labor-management cooperation, his position in the world created by his rhetoric, his job in the union, and the position of the businessman in the American system."[102] By integrating their members into the work process according to the impetus of management, unions effectively "rationalize[d] production without socializing it."[103]

If labor continued along its present path, Mills argued, there would be no halting the "main drift" toward a "corporate garrison state." Mills's description of this "main drift" was woolly, but it built on his wartime writings and foreshadowed his *Power Elite* thesis. The "main drift" was a plan by sophisticated conservatives among the business, military, and political elites to stabilize American society by creating a permanent war economy and expanding American influence abroad to ensure foreign markets for American goods. Such a program, Mills argued, would extend the monopoly features of the American social system, would result in rule by an elite group rather than a substantive democracy, and would involve the constant threat of war.

This scenario was bleak, but Mills had not abandoned his hope for labor radicalism altogether. *The New Men of Power* contains the most concrete program for radical social transformation of any of his writings. Throughout the 1940s Mills had offered only vague alternatives to the society that he had criticized. In *The New Men of Power*, however, believing that the labor movement could be an agent for social transformation, Mills made his radical political vision more explicit. In striking contrast to his later books, Mills offered a penultimate chapter entitled "Alternatives." Even though he would soon decide that labor was incapable of implementing this radical program, the vision he presented in *The New Men of Power* remained a powerful aspect of Mills's later social theory, offering him a standpoint from which to criticize contemporary American society. The crucial elements of this vision included widespread democratic participation, a dispersed power structure, avoidance of a military buildup, and meaningful work for all citizens.

The aim of the left, Mills wrote, was "to democratize the structure of modern society."[104] Its ultimate goal was "a society in which everyone vitally affected by a social decision, regardless of its sphere, would have a voice in that decision and a hand in its administration."[105] Though it is sometimes assumed that "participatory democracy" was an invention of the New Left, *The New Men of Power* demonstrates the idea's deep roots in socialist and radical labor traditions.[106] Mills argued that the left's program should begin with "the root of the matter: man in the process of his work."[107] In *The New Men of Power*, Mills advocated the position of workers' control that he had encountered in Shachtman's Workers Party and in the writings of British guild socialist G. D. H. Cole. He also drew on the historical example of the International Workers of the World (IWW), a radical syndicalist union that had reached the peak of its power at the beginning of the twentieth century and whose actions Mills admired (he often used "wobbly" as a term of praise). For Mills, workers' control meant that unions should expand their function beyond bargaining over wages and working conditions and move toward collective self-management: "Independence of labor action means continual workers' control at the point of production, which means that the union would attempt to replace management function by workers' control at every point where its power permits."[108] A union should thus act "as if it were going to become the organizer of work within this society and the basis for a social reorganization for a future democratic society."[109] Moreover, labor should not only strive for workers' control but should ultimately aim to alter the nature of work itself by "giving the impulses of man a chance to realize themselves creatively in work."[110] In order for this bold program to work, unions would have to organize the entire working class and form an independent political party.

Because Mills now advanced his most comprehensive and radical program for labor, his criticism of the existing labor leadership became more vociferous. If Mills concluded that the present labor leadership would likely follow the main drift rather than challenge it, he still entertained thoughts that his radical program might be realized during an economic depression that could radicalize the labor leadership. Mills's notion of a capitalism prone to serious crisis contrasted sharply with his wartime and 1950s views of a static corporate hegemony. In *The New Men of Power,* Mills wrote, "The liberal view of historical continuity should not obscure the fact that history, at times, is discontinuous."[111] Mills predicted that a "coming slump" would "implant the insurgent impulse into the American workers" and force the labor leadership to alter its character. If labor offered a compelling response to the new depression, others would rally behind it as "broad and energetic action properly communicated to the public would greatly enlarge the sphere of union influence and support."[112] A mass base could be found for a left-wing program among the middle class, as "All those who suffer the results of irresponsible social decisions and who hold a disproportionately small share of the values available to man in modern society are potential members of the left."[113]

Mills's belief that a slump could lead to a radical labor movement was based on a faith in both the latent radicalism of the working class, and the potential power of the labor intellectual. The coming slump would provide the opportunity for what Mills termed the "union of the power and the intellect."[114] Always inclined to place a high value on ideology, Mills argued that in an economic downturn, power would shift "toward those who are ideologically and strategically prepared for it."[115] Sophisticated conservatives and the left would emerge as the two groups with the most coherent programs, and labor would be forced to choose between them. Under slump conditions, the intellectuals of the independent left, often "a powerless third camp of opinion, oscillating between lament and indignation," could acquire new political relevance.[116] In a slump, left-wing intellectuals would be able to offer "counter-symbols that will focus the deprivation politically, inculcate the truth about common interests and common struggles, and offer some hope of winning a better tomorrow."[117] If labor leaders listened to such intellectuals, Mills suggested, they might be able to combine the vision and the willpower necessary to implement a truly democratic socialist alternative to the main drift.

Mills's reflections on the labor intellectual in the concluding chapter of *The New Men of Power* owed a great deal to his experience with the IUI and his relationship with Hardman. Mills's call for a union of power and intellect was also heavily influenced by his attendance at a November 1947 United Automobile Workers (UAW) convention while revising the book. Mills attended the convention at the invitation of Nathan Glazer, then an editor at *Commentary,* and he reported on it in an article, "'Grass-Roots' Union with Ideas," several parts of which he incorporated into *The New Men of Power*. UAW president Walter Reuther's bold leadership, socialist background, and third-party inclinations made him an attractive figure for all those left of center. Irving Howe and B. J. Widick, for instance, hoped that the UAW under Reuther would "use its vast resource of energy and power to become a new social force in American life."[118] After Reuther won the union's presidency at the 1946 convention, Mills sent him a telegram: "Congratulations. We all expect the UAW under your leadership to become the center of progressive labor in the U.S."[119] With Reuther's reelection a foregone conclusion, the 1947 convention was not as exciting as the previous year's meeting. Mills was nevertheless energized by what he saw.

In "'Grass-Roots' Union with Ideas," Mills expressed concern that the UAW might fall prey to the sophisticated conservatives, worrying that there might be an "unconscious temptation" for Reuther "to become a human engineer for some sort of state capitalism guaranteeing industry disciplined workers and in effect, by drawing the teeth of the rank-and-file, making them easy prey to an American variant of a corporative set-up."[120] Nevertheless, Mills argued that with its militant membership and organic union intellectuals, the UAW could be at the forefront of a revitalized left-labor movement, embodying an ideal of "ideas in live contact with power." Though lukewarm on Reuther himself ("He gets close enough to satisfy . . . your social emotions, but not your social intelligence"), Mills lauded the UAW rank and file, seeing them as possessing a collective spirit and a militantly democratic "wobbly" impulse. "These men are not only organized they are also unionized," he exclaimed.[121]

While he praised the UAW's "vigorous rank-and-file democracy," Mills concentrated his attention on a phenomenon that he saw as new in American unionism: the presence of "union-made intellectuals" within the UAW. Mills was thinking here of a specific set of men, including Francis Downing, in the education department; Victor Reuther, Walter's more left-leaning brother; Frank Winn, who edited the union's newspaper; and especially Nat Weinberg, the research director. These men helped Mills find his way around the 1947 convention, and Mills later sent a draft of his article to them for comments, joking that one of their tasks was to "make sure uninformed people like myself don't write up weird accounts of the UAW after one week of 'field' experience."[122] In these organic union intellectuals Mills found refreshing counterexamples to New York intellectuals, whom he mocked for embracing a "politics of hopelessness." Union-made intellectuals, Mills wrote, were "intellectuals without fakery and without neuroticism," and they did not "compete with one another in the small ways common to so many academic and other circles."[123] Their combination of professional experience in trade unions with broad political vision provided a crucial link between bread-and-butter unionists and the world of broad political ideas. Borrowing a phrase from the BASR's two-step model of communication, Mills argued that union-made intellectuals enabled the UAW to be an "opinion leader" within the ranks of labor. They thus provided "the only guarantee that the UAW will be the vanguard union long enough to provide results, not only to its members, but to all those who hope for a radical shift in American politics."[124]

"'Grass-Roots' Union with Ideas" contained a positive laborite vision of a union of power and intellect that also found expression in *The New Men of Power*. However, the book also foreshadowed Mills's later rejection of the "labor metaphysic"—the notion that the labor movement could serve as the principal agent of left-wing social transformation. Even as Mills wrote The *New Men of Power,* labor's bid for a more progressive social order was faltering on anti-Communist politics, internal divisiveness, the entrenchment of the labor leadership, and a determined business counterattack. Mills's slump scenario had allowed him to argue that his radical program for labor was not a utopian one. Yet his predictions of a coming slump proved a fantasy. In *The New Men of Power,* Mills placed his hope not in labor as it was presently constituted, but in external circumstances that might produce changes within the labor movement. He was adopting a tone of frustration, seeing the resurgence of labor radicalism as necessary but increasingly impossible. *The New Men of Power,* which vacillated between hope and disenchantment, ended on a note of tragedy: "It is the task of the labor leaders to allow and to initiate a union of the power and the intellect. They are the only ones who can do it; that is why they are now the strategic elite in American society. Never has so much depended upon men who are so ill-prepared and so little inclined to accept the responsibility."[125]

To be sure, Mills's political hopes for labor had been extravagant. If there were a real lost opportunity for the labor movement in the postwar years, it was along the social-democratic lines advanced by Hardman and others rather than the radical program advocated by Mills. His attack on the labor metaphysic inadequately accounted for labor's accomplishments and continued aspirations. In the postwar period, unions played a vital role in securing a decent standard of living for their members and protecting them from the arbitrary acts of management. While Mills failed to recognize that labor is always part social movement and part interest group, he correctly understood that the balance had shifted decisively in the postwar years. By the 1950s, even those unions that supported a broad political agenda found themselves trapped by larger political structures and their own desire to wield power within that system.[126] Moreover, Mills's critique of labor leaders for failing to politicize their battles has proved prescient. Though labor unions won important benefits for their members in the postwar period, since the 1970s they have been unable to withstand a decades-long decline that has accompanied an increasingly conservative political environment.[127] Just as his growing estrangement from professional sociology in the wake of his conflict with Lazarsfeld shaped his mature social criticism, so did Mills's eventual renunciation of the "labor metaphysic," already foreshadowed in *The New Men of Power*. Lacking the connection to a social movement that labor had briefly provided and yet unwilling to give up his radical ambitions, Mills returned to and expanded upon his disillusioned radicalism in his next book, *White Collar*.

CHAPTER 4

The New Little Men

'White Collar'

"The white-collar people slipped quietly into modern society."[1] So began *White Collar*. A fundamental occupational shift had occurred: the rise of a new middle class of dependent, salaried employees and the decline of a propertied old middle class. Grasping the significance of this transition required examining white-collar workers in their various guises as corporate managers, bureaucratic professionals, salespeople, and clerical workers. This investigation of the "occupational salad" of the new middle class revealed a new picture of American society "as a great salesroom, an incorporated brain, a new universe of management and manipulation."[2] It was the novelists who had best captured this world's antiheros, the "new little men." White-collar alienation symbolized "those psychological themes that characterize our epoch."[3] Hence, one could look to the new middle class to understand "modern society as a whole."[4] For the "new little men," Mills concluded, were the "unwilling vanguard of modern society."[5] As its introduction intimated, *White Collar* offered an unsettling depiction of modern society as one in which powerful large bureaucratic organizations dwarfed the new little men.

White Collar established Mills's national reputation as a social critic. Published in 1951, it joined an anxious postwar conversation about the middle-class American character, a discourse in which sociological works figured prominently. The book earned the status of a classic work of American social analysis. Even a recent critic of *White*

Collar called it "the most important book we have about the American middle classes."[6] It was the most ambitious book Mills ever wrote. The disparate aims of *White Collar* were captured in a 1946 letter that he wrote to Gerth:

> I wish I cd have a long talk with you about the New Middle Class book. I'm in quite an upset condition about it. You see, I am trying to do five things at once, and it may be too ambitious of me: (a) to be absolutely definitive so far as factual materials existent are concerned (b) to exploit fully . . . the newer techniques, especially the intensive interview and (c) to write it in such a way as [to] be "literature" (d) fourth to be really informed without being obvious about it in terms of deep deep radical slant especially on the psychological side and (e) fifth to weave into it all, the themes that are really major in 20th century U.S.A.[7]

Even when understood in its most limited sense as a sociological treatise on the historical formation, objective class position, and psychological and political outlook of the new middle classes in the modern United States, the book's scope was impressive. Yet Mills also sought to provide a total picture of modern society from an unflinchingly radical point of view. Moreover, he attempted to craft his insights with a new type of writing, a "sociological poetry" that could both convey a personal vision and attract a nonprofessional public audience. His goals may well have been "too ambitious," as he worried they might be. The result was a portrait of white-collar workers and American society that, despite its brilliance, was often disjointed, confused, ambivalent, and exaggerated. *White Collar* contained a contradictory jumble of insights, reflecting the moment of uncertain transition in which it was written. If Mills's range of competing ambitions produced an uneven work, their interplay was the source of much of what was original in it.

White Collar marked both the culmination of Mills's 1940s sociological work and a new direction. More than any of his other works, *White Collar* revealed his long-standing interest in social psychology, in the relationship between individual character and social structure. Yet *White Collar* was fundamentally affected by the rapidly shifting intellectual and political environment of the late 1940s. Particularly for a prolific author such as Mills, writing *White Collar* proved to be a protracted and painful process that reflected an intellectual crisis caused by his separation from the political and intellectual forces that had earlier sustained him. Written in the wake of Mills's disenchantment with organized labor and his increasing distance from professional sociology, *White Collar* was the work of an increasingly isolated man grasping for new means of understanding his world.[8]

SOCIAL PSYCHOLOGY AND POLITICAL DEBATES

The idea for *White Collar* emerged at least as early as 1944. In that year, Mills shared his concept for a book on the contemporary American middle class with friends and submitted a successful application for a Guggenheim fellowship to begin research. Although Mills already sensed that this would be his first major work, his conception of the project was fairly vague at this point. His application for the Guggenheim fellowship, for instance, merely noted that he would seek "to understand white collar people and their role in American life" by examining popular images of them, by gathering systematic occupational data about them, and by developing "techniques for analyzing psychological types on the basis of occupational and communicational data."[9]

White Collar displays Mills's long-term interest in social psychology. The psychological approach that Mills adopted in *White Collar* emerged from a set of interlocking yet distinct theoretical, empirical, and political commitments that he developed during the 1940s. From his engagement with pragmatism at the University of Texas, Mills had learned that psychology was deeply *social*. In his writings of the late 1930s and early 1940s, Mills emphatically rejected the notion that timeless biological constants defined human nature. Accordingly, Mills supplemented the pragmatist psychological tradition with the sociological content that he felt it lacked. In *White Collar*, Mills applied his sociology of knowledge—tracing the sociological and historical context in which ideas arose—to the study of the individual psyche. Like the sociology of knowledge, social psychology appealed to Mills as a hybrid mode of study allowing him to transcend narrowly construed boundaries of disciplinary social science in order to ask fundamental questions about man and society.

By focusing on social psychology, Mills participated in a prevailing trend of American social science. Within sociology, social psychology was becoming an important subdiscipline, pursued both by functionalists such as Talcott Parsons and Robert Merton and by a group of symbolic interactionists in the Chicago tradition led by Herbert Blumer. Like the symbolic interactionists, who studied human interaction in specific interpersonal environments, Mills was influenced by the pragmatist philosopher George Herbert Mead. In applying the methods of psychology to the study of national societies, Mills's work also paralleled that of the "culture and personality" school developed by interwar anthropologists such as Margaret Mead and Ruth Benedict, which became increasingly influential during World War II. Like the culture and personality theorists, Mills drew upon the work of Freudian revisionists such as Henry Stack Sullivan and the German émigrés Erich Fromm and Karen Horney, who relativized the insights of psychoanalysis by grounding Freud's insights in history and culture.[10]

Though Mills's work reflected this social scientific trend, his focus on the determinative role played by institutions in shaping individual character distinguished his approach to social psychology. Criticizing the "milieu" approach of the symbolic interactionists, Mills's social psychology entailed the macroscopic study of total societies, and the contemporary United States in particular. Rather than situating the individual in a particular interactional setting, Mills traced the influences of larger and more impersonal forces on the individual. And, unlike the cultural and personality school, which often relied on oversimplified notions of "national character," Mills identified ways in which societies are stratified along lines of class, status, and power. Hence he promised a more differentiated account of the various types of men and women who lived in complex modern societies.

Mills's institutionalist approach to social psychology emerged through his engagement with Weberian sociology under the influence of Hans Gerth. Mills worked out his social psychology in the textbook that he coauthored with Gerth, *Character and Social Structure: The Psychology of Social Institutions*. Although *Character and Social Structure* was not published until 1953, Mills and Gerth had conceived the basic ideas of the book before Mills completed *White Collar*. As discussed in chapter 2, they drafted an extensive outline of the book in 1941.[11] Though written as an undergraduate textbook, and often neglected in studies of Mills's corpus, *Character and Social Structure* is an important work of social psychology that helps us to understand his linking of character and social structure in *White Collar* and other works.[12] Much of *Character and Social Structure* dealt with "character" or "social structure" on its own terms, but the fundamental contribution of the book was its provision of a "working model" connecting the "structural and historical features" of society to "the most intimate features of man's self."[13] Gerth and Mills identified this link in their concept of "role," a set of social expectations for behavior. Social institutions organized roles to shape "persons," defined as the collection of roles each individual played. Thus, Gerth and Mills suggested that social psychologists should carefully examine "institutions [that] select and form persons by means of the roles persons enact and the traits they internalize."[14] Once sociologists understood how institutions shaped persons, they could investigate the relationship between the person and the "self," defined as the inner feelings and consciousness of each individual. Gerth and Mills stressed the ways in which persons and selves were formed by institutions, which fundamentally reflected distributions of authority in the political, economic, military, religious, and kinship orders. Yet they also sought to provide a means for talking about large-scale historical and political developments without losing sight of the unique individual.[15]

The theoretical framework developed in *Character and Social Structure* led Mills to pursue at least three social psychological lines of inquiry for which he believed a study of white-collar workers would provide the best answers. The first investigated the "psychological aspects of bureaucracy," or how the increased power of large-scale institutions in the modern world affected the lives of individual men and women.[16] In *White Collar*, Mills studied the managers, professionals, clerical workers, and department store clerks who worked in massive organizational structures. Second, Mills examined the effects of modern capitalism on individuals—how an increasingly commercialized world shaped modern persons. Thus, *White Collar* investigated alienation and the psychology of salesmanship. Finally, Mills explored how unstable and quickly changing role expectations created what he referred to as a "status panic." *Character and Social Structure* identified the sources of modern anxieties as the "unpredictable drift of the social structure and the similarly unstable dynamics of interpersonal relations," and referred to "the status-ridden man's frantic attempt to get others to confirm his self-image in a society in which there is no common career pattern, no harmony in the shifting expectations and appraisals by others."[17]

Beginning in 1945, Mills collected empirical information to help him sketch the social psychology of the American middle class. In several studies he conducted during the mid-1940s, he "kept his eyes open for 'white-collar material.'"[18] He devoted much of his energy to the most straightforward research task: gathering and systematizing occupational data for white-collar workers. At the Bureau of Applied Social Research (BASR), he amassed and tabulated a wide range of statistics from government and business sources. For instance, he and his staff examined detailed census data to understand objective features of white-collar social stratification such as occupation, trade-union membership, and income.[19] To get at more subjective psychological features of white-collar life, Mills proved resourceful. He drew upon his interviews for the *Small Business and Civic Welfare* report for insight into the psychology of the old middle class of small businessmen and collected material from the Decatur study (including the forty-five "open-ended" interviews he conducted that were not part of the study's original design).[20] Most intriguingly, Mills commissioned ethnographic observations. He drew heavily from a memo on different types of Macy's salespeople written by a former University of Maryland student, James B. Gale, and he also paid one researcher, Helen Powell, to report to him on her experiences as a Macy's saleswoman.[21]

For *White Collar,* Mills also conducted a series of intensive interviews as part of "Everyday Life in America," a study he directed under the auspices of the BASR in the fall of 1946. Mills modeled the "Everyday Life" project on previous studies conducted at the bureau. The willingness of the bureau to conduct qualitative research was greater than is sometimes assumed; in addition to quantitative studies, the BASR sponsored projects that relied on techniques designed to foster a deeper understanding of social psychology. The "Everyday Life" study was likely most closely modeled on Robert Merton's *Mass Persuasion,* a study of a 1943 marathon radio broadcast to sell war bonds featuring the celebrity singer Kate Smith. *Mass Persuasion* employed the focused interview, a forerunner of the contemporary focus group. While the focused interview used a set questionnaire and generated statistical results, it was also open-ended enough to allow the interviewer to explore the subjects' psychology in greater depth. Mills's "Everyday Life" study used a similar technique. Bureau staff member Jeannette Green, who worked on the *Mass Persuasion* study, also directed the interviews for the "Everyday Life" project. *Mass Persuasion* also contained two features notable in Mills's "Everyday Life" study: an attempt to relate individual psychology to the larger social structure, and an embrace of the critical function of social research. Not simply analyzing which techniques of mass persuasion were most effective, Merton began his book by emphasizing that the social psychology of its subjects could be comprehended only by placing them in the context of a "manipulative society" in which the value of salesmanship was pervasive. He ended

Mass Persuasion by arguing the need for a social science "oriented toward . . . democratic values."[22]

For the "Everyday Life" project, Mills's team conducted 128 interviews of white-collar workers in New York City. The interview pool was a heterogeneous group of men and women with different occupations and ranks. It included people who worked as middle managers, professionals, secretaries, and sales clerks in different work environments such as law firms, insurance companies, universities, governments, and department stores. Many questions in the "Everyday Life" questionnaire dealt with how workplace institutions shaped white-collar lives. Interviewers asked questions about occupation-related topics such as relations with co-workers, supervisors, and customers; job history; potential for job ascent; levels of job satisfaction; and how the passage of time was experienced during the workday. The study was also designed to collect information about the subjects' lives outside work and included a series of questions on friendship, leisure time, self-perceptions of social status, political views and "images of social reality," and attitudes toward unions.[23] Had respondents merely answered the seventy-three set questions, Mills would have amassed a large body of material on white-collar workers. However, he also encouraged interviewers to rely on their intuition to ask "prob[ing] questions . . . to allow the individual's experience to enter fully into the answers given."[24] Although the responses could be tabulated statistically, Mills encouraged interviewers to use their imaginations to develop a qualitative sense of the psychology of each individual—something that statistics alone could never capture. In particular, Mills sought to understand the "dream life" of white-collar workers, their deepest thoughts and feelings. As he instructed his interviewers, "You've found out what he is most concerned with when he is awake; now you want to know what he dreams of when he goes to sleep. What is the focus of his life, if he has one? What purpose does he feel he serves, if any?"[25] With so much to uncover, these interviews were "intensive" indeed. They often lasted several hours and were frequently conducted in two sittings.

White Collar emerged out of the theoretical and empirical commitments Mills developed in social psychology, but he also intended to offer a "deep radical slant" on social psychology. Here Mills drew upon an extensive left-wing literature on white-collar workers. As Mills pointed out, "There is no doubt that throughout this century, the center of theoretical initiative for political thought has been on the left, its 'thinkers' first discovered the new middle class."[26] A substantial German sociological literature on white-collar workers influenced Mills. No doubt Gerth had helped introduce this body of scholarship to Mills. In addition, a number of the key participants in these earlier debates, such as Emil Lederer and Hans Speier, were now teaching in New York at the New School for Social Research, a haven for German émigré scholars. Key German works had been translated into English during the 1930s as part of a Works Progress Administration project. Mills also knew American leftists' work on white-collar workers, including the books of Alfred Bingham, Lewis Corey, and William English Walling.[27] Mills echoed the analysis of many of these earlier writers, both German and American, when he argued that the new middle class needed to be understood in psychological terms. Many analysts saw white-collar workers as a particularly status-conscious group, juxtaposed between manual workers on the one hand and businessmen on the other. German writers had described white-collar workers as a *neue Mittelstand,* a new "status group" whose anxieties and aspirations needed to be understood in more than economic terms. Mills's analysis of white-collar workers drew heavily from German traditions; his use of the phrase "new little men" referred to the title of Hans Falluda's Weimar novel *Little Man, What Now?*[28]

For Mills, as for earlier leftists, white-collar workers proved a barometer for political hopes and fears. The emergence of white-collar workers as a large stratum in modern society forced left-wing thinkers to reconsider Marx's assumption that the industrial world would become increasingly divided between proletarians and bourgeoisie. Earlier writers had predicted that the political decisions made by the new middle classes would determine the future shape of the social world. Would white-collar workers ally with the working class to create socialism, or perhaps even develop their own distinctive brand of radical politics? Alternatively, would they play a reactionary role by joining with the bourgeoisie against labor or supporting right-wing movements such as fascism? In the Old Left discourse of the 1930s, American thinkers often claimed that the new middle class faced a stark choice between fascism and socialism. As Alfred Bingham put it, the American middle class was "ripe for Fascism," but it also had "an amazing ripeness for a really constructive and intelligent change."[29]

Mills's psychological focus distinguished him from more orthodox materialist analysts on the left. For instance, in a speech to the Workers Party on January 5, 1947, Mills urged the Trotskyists in the audience to recognize the failure of Marxist ideas to take hold in the twentieth century. According to Mills, rather than relying on faith that individuals would automatically act in their objective class interests, socialists needed to better understand the psychology of those whom they hoped to recruit. They particularly needed to study the new middle class, which was central to understanding "psychological problems of class, class consciousness, and politics." Addressing "the remnants of a vast defeat," Mills claimed that the failure of revolutionary socialism could be explained not only by "economic and political mistakes," but also by "miscalculation of the psychology of the masses." "The misery of 20th century man is psychological and cultural," Mills declared, "even more than it is material, at least here in America." Socialists needed to remember that their goal was not material abundance but the creation of a social structure that could produce the "unalienated man: man exuberant in work and love."[30] Mills's use of psychology thus had much in common with a similar psychological turn among European Western Marxists, who challenged the traditional materialism of orthodox Marxism by stressing the importance of superstructural elements such as culture and psychology. Like Western Marxists, Mills evinced a fundamental concern with alienation rather than mere economic exploitation, and he focused on the false consciousness of workers—their inability to realize their objective class interests—as an explanation for the failure of a socialist revolution to materialize.[31]

As Mills worked on *White Collar* in the mid- to late 1940s, he alternated between two different models of providing a "radical slant" on the social psychology of white-collar workers. On the one hand, consistent with Mills's laborite vision in those years, he followed an earlier strand of left-wing analysis in hoping that white-collar workers might realize their shared class interests with blue-collar workers and join a radicalized labor movement. In *The New Men of Power,* for instance, published just three years prior to *White Collar,* Mills argued that an assertive labor movement could win "allies of pivotal importance" among white-collar workers.[32] Although it employed a neutral social scientific tone, Mills's first sociological investigation of white-collar workers, "The Middle Class in Middle-Sized Cities," published in the *American Sociological Review* in 1946, advanced the same argument. Here, Mills asserted that, of all the strata, "the small businessmen and the white-collar workers occupy the most ambiguous and least clearly defined social position," an amorphous position between big business and labor.[33] Small businessmen based their unstable prestige claims on

an identification with "business as such," making them far more likely
to ally politically with large business than with labor. The political loyalties of the heterogeneous white-collar workers, however, were more
up for grabs, and Mills envisioned them following labor if it proved
able to achieve "civic power and prestige."[34]

Mills hoped that his research on white-collar workers could aid the
practical goal of union organizing. If he could understand how status
aspirations led white-collar workers to forgo their objective economic
interest in joining unions, perhaps he could help union organizers discover better ways of overcoming these obstacles to unionization. Many
questions in the "Everyday Life" questionnaire dealt with labor unions,
and Mills described the study to a union official as a "pilot study on
the psychological resistances which people in white-collar work have
against unionization" that would help "develop more systematic
devices to overcome them in unionization drives."[35] Indeed, in late
1947, the research director of the UAW, Nat Weinberg, invited Mills to
play a direct role in unionizing white-collar workers. Weinberg wrote,
"We might bring you out here to talk to some of the international reps
on the organization of white collar workers. Maybe we could have a
week's seminar on the subject for those reps who are directly involved
in organizing and servicing office workers. What do you say?" Mills
agreed.[36]

However, Mills was also drawn toward a different way of providing
a "radical slant" on psychological issues. Throughout the 1940s, Mills
was influenced by the emerging left-wing analysis of the United States
as a "mass society" whose population was apathetic and politically
passive. This view appealed to Dwight Macdonald's *politics* circle and
was also advanced in sophisticated theoretical form by members of
the Frankfurt School. Mills probed the extent of American middle-
class apathy by encouraging interviewers to explore the alienation of
white-collar workers in the "Everyday Life" study. For instance, one set
of questions listed under the category of "political apathy" included,
"Do you feel you have any say-so in how things are run? Does it make
any difference to you whether your say-so counts?" Mills described the
intention of these questions as "search[ing] out the roots of political
indifference" and instructed interviewers to focus their attention on
"the reasons why respondent is a clock with no political mainsprings
at all—as the case may be—rather than in what respondent thinks."[37]
Whether Mills's political analysis of white-collar worker psychology
would be guided by laborite hopes or by mass society pessimism would

prove decisive in the formulation of *White Collar*. Here the political
and intellectual events of the late 1940s proved pivotal.

THE ISOLATION OF C. WRIGHT MILLS

By 1948 Mills had gathered extensive research material for *White
Collar* and had written some sections of it, but the book was decisively shaped during the period from 1948 to 1950, when most of
the text was written and revised. Events of the late 1940s shaped the
final text in two important respects. As Mills distanced himself from
the sociological profession, *White Collar* became less the result of
disciplinary research, such as that conducted in the "Everyday Life"
study, and more a work of what Mills called "sociological poetry." As
Mills's hopes in the postwar labor movement were dashed and much
of the intellectual left was deradicalized, Mills returned to a stance
of disillusioned radicalism. Both developments left Mills increasingly
isolated as he completed *White Collar*, lending the book much of its
character as an imaginative and despairing portrait of the American
middle class.

From the beginning, *White Collar* was to be not only a theoretically
sophisticated and empirically rich contribution to social science, but
also a trade book with the potential to reach a mass audience.[38] As
Mills explained to his parents in 1946, "After all the translation Gerth
and I did *[From Max Weber]* was a book for specialists . . . but this
white collar book: ah, there's a book for the people; it is everybody's
book."[39] The book was not just about white-collar workers, but for
them as well: "It is all about the new little man in the big world of the
20th century. It is about that little man and how he lives and what
he suffers and what his chances are going to be; and it is also about
the world he lives in, has to live [in], doesn't want to live in. It is, as
I said, going to be everybody's book. For, in truth, who is not a little
man?"[40]

In order to reach this broader audience, Mills created a style blending
sociological argument and poetic vision. One of Mills's stylistic models
was James Agee and Walker Evans's *Let Us Now Praise Famous Men*,
a work that Mills described as "sociological poetry" in a 1948 essay in
politics. The social scientific perspective, Mills argued, was ill equipped
to handle the problem of modern alienation because it was too comfortable with its detachment from its subject matter. Social scientists,
he claimed, "make up a rationale and a ritual for the alienation inher-

ent in most human observation and intellectual work today. They have developed several stereotyped ways of writing which do away from the full experience by keeping them detached throughout."[41] Sociological poetry required not only the objectivity of the trained scientist, but also the imagination of the artist. Mills thus came to see his task in *White Collar* as similar to that of a novelist. Nevertheless, Mills insisted on the virtues of a social scientific approach. Mills's sociological poetry did not dispense with the theories and methods of social science. Rather, it stood "somewhere between the thick facts and thin meanings of the ordinary sociological monograph and those art forms which in their attempts at meaningful reach do away with the facts, which they consider as anyway merely an excuse for imaginative construction."[42]

No doubt, Mills's experience at the BASR convinced him that sociological works needed to express a personal and critical vision—indeed, it was exactly these elements that Lazarsfeld sought to excise from Mills's drafts of the Decatur report.[43] The Decatur dispute, which precipitated Mills's isolation from professional social science, continually resurfaced throughout the late 1940s and early 1950s. After completing the bulk of the work on *The Puerto Rican Journey*, Mills left the bureau in late 1948, glad to move on with his own work. In the spring of 1949, Mills was a visiting professor at the University of Chicago, and he explored the possibility of a permanent position there. Unsatisfied with the general education curriculum at Chicago, Mills patched things up with Columbia and Lazarsfeld, then serving as department chair.[44] Yet Lazarsfeld periodically asked Mills to write new drafts of the Decatur report, which remained a constant source of tension between Mills and the department. "God, will I ever get that crap off my desk," he wondered in 1950. "It is continually in my hair. I just hate to work on it."[45] Finally, in early 1952, just months after the publication of *White Collar* and more than six years after the fieldwork for the report had been concluded, Mills refused to work on the project any longer. "I've worked on that crap more than on any other book with which I have been associated," he wrote, "and of course he [Lazarsfeld] will now take it away, but I do not care." Mills's refusal marked a definitive break with academic sociology as a whole. "To hell with the professional acclaim I loose," he concluded. "Nothing is worth the continual feeling that youre not your own man."[46]

After leaving the bureau, Mills effectively retreated into Columbia College, the undergraduate wing of the university. Other distinguished faculty members taught there at the same time, including Jacques

Barzun, Daniel Bell, and Lionel Trilling.[47] Although Mills's original appointment at Columbia had been in the undergraduate college, he did teach graduate students and was clearly expected to play a prominent role in the research activities and graduate training of Columbia University's Department of Sociology. That he no longer did so following the Decatur dispute was a good indication of his place not only at Columbia, but also in the profession at large: he was still a part of one of the nation's centers for sociological research, but he was decidedly on its margins.

Mills's relationship with Robert Merton was a good barometer of his increasing ambivalence about and alienation from Columbia sociology and the profession at large. To some degree, Mills continued to respect and admire Merton's work, indicating that he still found much of value in mainstream sociology. In late 1949, Mills sent Merton a note praising his influential *Social Theory and Social Structure:* "I hadnt realized . . . how far I'd wandered from really serious work in our discipline."[48] Yet Mills also began increasingly to criticize Merton. "Merton teaches nothing practically, but technique," Mills complained in 1950, adding, "I can't understand his subjection to PFL [Lazarsfeld], which is embarrassing."[49]

Mills's judgment was not entirely fair, for Merton remained a theorist with an extraordinarily wide range. However, Merton was heavily influenced by his work with Lazarsfeld during the 1940s. By the end of that decade, Merton had moved away from his earlier works of social theory, which contained important elements of social critique, to a more narrowly construed effort to define the limits of professional sociology. In his influential introduction to *Social Theory and Social Structure,* Merton (one of the most graceful scholarly essayists of his generation) cautioned that sociologists should follow the physical sciences in avoiding a "misplaced concern with the literary graces." Merton believed that sociology should be "public," but he did not mean that sociologists should seek to communicate directly with nonprofessionals but instead that sociological insights needed to "be standardizable and the results of their insights testable by others," even when they emerged from an "intensely private experience."[50] Merton's definition of professional sociology, accepted by many of his contemporaries, excluded exactly those elements that Mills found essential for *White Collar:* social critique, personal vision, and an attempt to reach a nonprofessional audience. Mills and Merton maintained cordial contact, at least until Mills's publication of *The Sociological Imagination* in 1959, but their relationship was no longer marked by the intellectual exchange and camaraderie that characterized it in its early years.[51]

In the profession as a whole, postwar leaders expressed a renewed confidence in the ability of sociological knowledge to achieve scientific status as they worked to build a consensus uniting theoretical and statistical strands of the discipline. At Harvard's influential Department of Social Relations, an alliance between theorist Talcott Parsons and statistician Samuel Stouffer paralleled the one between Merton and Lazarsfeld at Columbia. Mills was skeptical of developments at Harvard from the beginning, writing in a letter to Gerth, "People are talking a lot about the new Harvard set-up, think that parsons and stouffer will integrate 19th c theory and 20th c technique into a new grand thing (of this I am doubtful on two counts: S[touffer] and P[arsons]) but they do have plenty for research and god knows it costs plenty."[52] Postwar sociology in the United States was never as unified as its proponents portrayed it, nor was it as monolithic as later critics, Mills included, alleged. There were significant differences in approach among disciplinary leaders, and alternative traditions persisted, as reflected in the work of Mills, among others. Nevertheless, the commitment of disciplinary leaders to achieve scientific status for the discipline meant that there was less of room for Mills's kind of work—public, humanistic, and explicitly leftist—than there had been before. Indeed, postwar sociologists often made explicit pleas to suppress overtly critical viewpoints of American society. In the 1948 survey *The Present State of American Sociology,* for instance, influential University of Chicago sociologist Edward Shils called on his colleagues to take a "more responsible attitude to political power." In a barb that Mills easily could have taken as directed at him, Shils wrote, "Chronic oppositionism will not make social science more realistic, however much their proponents talk of bureaucracy, power, alienation, and the other things which are fashionable among disillusioned Marxists."[53]

At the same time that Mills was distancing himself from the sociological profession, he was also growing disenchanted with the prospects for left-wing politics. The political and cultural power of the American left, which had risen in the 1930s, faded sharply by the end of the 1940s. Historians have long pinpointed the post–World War II red scare, or McCarthyism, as the principal reason for the decline of the left during this period. Indeed, powerful anti-Communist conservatives targeted not only Communists but also liberal and left-wing ideas and activism as a whole.[54] For their part, many liberals drew sharper

divisions between their politics and more radical alternatives that had
not been drawn before, leaving proponents of the left increasingly marginalized. Arthur Schlesinger Jr., for instance, influentially redefined
liberalism as part of a "vital center" standing between radical extremes
of the right and the left.[55] Mills tended to discount the significance
of the postwar red scare in suppressing the left. In large part, this is
because of the particularities of his political journey. Because Mills was
always an anti-Stalinist who had no connections to the Communist
Party or Popular Front organizations, he did not fear becoming a target
of McCarthyist repression.

Though he underestimated the effects of McCarthyism, Mills nevertheless recognized how the emerging cold war political order threatened
the chances for a left-wing revival, as is evident from an unpublished
radical manifesto, "A Third Camp in a Two-Power World," that he
wrote with fellow anti-Stalinist radicals Irving Sanes and Lewis Coser
and intended to publish in *politics*. The authors appropriated the term
"third camp" from Max Shachtman, head of the Workers Party, who
had used it since the early 1940s to refer to the formation of a socialist
bloc independent of the capitalist West and the Stalinist Soviet Union.
The manifesto addressed itself to what, from an independent radical
point of view, could only be seen as a depressing state of world affairs.
"What an endless, empty thing the war . . . turned out to be for the
20th century world," the authors ruminated.[56] Increasingly, the world
was being divided up between the two antagonistic superpowers, neither of which offered a progressive model for the future. Decimated by
war, Europe lacked the potential to serve as a third force, and the rise
of independent nations in the post-colonial world was spoiled by their
need to offer allegiance to one side or another of the cold war. The
Soviet Union was firmly in the clutches of the Stalinist bureaucracy.
Finally, manifestations of democratic tolerance in the United States
were superficial, "mainly a reflection of oppositional weakness on the
one hand and the power and relative richness of the American political
economy, on the other."[57] Theirs was an oversimplified analysis, to be
sure, and one that severely underrated the significance of democratic
institutions in the United States. Yet the authors clearly grasped that the
emerging cold war meant that as the world chose between two alternatives—a liberal, formally democratic capitalism or an authoritarian
Soviet-style communism—the potential for pursuing other political
alternatives would sharply decline. Indeed, the rapidly emerging cold
war order, with a series of defining events in 1947 and 1948—from the

announcement of the Truman Doctrine in March 1947 to the Berlin airlift beginning in June 1948—worked to close off the sort of political opportunities that had excited Mills in the early postwar period.

Mills experienced the confining effects of the new cold war environment through developments in the American labor movement. The manifesto's authors still hoped for a political interlude in which to organize a broadly based labor party that would allow radicals "to raise such questions as the removal of occupation forces in Europe, nationalization of property without the loss of parliamentary democracy, and opposition to Russia that is not based on the need for the expansion of American capitalism." The authors claimed to write not "of the chances for such forces to emerge, but of their necessity."[58] Yet such hopes were increasingly unrealistic. There were few indications that the non-Communist leaders of organized labor were willing to challenge the Truman administration's foreign policy. By the time the manifesto was written, organized labor had wholeheartedly embraced the goals of the Marshall Plan, and its leaders were on the political defensive following the passage of the 1947 Taft-Hartley Act, which required them to pledge their loyalty to the government and led them to purge from their own ranks Communist-associated radicals, who were labor's strongest critics of U.S. cold war policies.[59] Coser, Mills, and Sanes were grasping at straws if they expected American labor single-handedly to prevent the cold war and reverse the direction of international politics. It was probably for this reason that the article was withheld; Sanes wrote Mills that their manifesto should be "held back," as it was "a little naive . . . and not really too convincing." Although the winter 1948 issue of *politics* advertised the article's appearance in a forthcoming issue, the authors decided not to publish it, though Mills did not give up easily, sending drafts to friends as late as September 1948.[60]

As a number of drafts of another unpublished manuscript, "Notes on the Meaning of the Election," make clear, the 1948 presidential election caused Mills to lose all hope for leftward political change in the United States. Mills had already noted in *The New Men of Power* that Henry Wallace's third-party campaign, widely viewed as a Communist front, discouraged labor leaders from forming their own independent political party. Now he argued that the unexpected victory of Truman had foreclosed the possibility of CIO leftists forming a labor party. Indeed, the UAW, which had planned a blockbuster educational conference to discuss the possible formation of a third party for the day after the anticipated Republican victory, quickly abandoned the idea following Truman's election.[61] Since Truman won in large part because of the labor vote, labor leaders now seemed little inclined to start their own party. It increasingly appeared to Mills that organized labor was devoid of radical potential, and he found himself lamenting what might have been: Truman's defeat could have caused a "general exodus of liberal and labor elements from the Democratic party into the ranks of the new party." Mills imagined that "had the Democratic Party dissolved and a new, non-Communist labor party been founded, and had a conservative Dewey administration hung on long enough to confront another economic slump, the new party might have come roaring into the political arena with a voice that would make FDR's New Deal seem lamb-like." This was a long string of what-ifs for a series of opportunities whose time had already passed.[62]

In his final article for *Labor and Nation,* published in early 1949, Mills examined white-collar unionism. Just a few years before, when he was directing the "Everyday Life" study, Mills hoped that an analysis of white-collar workers' reactions to unions could uncover information that would assist in labor organizing. By 1949, however, Mills had become so pessimistic about the state of labor that he argued that unionizing white-collar workers would not affect the wider political climate. Though he predicted that organization drives among white-collar workers would become increasingly successful, he argued that their unionization would not improve the "possibilities of a broadly democratic political economy." Mills maintained that "the larger meaning of unionism involves the question of whether the unions are to become a movement, or whether they are going to become another vested interest, an agency of political regulation at an economic price." Convinced that the latter was the case, Mills argued that the organization of white-collar workers could only be a "unionization into the main drift: it will serve to incorporate them as part of the newest interest to be vested in the liberal state." To Mills, the consequences of labor's transformation were profound: "If the future of democracy in America is imperiled, it is not by any labor movement, but by its absence, and the substitution for it of a set of new vested interests."[63]

Much of this *Labor and Nation* article was incorporated into *White Collar.* The book expressed a profound disillusionment with the labor-based social change hoped for by the Old Left, since Mills no longer believed that unions might engage in a "cultural and political struggle . . . that would re-order U.S. society."[64] Mills's dismissal of the possibility of a "union of the power and the intellect" reflected larger trends within the postwar labor movement, as intellectuals who previously identified with labor now came to see it as hopelessly embedded in the dominant political order. Even those who continued to write about labor, such as Mills's friend Harvey Swados, adopted an increasingly frustrated tone.[65] The last issue of *Labor and Nation* was published in January 1952. A casualty of labor's postwar transformation, the magazine had relied upon financial backing from unions that supported its vision of union leaders and intellectuals working together to create an American social democracy. By the early 1950s, this funding was dwindling.[66] Though the union-made intellectuals that Mills had earlier found so inspiring such as Frank Winn and Nat Weinberg remained on the UAW staff until the 1960s, they became increasingly frustrated with the political compromises made by the labor movement.[67] Even though *White Collar* was shaped by Mills's rejection of the labor metaphysic, it was still deeply influenced by Mills's earlier engagement with the labor question. After all, this was a book about white-collar *workers*. In criticizing the alienating features of modern work in *White Collar,* Mills employed ideals that he had earlier praised in movements for workers' control.

If a union of power and intellect had not come to pass, Mills might at least have drawn support from interacting with a community of like-minded left-wing intellectuals, such as the one that nurtured his nascent radicalism during the early 1940s. Even when the political fortunes of the independent left seemed dim, the 1940s had seen a vibrant debate among radical intellectuals.[68] In the "Third Camp" manifesto, the authors had called for "a rethinking of the socialist ideal in connection with the experiments in modern social structure that have emphasized economic categories to the exclusion of political freedom and human dignity."[69] The manifesto itself was intended to promote this discussion. The authors proposed guest editing an issue of *politics* devoted to the issues raised in their manifesto, and they planned to solicit responses from a wide range of intellectuals, including Hannah Arendt, Sidney Hook, George Orwell, Arthur Schlesinger Jr., and, surprisingly, Mills's Columbia colleagues Lazarsfeld and Merton.[70]

Sadly, even the modest goal of finding a group willing to discuss the possibilities for a left-wing revival proved unattainable for Mills in the late 1940s. By the end of the decade, most New York intellectuals had abandoned their radical beliefs.[71] Mills was the primary organizer of "Dialogs on the Left," which were recorded in 1949. The dialogues, which featured Lewis Coser and Meyer Schapiro, among others, had the goal of "reviving radical criticism and reestablishing contact among those believing in its values." However, only a handful of intellectuals attended, and a proposed book and magazine never materialized.[72] One sign of the times was Dwight Macdonald's decision to stop publishing *politics* in 1949. To be sure, in the postwar period Mills disagreed with much of the magazine's content. Still, he considered it "the publication closest to my own confusions."[73] In 1948, tiring of his editorial duties, Macdonald sought to reconstitute the magazine by inviting Mills, Irving Howe, and Mary McCarthy to join him as editors. Mills considered the offer a means to keep alive a critical voice on the left.[74] In the end, however, Mills decided not to accept Macdonald's offer. In addition to his concern about the time commitment required, Mills claimed that he was so uncertain about his own political stance that he would feel uncomfortable in the role. Given that he was "not now clear on so many of the issues," Mills wrote Macdonald, he "shouldn't be a miserable editor but a miserable contributor."[75] Following the collapse of *politics,* Macdonald followed the widespread trend toward deradicalization. In 1952, he famously declared that he "chose the West" in the cold war.[76]

With so many of his former friends moving away from the left, why did Mills maintain his commitment to radical social critique? Certainly, Mills was psychologically well equipped to be a lone rebel, having played that role before. However, certain features of Mills's radicalization in the early 1940s also prevented him from following the trend toward deradicalization. For many New York intellectuals, having been among the first leftists to recognize the perils of Stalinism, the logic of their single-minded anti-Communism led them to identify with the United States now engaged in a cold war against the Soviet Union. Though anti-Stalinist, Mills was not part of the left during the Moscow show trials and the Hitler-Stalin pact and did not share a similar preoccupation with Communism. He was thus better situated to maintain a stance of independent radicalism during the postwar period, since he did not feel compelled (as Macdonald and others did) to choose between the West and the Soviet Union. Moreover, as argued in chapter 2, Mills's radicalism was born out of disillusionment. He joined the left at a moment when he was pessimistic about its capacity for political transformation. Though Mills grew more optimistic about the left's chances during his postwar stint as a labor intellectual, he came to radicalism as an intellectual stance, and his commitment was thus not tied to the success or failure of any particular political movement.

Inevitably, the sharp decline of the left at the end of the decade shaped Mills's mature social criticism, making *White Collar* a work of thoroughly disillusioned radicalism. The demise of the Old Left, which corresponded with his increasing marginalization from the sociological profession, left Mills isolated, confused, and angry. "I am really very lonesome intellectually," he wrote to Gerth in 1950, reporting that the only thinkers with whom he had much contact were Macdonald and Frankfurt School theorist Leo Lowenthal.[77] His intellectual and political isolation made it difficult for Mills to complete *White Collar* and to achieve the wide range of ambitious sociological and political goals he had set for the project. In 1949 Mills complained to Irving Sanes that finishing the book was like "wallowing in this dark chaos."[78] Similarly, he wrote to his friend William Miller:

> I am disillusioned about *White Collar* again. I can't write it right. I can't get what I want to say about America in it. What I want to say is what you say to intimate friends when you are discouraged about how it all is. All of it at once: to create a little spotlighted focus where the alienation, the apathy and dry rot and immensity and razzle dazzle and bullshit and wonderfulness and how lonesome it is, really, how terribly lonesome and rich and vulgar and god I don't know. Maybe that mood, which I take now to be reality for me, is merely confusion which of course might be so and still worthwhile if one could only articulate it properly.[79]

Mills's intellectual isolation also led him toward a particular solution to his revision problems that shaped the text in important respects. He cut much of the statistical material he had originally included, deciding to emphasize his personal sociological vision over the inclusion of data that might support and complicate his claims. Most important, he wrote the work not as a plea for radical urgency, as was *The New Men of Power,* but as a moral condemnation. As he explained to Miller, "It is a total damnation of everything in this setup. If it is so, then one has to ask how and why the damn setup continues. It can't be so; and yet it seems to be just so to me."[80]

'WHITE COLLAR'

White Collar: The American Middle Classes appeared in September 1951. It consisted of fifteen chapters divided into four sections: "Old Middle Classes," "White Collar Worlds," "Styles of Life," and "Ways of Power." The book was a distinctively Millsian mixture of sociological classifications, sharply etched ideal types, and bold political analysis. More than any of Mills's other books, *White Collar* was written in a self-consciously literary style, chosen to achieve the ideal of "sociological poetry." Mills's language succinctly conveyed his analysis while simultaneously capturing the readers' attention, as in chapter titles such as "The Great Salesroom" and "The Enormous File." The text combined many of Mills's writings from the previous decade, though these were not always successfully integrated into a coherent whole. For instance, readers might have been surprised to find a chapter on intellectuals, "Brains Inc.," consisting in part of Mills's 1944 essay "The Powerless People," wedged in between a chapter on professionals and another on salespeople.

In section one, Mills described a historical transition from the old middle classes to the new. With diffuse property ownership providing the economic base, Mills claimed, nineteenth-century America had been a middle-class society closely approximating the classic liberal ideal of a self-regulating market, in which competition offered individuals the opportunity to become free men. "With no feudal tradition and no bureaucratic state, the absolute individualist was exceptionally placed in this liberal society that seemed to run itself and in which men seemed to make themselves."[81] By depicting a society that was, in Louis Hartz's phrase, "born liberal," Mills's interpretation of nineteenth-century American history resembled notable works of the postwar consensus school of history. Like consensus historians, Mills stressed the absence of feudal hierarchies in the United States and concluded that a liberal individualist ideology pervaded American society. The ideological valence of consensus history ranged from the celebratory conservatism of Daniel Boorstin's *The Genius of American Politics* to the radical critique of Hartz's *The Liberal Tradition in America* and Richard Hofstadter's *The American Political Tradition*, which sharply criticized what they saw as a hegemonic liberal capitalist political culture running throughout the course of American history. Though the overall mood of disillusioned radicalism in *White Collar* had much in common with Hartz and Hofstadter, Mills's laudatory depiction of the nineteenth century was closer to that of Boorstin.[82] Not only did Mills present a harmonious vision of the workings of the free market, but he also offered a passing reference discounting the historical significance of slavery (which, he claimed, "did not loom so large as is often assumed") and neglected to mention the forcible expropriation of land from Native Americans and Mexicans (referring instead to the "exhilaration of expansion across the gigantic continent").[83]

To some extent, Mills was aware that the first part of the book "sets forth [a] utopian past."[84] Richard Gillam argues that Mills's historical account of nineteenth-century American capitalism failed as "scholarship" but succeeded as "radical mythology" by envisioning the possibility that American society could once again recapture its republican roots.[85] It is difficult to accept Gillam's claim. Though there were many mythic elements in Mills's historical account, there was nothing specifically radical about his nostalgia for a society consisting of small property owners. Indeed, there was almost a conservative flavor to the way that Mills contrasted the bold entrepreneurs of the past to the security-conscious bureaucrats of the present. Mills even included a barb against New Deal social insurance policies, sarcastically remarking, "Thus do governments intervene to keep men more equal."[86] Yet, despite striking such conservative notes, *White Collar* was hardly a conservative book. Rather, it fit within a left-wing tradition of critiquing corporate America by contrasting it with an idealized republican past. As Michael Denning has argued, native-born American radicals often favored the trope of a once-promising democracy in decline. John Dos Passos's *USA* trilogy, for instance, told the story of the "decline and fall of the Lincoln Republic" in order to critique the dominance of "the big money" in the modern United States.[87] Rather than a hopeful radical mythology, Mills's nostalgia represented the hopelessness of a disillusioned radicalism. Whereas left-wing consensus historians Hofstadter and Hartz projected their felt lack of political alternatives onto the American past, Mills romanticized the earlier republican period in order to more sharply condemn a contemporary period of corporate hegemony

Even while Mills lamented the decline of an independent producing class, he convincingly debunked the notion that twentieth-century politics were based on the free-market liberalism of the old middle class. In the modern world, Mills contended, the ideology of free-market liberalism no longer expressed possible social ideals. Rather, it provided an ideological cover for corporations, leading the old middle classes to misdirect their resentment against labor unions and the welfare state. Mills thus argued that any serious twentieth-century democratic movement must address the "basic relations of capitalism."[88] His examination of the modern fate of old middle-class "heroes," the farmer and the small businessman, demonstrated that even those who controlled

their own property and labor in the contemporary United States could
no longer act independently. Though small businessmen persisted as a
class, they were deprived of their "entrepreneurial function," forced to
operate in a market whose dynamics were set through the economic
and political machinations of large corporations. Rather than personi-
fying the republican virtue of independence, Mills argued, contemporary farmers had become a dependent class reliant on the state to set
prices via farm subsidies designed to curtail production.

Dependence on larger bureaucratic institutions was the fate not only
of the old middle classes, but also of the new middle classes, as Mills
explained in the second section of his book, "White Collar Worlds."
The six chapters in this section constituted the empirical, sociological
heart of the book. When defining and describing the new middle class,
Mills was at his most analytical, offering a range of careful distinctions
and definitions. Though he cut much of the statistical apparatus of the
book prior to publication because of space considerations, he nevertheless documented a momentous shift from an entrepreneurial old middle
class of farmers, small businessmen, and independent professionals to a
new middle class of employees—managers, salespeople, office workers,
and salaried professionals. According to Mills's statistics, from 1870
to 1940 the percentage of the U.S. population in the old middle class
declined from 33 percent to 20 percent, while that of the new middle
class rose from just 6 percent to 25 percent.[89]

Mills has been accused of lumping the new middle classes together
into one overarching, homogeneous category.[90] In fact, however, he
carefully guarded against such oversimplification, explicitly stating
that "white collar people are not . . . one compact horizontal stratum."[91] Compared to the old middle classes, they were defined by their
lack of property, and were hence stratified by occupation. Compared
to wage workers, they were defined by the nature of their work: they
worked not to produce things, but instead with "paper and money and
people."[92] Compared to the upper classes, they lacked ultimate deci-
sion-making powers. Yet within this broad stratum of the new middle
classes, Mills saw varying degrees of income, prestige, and power.

One of the most valuable contributions of *White Collar* was its
identification of hierarchies within the white-collar workplace. Mills
described a "white collar pyramid," ranging from managers and professionals at the top to salespeople and clerical workers at the bottom.
In one of the few instances in which he brought gender into his analysis,
Mills described a world in which authority was "roughly graded by age

and sex: younger women tend to be subordinated to older men."[93] Mills might have made much more of gendered divisions within the white-collar pyramid. Interestingly, he actually had the material to do so. The "Everyday Life" project contained a series of questions for female respondents about domestic and career ambitions and the prevalence of sexual propositioning in the workplace. He had planned to include in *White Collar* a chapter titled "Sexual Exploitation in White-Collar Employment," but in the end, it was not published in the book. In his notes, Mills went further than he did in the final text, describing the white-collar world as a "commercialized patriarchy."[94]

The organization of "White Collar Worlds" proceeded from the top of the pyramid to the bottom, with separate chapters devoted to managers, professionals, intellectuals, salespeople, and lower-level office workers. To capture the variety of white-collar life, Mills offered snapshots of the different levels, using a range of sources. He drew from statistical calculations, intensive interviews, historical studies, and ethnographic observations, as well as from personal experience and works of fiction. Mills rendered these depictions with a dose of poetic vision, providing compelling vignettes of historical events marking the transition to a society in which the new middle classes predominated, as in his accounts of the mechanization of the office and the development of the modern department store. He also offered a series of fascinating ideal types of white-collar workers. For instance, drawing heavily on the experiences of a former student at Maryland, James Gale, who had worked at Macy's, Mills classified different kinds of saleswomen found in urban department stores: the Wolf (aggressively on the prowl for customers); the Charmer (who uses her personality to sell goods); the Ingenue Salesgirl (amateurish and self-effacing); the Drifter (who communicates gossip from department to department); the Social Pretender (who claims higher status); and the Old-Timer (a veteran who has become either disgruntled or subservient).[95]

Though Mills portrayed the richness and diversity of white-collar worlds, he nevertheless offered a consistent analysis of what was happening in the white-collar workplace. At all levels of the pyramid, workers were struggling to maintain a distinctive skill or craft and were hence losing their independence. Large, impersonal, bureaucratic organizations were increasingly seizing control of their work via a pervasive "managerial demiurge" that organized their functions from the top down. In the modern workplace, Mills argued, "more and more areas become objects of management and manipulation."[96] For example, as advertising became standardized in regional or national campaigns, salespeople had less autonomy to make sales. Even the salespeople themselves became standardized as organizations looked to hire and train a particular type of person to ply their goods. This trend toward investing more and more control in organizations and less and less in the individual worker affected even those at the top of the white-collar pyramid. Lawyers, for instance, were more likely to work for large corporate "law factories" rather than to set up practice on their own. Middle managers were merely the "cog and beltline of the bureaucratic machinery itself."[97] Reprising his critique of the managerial thesis of James Burnham, Mills argued that top managers of corporations lacked significant autonomous power because they were reliable servants of the owners of large property. At times Mills carefully qualified his description of the bureaucratization of white-collar worlds, noting the persistence of entrepreneurialism in large corporations and the incompleteness of the trends he identified. Other times, he portrayed this shift in more hyperbolic terms. At one point Mills remarked, "It is as if rationality itself had been expropriated from the individual, and been located as a new form of brain power, in the ingenious bureaucracy itself."[98] At another, he concluded, "the alienation of the wage-worker from the products of his work is carried one step nearer to its Kafka-like completion."[99]

Mills's analysis of the deskilling of American work was a key contribution of *White Collar* and pointed the way to later critiques such as Harry Braverman's *Labor and Monopoly Capital*.[100] Though Mills had by this point given up on the labor movement, *White Collar* was still very much a book about labor. Despite his inability to identify any political force or immanent historical development that might counteract the pernicious trends he identified, Mills raised the crucial issue of the meaningfulness of modern work. In criticizing the alienation of modern work, he advanced an ideal of craftsmanship that allowed him to imagine what unalienated labor would look like: this ideal included control over one's work and the notion that work should be individually meaningful and creative. Mills cited Karl Marx, William Morris, John Ruskin, Leo Tolstoy, and Thorstein Veblen as thinkers who had elaborated this ethic of craftsmanship. Yet he pessimistically concluded that this ideal had become "an anachronism" in modern times.[101]

If *White Collar* succeeded as a critique of the bureaucratization and deskilling of work under modern capitalism, its other accomplishments were mixed according to the goals Mills had set himself: to describe the psychology of the new middle classes and to capture their work worlds and their "styles of life," as section three of the book was titled. Mills followed a sociological tradition in arguing that the new middle classes displayed "a psychology of prestige striving," a reliance on their social status for a sense of identity and self-worth.[102] White-collar workers, Mills argued, "borrowed prestige" from their social superiors, as when salespeople identified with wealthy clientele, or when corporation men tied their identities to the names of their prominent companies. Historically, Mills noted, white-collar workers claimed status over blue-collar workers on the basis of several factors: their higher income, paid in salary rather than by the hour; the nonmenial character of their work; their higher educational background; and the ethnic and racial exclusivity of white-collar work (a factor he might have emphasized more). But as an organized working class gained increasing economic and political power, Mills contended, the material bases for prestige were eroding, resulting in a "status-proletarianization" for workers at the bottom of the white-collar pyramid. Such workers, Mills argued, were vulnerable to a "status panic" in which their insecurities and anxieties would surface as they clung to shrinking fragments of prestige.[103]

In *White Collar* Mills endeavored to link character and social structure by envisioning what type of people these new bureaucracies would create. Here, Mills offered a consistent portrait of white-collar workers as "new little men": alienated victims who did not actively participate in the making of their worlds, but who were acted upon by larger social forces that they could not control. Because decisions seemed to emanate from an impersonal bureaucracy, white-collar workers could not even understand the causes of their alienation. "Impersonal manipulation is more insidious than coercion," Mills concluded, "precisely because it is hidden: one cannot locate the enemy and declare war upon him."[104] From this, Mills drew the larger insight that in the modern world, "exploitation becomes less material and more psychological."[105] "One of the characteristic psychological features of the American social structure today," Mills argued, "is its systematic creation and maintenance of estrangement from selfhood and society."[106]

Mills, however, did not consistently treat bureaucratic centralization as the root of psychological alienation. In particular, Mills remained uncertain about the extent to which alienation might also be caused by the continued prevalence of capitalist market relations. He relied heavily on a Marxist tradition that stressed a psychological critique of capitalism, particularly evident in Marx's early writings and in his famous analysis of the "fetishism of commodities" in *Capital*.[107] Echoing Marx, Mills maintained that the priority of the "cash nexus" in modern society meant that "men are estranged from one another as each secretly tries to make an instrument of the other. . . . One makes an instrument of himself, and is estranged from it also."[108] "The market now reaches into every institution and every relation," he asserted.[109] Thus, Mills complained, "men are cogs in a business machinery that has routinized greed and made aggression an impersonal principle of organization."[110] In contrast, Mills continually compared working in modern bureaucracies unfavorably to independent entrepreneurial work in the previously open market. In this sense, the problem resided not in capitalist relations themselves, but in a modern corporate society that had rendered Marx's analysis obsolete. At one point, Mills contended, "The world market, of which Marx spoke as the alien power over men, has in many areas been replaced by the bureaucratized enterprise."[111]

Mills's confusion about the source and nature of white-collar alienation was reflected in his ambivalence about the validity of the Marxist humanist work of Erich Fromm, a German émigré and revisionist psychoanalyst associated with the Frankfurt School. In *Man for Himself*, widely read by American intellectuals, Fromm described a "marketing personality" that conformed in order to avoid the existential dilemma of human freedom.[112] Fromm believed that beneath the marketing personality lay an authentic self. When Mills spoke of white-collar workers being alienated or estranged "from themselves," he implied that he agreed with Fromm. In fact, Mills doubted the existence of such an authentic self. In an unpublished note, Mills rejected Fromm's statement that the marketing personality's misery was due to the fact that "a person is not concerned with his life and happiness, but with becoming saleable." Mills replied, "Isnt all this romantic humanism . . . bullshit . . . dont they get happiness ut of being such good sellers."[113] In *White Collar*, it was unclear whether modern salesmen were alienated because their constant need to market themselves estranged them from their true selves, or because the modern machinery of commercial advertisement had expropriated their entrepreneurial function of deciding how best to sell their goods. Committed to a radically *social* view of the self, Mills found it difficult to fully accept the notion that there was an authentic self from which one could be alienated.[114] In fact, Mills's greatest fear was that white-collar workers might not be able to experience any sense of alienation. If human nature were infinitely malleable, Mills thought, then white-collar workers were possibly the vanguard of a new type of human created by oppressive modern bureaucratic organizations: the "cheerful robot."[115]

For Mills, alienation pervaded not only the work lives of white-collar workers, but their "styles of life" as well. The split between work and leisure activities, Mills argued, fragmented the identity of white-collar workers: they developed an "everyday self" at work and a "holiday self" on nights and weekends. Mass culture, he hypothesized, "diverts them from the restless grind of their work by the absorbing grind of passive enjoyment of glamour and thrills."[116] If work held no inherent meaning for white-collar workers, their free time would be spent largely in "mass leisure activities" that "astonish, excite, and distract" but "do not enlarge reason or feeling, or allow spontaneous dispositions to unfold creatively."[117] "Each day," Mills wrote, "men sell little pieces of themselves in order to buy them back each night and weekend with the coin of 'fun.'"[118] Escapist mass culture, Mills argued, created an "illusory world in which many white-collar people now live."[119] Mills drew here on a mass culture critique common among midcentury leftists and advanced by Frankfurt School intellectuals as well as American authors such as Clement Greenberg and Dwight Macdonald. Mills raised serious questions about the ways mass leisure activities compensate for the lack of meaningful work. Yet, as with other midcentury critics of mass culture, he caricatured the consumers of mass culture as wholly manipulated, passive, and apathetic.[120]

Though Mills attempted to understand the everyday lives of white-collar workers, he neglected factors that may well have given meaning to their lives, such as family and religion. The "new little men" of *White Collar* were more a symbol of larger historical shifts than an accurate representation of how individual white-collar workers lived. Those readers who wanted to know how individuals really behaved in these new bureaucratic organizations would have to turn to other sociologists, such as Erving Goffman.[121] Gerth and Mills's *Character and Social Structure* proposed a model to capture a continual process of interaction between character and social structure. Yet *White Collar* concentrated its attention almost entirely on how social structure shaped character. Mills often inferred the effects on character from his understanding of social structure rather than capturing the interaction between the two. He depicted white-collar workers with sympathy, but nevertheless as victims—"the small creature who is acted upon but who does not act."[122]

Mills's portrait of white-collar workers also suffered because he made scant use of the BASR "Everyday Life" study. The interviews did offer Mills a key source of empirical material for his imaginative depictions and critiques of white-collar worlds and styles of life. But he used this material "only as a source of quotations and an informal limit to psychological statements," promising that the results of the study would be reported in a "later volume on qualitative method" (that volume never appeared).[123] Mills's decision not to take advantage of this rich material reflects the way in which his increasing distance from professional sociology, even as it opened him up to creative possibilities and new audiences, negatively affected his social analysis. The interviews would have offered more evidence for Mills's analysis of white-collar alienation and anxiety. But they also would have allowed him to portray white-collar workers as possessing agency of their own.[124]

Ultimately, Mills's depiction of the expropriation of individual freedom and rationality by large bureaucracies, a process that rendered white-collar workers powerless, revealed his deep disillusionment with political alternatives at the end of the 1940s. Though *White Collar* contained traces of Mills's postwar hope that white-collar workers would align themselves with a politically progressive labor movement, he now saw very little chance of this happening. Nor did Mills fear that American white-collar workers were ripe for joining a right-wing movement, as earlier leftists had worried. In the book's final section, "Ways of Power," he concluded that the new middle classes were politically indifferent, "alienated from politics as a sphere of loyalties, demands, hopes."[125] Passive and apathetic, white-collar workers functioned decisively as a political group not through their actions, but through their inaction: "They are not radical, not liberal, not conservative, not reactionary; they are inactionary; they are out of it. If we accept the Greek's definition of the idiot as a privatized man, then we must conclude that the U.S. citizenry is now largely composed of idiots."[126]

Mills's portrayal of white-collar workers was a Deweyan nightmare. Like Dewey and other progressives, Mills possessed a normative commitment to a deliberative democracy in which individuals would rationally control the social structures that affected their individual lives. Yet, in his empirical description of American society, Mills agreed not with Dewey, but with one of Dewey's most famous critics, Walter Lippmann. According to Mills, Lippmann, whose analysis no liberal could refute, had demonstrated that in the modern world, "the citizen was unable to know what was going on politically, to think about it straight, or to act upon it intelligently."[127] The new little men, Mills argued, were not engaged citizens but "political eunuchs," unwilling and incapable of exerting collective rational control over history and society. Hence, Mills described what he saw as a central irony of modern America: "By virtue of their increased and centralized power, political institutions become more objectively important to the course of American history, but because of mass alienation, less and less of subjective interest to the population at large."[128]

In such a world, the intellectual was also a powerless person. When Mills referred in *White Collar* to "a malady that is particularly acute in the intellectual who believed his thinking would make a difference," he described himself.[129] Nevertheless, Mills attacked those intellectuals who had too easily given up on the "optimistic faith in man's rationality" once common among left-leaning intellectuals.[130] Despite its bleak depiction of white-collar workers as cheerful robots and political eunuchs, *White Collar* contained at least a glimmer of optimism. As he would soon elaborate upon in his essays of the early 1950s, Mills believed that by exposing the faults of American society, intellectuals could help generate democratic debate. The harshness of Mills's portrayal of the "new little men," in a book written not just about them but also for them, was partly intended to strip white-collar workers of their illusions and to spur them to self-consciousness. However disillusioned he was, Mills remained committed to his version of a radicalized "modern sociology," the "first lesson" of which was "that the individual cannot understand his own experience or gauge his own fate without locating himself within the trends of his epoch and the lifechances of all the individuals of his social layer."[131] Even so, it was easy for readers to conclude that such lessons would be lost on the new little men.

'WHITE COLLAR,' 'THE LONELY CROWD,' AND POSTWAR AMERICAN SOCIAL CRITICISM

Scholars have viewed *White Collar* in retrospect as a classic work of social criticism of the 1950s. As I have indicated, the roots of the book actually lay deep in the 1940s. Nevertheless, the publication of the book in 1951 did touch a nerve in American culture of the time. *White Collar* may not have become "everybody's book," as Mills had hoped, but it did make an impact. Widely reviewed in major newspapers and journals of opinion, the book, published by Oxford University Press, sold out its original print run of 3,500 copies in just one month.[132]

Mills reached an audience much larger than professional social scientists and a small coterie of left-wing intellectuals. In large part, this success testified to Mills's talent for conveying sociological insight and radical social critique in clear and vivid prose. The popularity of *White Collar* also offered evidence of what Wilfred McClay has described as "a subterranean stream of doubt that ran beneath the triumphant surface of postwar American culture."[133] The book contributed to a postwar discussion about the meaning of the American dream and the American character, a discourse that focused on the loss of autonomy for middle-class men. Arthur Miller's play *Death of a Salesman* had already appeared in 1949; Sloan Wilson's novel *The Man in the Gray Flannel Suit* would be published 1955; and William H. Whyte's *Organization Man* would appear in 1956, the same year as the release of the classic horror film about conformist "pod people," *Invasion of the Body Snatchers*.[134] Because *White Collar* meshed with a larger discourse about psychological conformity in a new era of affluence, reviewers were less likely to accuse Mills of being an irresponsible radical, an assertion that was more frequently expressed in the reactions to *The Power Elite*.

That said, few reviewers saw American society as bleakly as did Mills. Almost universally, reviewers praised the work as an important jargon-free work of sophisticated sociology and social criticism, yet they rejected its unrelentingly dark portrait of white-collar alienation. The *New York Times* review by Horace Kallen was typical. Kallen praised the book as a "mid-century portrait of the species *homo Americanus*" and recommended it to white-collar readers to alert themselves to "their remoteness from ultimate salvation." Yet Kallen also dubbed Mills "an authentic voice of the futility he portrays" and concluded that *White Collar* was "more a composition produced by paranoid rancor than a configuration emerging from the subject matter itself."[135] Writing in *Commentary*, University of Chicago sociologist Everett C. Hughes found *White Collar* to be "such a combination of facts, brilliant lines and paragraphs, metaphors, tendentious reasoning, and sardonic contempt" as to confound any reviewer. Hughes criticized the book for offering too dehumanizing a portrait of white-collar workers, claiming that Mills had some "cruel fun" at their expense.[136] Reviewers like Kallen and Hughes correctly perceived that Mills's portrait of white-collar workers often verged on caricature, but they failed to grapple with the full force of Mills's critique. Rather than addressing Mills's analysis of the changing institutional structure of American work and

its political implications, these reviewers scored easy points by noting
hat not all white-collar workers were miserable.

Reactions to *White Collar* revealed the distance that Mills had traveled in the early 1950s away from both professional sociologists and
formerly anti-Stalinist radicals. Referring to *White Collar* at a gathering at Harvard, Talcott Parsons apparently remarked, "Well, the man
[Mills] can write some, but it is all impressionistic stuff."[137] Writing
in *Partisan Review*, Dwight Macdonald viciously and indiscriminately
attacked *White Collar,* signaling his own retreat from his former
radicalism and putting an end to his already strained friendship with
Mills. Macdonald's criticisms were harsh and often unjustified. For
instance, he called the book "boring to the point of unreadability" and
inexplicably concluded that Mills was "indifferent" toward American
society. Mills was deeply wounded by Macdonald's negative judgment
and wrote to several close friends and colleagues seeking assurance that
Macdonald's critique had missed its mark.[138]

The most astute review of *White Collar* was written by David Riesman
and appeared in the *American Journal of Sociology*. Riesman began by
commending Mills's "grasp of the jugular" and ended by praising the
book for dealing "resourcefully with the big questions of our day."[139]
Perhaps more important, Riesman assured the journal's readership
that Mills's sociological methods were sound, anticipating the criticisms voiced by professional sociologists such as Parsons. Yet Riesman
criticized the book's portrait of the "new little men," which he believed
missed much of the complexity of white-collar life. For instance, Mills
neglected white-collar agency at work: "He may possibly underestimate
their powers of sabotage, accommodation, and even *joie de vivre,*"
Riesman wrote.[140] Riesman identified the telling absences in Mills's
picture of white-collar "styles of life," which had focused largely on
mass culture. "By robbing the white-collar people . . . of any ethnic,
religious, or other cultural dye," Riesman noted, "the white collar itself
assumes a more wan and celluloidal look than is, on the whole, probably
warranted." Comparing the pessimistic vision of *White Collar* with the
laborite hopes of *The New Men of Power,* Riesman was almost alone
in recognizing *White Collar* as a work of disillusioned radicalism. With
some justice, Riesman contended that Mills's political disenchantment
distorted his picture of white-collar workers: "I think that Mills holds
against the white-collar 'proletariat' not only the actual banalities and
miseries of its life, but also its uselessness in political insurgency . . . and
that this in turn leads him to see even more banality and misery than is

actually there."[141] Mills himself respected Riesman's review. Favorably comparing Riesman to other reviewers who had ducked the main issues raised by the book, Mills wrote Riesman, "It's just plain good to know that at least one man understands what one is about."[142]

It was no accident that, of all the reviewers, Riesman had understood *White Collar* the best. In 1950, Riesman, in collaboration with Nathan Glazer and Reuel Denney, published a pathbreaking sociological study of the new middle classes, *The Lonely Crowd*. *The Lonely Crowd* famously concluded that American society was in the midst of a momentous shift from inner-directed to other-directed character types. Inner-directed types were self-reliant individuals who had clear goals, having internalized their values during childhood; other-directed types were outwardly conformist, constantly looking to other people and to mass culture for guidance.[143] *White Collar* and *The Lonely Crowd* had much in common besides being frequently lumped together by contemporaries and historians as works that criticized 1950s "conformity." They were similar works of sociology: public, humanistic, and overtly critical. Trained as a lawyer and lacking a professional degree in the social sciences, Riesman, like Mills, remained aloof from the dominant postwar mood of sociological professionalism. Like Mills, Riesman communicated sociological insights to a mass public. In this regard, *The Lonely Crowd* was a spectacular success. *The Lonely Crowd* sold half a million copies in the 1950s, making it probably the best-selling work of American social science of all time and landing Riesman on the cover of *Time* in 1954.[144] *The Lonely Crowd* and *White Collar* utilized their authors' imaginations and relied primarily on qualitative sources, including readings of novels and works of mass culture, for their sociological insights. Written at a time of historical transition, as the postwar social order unfolded, both books focused on the connections between character and social structure, and they raised similar questions about the desirability of the new types of people being created. Neither presented unambiguous answers. The works were also similar in what they ignored, particularly issues of poverty, race, and gender.

Interestingly, Mills wrote part of *White Collar* while subletting David Riesman's house in Chicago in 1949. More significantly, the books had a common origin in the "Everyday Life" study that Mills conducted at the BASR. In the spring of 1947, Nathan Glazer, a graduate student in sociology at Columbia and Riesman's eventual collaborator on *The Lonely Crowd*, took a seminar with Mills in which students analyzed the "Everyday Life" data: Glazer was assigned the questions on "political apathy."[145] Mills also shared transcripts of the intensive interviews with Riesman. On the basis of these transcripts, Riesman classified the respondents into three types—the Protestant ethic, marketing ethic, and rational ethic—and suggested that the country was in the midst of a transition from the Protestant ethic to the marketing ethic. These categories were clearly forerunners to those employed in *The Lonely Crowd:* inner-directed, other-directed, and autonomous.[146] Hence, the "Everyday Life" study offered both Riesman and Glazer important hypotheses, which they tested in their own intensive interviews, in which they asked their respondents many of the same questions that Mills had. Indeed, the third author of *The Lonely Crowd,* Reuel Denney, criticized Mills for failing to make greater use of the "Everyday Life" material in *White Collar.* In a March 1952 review titled "Not All Are Victims," he complained, "This reader is left with the impression that Professor Mills has mistakenly edited out of his book a wealth of characterization and anecdote that his original research must have provided."[147]

Riesman's portrayal of the other-directed personality type resembled Mills's critique of the new little men. For Riesman as for Mills, an anxious and politically apathetic personality was emerging during the transition from a production-oriented society to a consumption-oriented one, from entrepreneurial capitalism to bureaucratic capitalism. Like Mills, Riesman believed that the major problems faced by modern men were increasingly psychological. Though middle-class Americans benefited from living in a society of increasing affluence and leisure, Riesman wrote, "They pay for these changes . . . by finding themselves in a centralized and bureaucratized society."[148] Describing the psychological problems created by a "society increasingly dependent on the manipulation of people," Riesman's critique of the other-directed type, who was unable to develop an individuated personality, was similar to Mills's account of the alienated white-collar worker.[149] Always looking to the group for direction, the other-directed type proved incapable of self-direction and self-expression. Riesman summed up his evaluation in a pithy commentary on a well-known rhyme recited by parents while playing with their children's toes: "The rhyme may be taken as a paradigm of individuation and unsocialized behavior among children of an earlier era. Today, however, all little pigs go to market, none stay home, all have roast beef, if any do, and all say 'we-we.'"[150]

The similarities between *White Collar* and *The Lonely Crowd* sug-

gest the extent to which Mills remained embedded within the discourse
of liberal social science. Howard Brick has suggested that Mills's work
bore resemblances to a "postcapitalist vision" shared by liberal social
scientists such as Riesman and Talcott Parsons, a vision that became
especially prevalent during the 1940s.[151] Postcapitalist theorists believed
that American society was undergoing an important transition beyond
traditional forms of capitalism, which required that they develop new
methods for understanding that society. Some of the most important
claims of *White Collar* resonated with postcapitalist discourse. Mills
certainly perceived a not-yet-completed, but fundamental, transition in
American society. Mills employed the term *capitalism* on a few occasions in *White Collar*. Nevertheless, he preferred the phrase *modern
society,* suggesting that he, like postcapitalist theorists, did not find
the word *capitalism* an entirely adequate description for "the outlines
of a new society."[152] Though he continued to argue against the thesis
that managers had replaced owners as the true sources of power in
corporations, like postcapitalist theorists Mills often downplayed the
importance of property relations in modern society, suggesting that
such trends as bureaucratization, rationalization, and centralization were more fundamental. Moreover, Mills believed that modern
society should be understood "in more psychological terms," as did
postcapitalist thinkers such as Riesman and Parsons who developed
a noneconomic conception of civil society.[153] Indeed, Mills's concept
of "status panic" in *White Collar* anticipated some of the social psychological insights of postcapitalist thinkers and leading liberal social
scientists, including Parsons, Riesman, and Daniel Bell.[154] It also influenced Richard Hofstadter's historical interpretation of progressivism as
a movement of the status-frustrated middle class in his influential 1955
book, *The Age of Reform.*[155] Thus, as Brick suggests, Mills might be
understood as offering a pessimistic version of the postcapitalist vision
optimistically expounded by postwar liberals.

There were key differences, however, between Mills's perspective
and that of liberal postcapitalist theorists. This was evident in the
important divergences between *White Collar* and *The Lonely Crowd.*
If *White Collar* was the product of a disillusioned radicalism, then
The Lonely Crowd was the product of a hopeful (though anxious)
postwar liberalism. Riesman placed his hopes on the development of
"autonomous" individuals who were free from both the self-repression
required of the inner-directed type and the desire to conform of the
other-directed type. He located the solution to middle-class confor-

mity within the postwar social order itself, in the "effort to develop a society which accepts rather than rejects new potentialities for leisure, human sympathy, and abundance."[156] Describing the development of autonomous personalities, Riesman focused on the realm of leisure and consumption, offering a more complex analysis of mass culture and middle-class leisure activities than did Mills. *The Lonely Crowd* contained a series of intriguing proposals for employing playful fantasy and active participation to foster more autonomous personalities through leisure activities.

Unlike Mills, however, Riesman often lacked a sense of the social and political obstacles that hindered the development of autonomous character types. Not only did Riesman largely ignore issues of work and focus almost solely on individuals, he often blunted his call for more autonomous personalities at leisure, reducing it to a mere plea for more sophisticated consumers. Calling market research "one of the most promising channels for the democratic control of our economy," Riesman proposed a scheme for creating autonomous character types by developing "free stores" in which children would be given fake money so that they could experiment with playing with different types of goods, while market researchers gauged their responses. If Mills's picture of white-collar alienation was often exaggerated because of its disillusioned radicalism, then Riesman's account was no less distorted by the wishful thinking of its optimistic liberalism. A similar dynamic was evident in the works of other liberal postwar social theorists. For example, Talcott Parsons's earlier critique of individualist society lost its edge in the postwar period when he increasingly identified American society as having superseded competitive individualism, ignoring the political steps necessary to realize the values he simply assumed were now part of the fabric of American life.[157]

White Collar and *The Lonely Crowd* both began as works intended to address the problem of political apathy, and it was on this subject that their differences were the greatest. Riesman treated political apathy as a genuine problem and even argued that utopian visions were necessary, yet his solution was to encourage political participation for individual psychological fulfillment.[158] According to Riesman, political apathy was a psychological problem but it was not a serious political one, because the contemporary United States had an indeterminate and amorphous power structure of countervailing "veto groups" in which power was evenly dispersed. Whereas Riesman psychologized politics, Mills politicized psychology, preserving the notion that a radi-

cal social transformation might abolish individual alienation. It was
Mills's recognition of the social psychological implications of unequal
power relations in American society that sharply distinguished his
work from that of postwar liberals such as Riesman. In his next book,
The Power Elite, Mills would resoundingly debunk Riesman's notion
that the United States no longer suffered from "the power hierarchy of
a ruling class."[159]

CHAPTER 5

The Politics of Truth

'The Power Elite' and 'The Sociological Imagination'

Shaped by the intellectual and political environment of the late 1940s, *White Collar* was the work of a professionally and politically isolated intellectual who espoused a fully disillusioned radicalism. The book thus marked the transition to Mills's influential social analysis of the 1950s. But it was also the product of methods and ideas that Mills had developed over the previous fifteen years. Like *White Collar, The Power Elite* (1956), Mills's influential book on American power and democracy, and *The Sociological Imagination* (1959), his classic critique of professional sociology, were not simply responses to the particular time in which they were written, but reflections of Mills's long-term engagements with social science and the American left. Mills's signature contributions to the discussions of the 1950s were based on the ideas he had developed in the late 1930s and 1940s.

In the early 1950s, Mills's political isolation led him once again to turn inward and consider the proper moral and political responsibilities of intellectuals, much as he had during the early 1940s. In essays published during the first half of the 1950s, Mills argued that in an age of sharply diminished possibilities for left-wing social transformation, the radical intellectual should practice a "politics of truth." The politics of truth provided a demystifying social analysis that debunked official definitions of reality. Truth-telling, in this sense, was automatically radical. Both the strengths and limitations of the politics of truth were evident in *The Power Elite*. As a critical stance, Mills's politics of

truth was well suited to the postwar period. *The Power Elite* successfully revealed the weaknesses of liberal postwar democratic theory and
exposed how American corporate and government institutions in the
cold war era had obtained an unprecedented power to officially define
social reality. Yet *The Power Elite* was limited not only by the bleak
pessimism of Mills's disillusioned radicalism, but also by the desperate
self-righteousness of an author overly confident in his own sense of
the truth. The most compelling contribution of *The Power Elite* was
its elaboration of an ideal of a politics of truth practiced collectively,
in which realities, values, and policies would be open to public debate
in a society organized around democratic participation. This vision
underlay Mills's most persuasive analysis of how American elites sub-
verted their nation's democratic promise. Mills's sharp condemnation
of the nation's power elite clearly distinguished his political stance
from that of postwar liberals. Indeed, many liberal social scientists,
including several erstwhile radicals, felt compelled to refute the claims
of *The Power Elite*. The liberal view of a mostly benign postwar consensus, reflected in the phrase "the end of ideology," contrasted sharply
with Mills's dystopian analysis of diminished American democracy.
Nevertheless, even though Mills evaluated postwar American society
differently than did liberals, his analysis resembled theirs in certain key
respects. Even Mills's critique of liberal ideas drew on values that he
shared with them. In this sense, Mills reflected his continued embeddedness in a discourse of liberal social science.

Of all of Mills's major works, the last one, *The Sociological Imagination*, elaborates upon themes that most closely resemble those he
developed in the late 1930s and early 1940s. Only by understanding his
earlier methodological and theoretical work is it possible to grasp his
influential critique of the discipline as split between Parsonian "grand
theory" and Lazarsfeldian "abstract empiricism." Mills's sense of isolation negatively affected *The Sociological Imagination:* he implied
that contemporary professional sociology as a whole had defaulted
on the classic promise of social science. Accordingly, he ignored alternative social scientific trends. The underlying structure of the book
contrasted his despairing portrait of contemporary sociology with his
inspirational vision of what social analysis could achieve—his compelling description of the "sociological imagination," built on his earliest
intellectual commitments developed through engagements with pragmatism, the sociology of knowledge, and Max Weber. Nevertheless,
The Sociological Imagination was much more than a treatise on socio-

logical methods and ideas. For the cultural promise that Mills saw in the expansion of the sociological imagination connected inextricably to the political promise that he saw in the politics of truth as a form of democratic participation. "The social sciences," he claimed, "are becoming the common denominator of our cultural period."[1] In *The Sociological Imagination,* Mills argued what was already implicit in *The Power Elite:* that sociological knowledge, made available for wider public debate, could provide the basis for a popular movement to reinvigorate American democracy.

THE RESPONSIBILITY OF INTELLECTUALS

Mills wrote *White Collar* in the rapidly shifting political landscape of the late 1940s, but by the first half of the 1950s the postwar political order had stabilized. As he feared, this new order excluded widespread discussion of radical political ideas. Mills spent much of the first half of the 1950s ruminating on one of his favorite topics, the proper role of the intellectual in society. As he had during his initial period of disillusioned radicalism, in the early 1940s, Mills formulated the responsibility of the intellectual in terms of the "politics of truth." Mills's politics of truth had two components: exposing the power of American leaders to manipulate the public's understandings of social reality, and asserting the intellectual's special responsibility to challenge that officially defined reality and to aid the formation of democratic publics.

Mills often expressed his politics of truth as a polemic against American liberals. Like many postwar thinkers, Mills viewed liberalism as the only significant American ideology and discounted the notion of a conservative intellectual tradition in the United States. "In America," Mills concluded, "liberalism—and the middle classes that bore it as a deep-seated style of thought—has become so paramount as to preclude any flowering of genuinely conservative ideology."[2] As such, Mills set the parameters of intellectual debate: his own form of radicalism, on the margin, and what he challenged as a "conservative liberalism," the product of postwar affluence and the past success of New Deal programs, at the center. This framed intellectual discussions about American politics in a way that established Mills as a steadfast champion of radical ideas against a compromised liberalism, but it ignored both conservative American intellectual traditions and the elements that liberalism and radicalism held in common.

Mills took particular aim at the deradicalized New York intellectuals. Perhaps his most famous attack against this group was his contribution to the 1952 symposium held by *Partisan Review*, "Our Country and Our Culture." As the symbolic organ of the New York intellectuals, *Partisan Review* embodied the postwar decline of the intellectual Old Left, a process already evident by the early 1940s, when Dwight Macdonald left the magazine to form *politics*. By the early 1950s, *Partisan Review* had completed its transition and become a central forum in the creation of a new cold war liberalism. Many of the intellectuals who played a key role in this development, such as Sidney Hook, Reinhold Niebuhr, David Riesman, Arthur Schlesinger Jr., and Lionel Trilling, contributed to the symposium.

Even in the postwar period, the *Partisan Review* circle believed that intellectuals should maintain adversarial roles as defenders of literary and artistic modernism against mass culture. The magazine, however, became a significant voice calling for intellectuals to abandon their earlier positions as alienated political radicals and to embrace a more optimistic view of American society. Introducing the symposium, editors William Phillips and Philip Rahv wrote, "American intellectuals now regard America and its institutions in a different way. Until little more than a decade ago, America was commonly thought hostile to art and culture. Since then, however, the tide has begun to turn and intellectuals now feel closer to their country and its culture."[3] A crucial feature of this shift was the sense among anti-Stalinist intellectuals that American society must be embraced as a bulwark against the Soviet Union. For example, Phillips and Rahv claimed, "There is a recognition that the kind of democracy which exists in America has an intrinsic and positive value: it is not merely a capitalist myth, but a reality which must be defended against Russian totalitarianism."[4] Not all contributors to the symposium viewed American society optimistically or embraced a complacent view of American politics. However, *Partisan Review* had clearly become entrenched in mainstream American politics. In the 1950s the magazine was aided in overcoming financial difficulties by secret grants from both media mogul Henry Luce and the CIA, each funneled through the cold war liberal organization the Congress for Cultural Freedom.[5]

Mills's response to the symposium solidified his status as the most prominent intellectual to maintain the older ideal of the radical intellectual. To Mills, the transformation of *Partisan Review* represented nothing less than the complete abdication of the intellectual's critical responsibility. "American intellectuals do seem to have quite decisively

shifted their attitudes toward America," he wrote in his contribution:
"One minor token of the shift is available to those who imagine 'the
old PR' running the title 'Our Country . . . ,' etc. in 1939. You would
have cringed. Don't you want to ask from what and to what the shift
has occurred? From a political and critical orientation toward life and
letters to a more literary and less politically critical view. Or: generally
to a shrinking deference to the status quo; often to a soft and anxious
compliance, and always a synthetic, feeble search to justify this intellectual conduct, without searching for alternatives."[6] Postwar liberals, Mills claimed, engaged in an "American celebration." Although
concerned about "the discrepancy between the enormous military and
economic power of the United States and its relatively low cultural level
and prestige," they avoided difficult and important questions about
the power structure of American society.[7] Given the lack of a left-wing
political movement, Mills concluded that the best course available to
the radical intellectual was to continue to raise the possibility of alternatives while discounting left-wing programs for action that were, at
least for the moment, utopian. "One just has to wait, as others before
one have," he wrote, "while remembering that what in one decade is
utopian may in the next be implementable."[8]

By the mid-1950s, Mills found that he was not entirely alone in his
adherence to radical ideas. Other intellectuals of Mills's generation
who maintained their allegiance to left-wing ideals similarly stressed
the special responsibility of the independent intellectual to criticize
American society. According to them, social analysis could preserve in
thought what could no longer be realized in action. The one-word title
of the magazine that Lewis Coser and Irving Howe founded in 1954
perfectly captured this attitude: *Dissent.* Coser had been one of the few
participants in Mills's "Dialogs on the Left" in the late 1940s, an early
attempt to keep left-wing ideas alive and rethink their significance for
the postwar period. Howe, however, was the principal force behind
Dissent. In 1952, convinced that the possibilities for creating a significant left-wing movement were dead, Howe left the Workers Party,
writing in his statement of resignation that "the major task of socialists
today is to engage in sustained intellectual activity, mainly with the end
of reorienting and reeducating ourselves."[9] Like Mills, Howe defended
in *Partisan Review* the ideal of the critical intellectual in a polemic
against deradicalized intellectuals. In his widely noted essay "This
Age of Conformity," Howe maintained his allegiance to "the idea of a
mind committed yet dispassionate, ready to stand alone, curious, eager,

skeptical." "The banner of critical independence," he declared, "ragged and torn though it may be, is still the best we have."[10] Designating the magazine a forum for discussion by "independent radicals," Coser and Howe founded *Dissent* with the frank recognition that "in America today there is no significant socialist movement and that, in all likelihood, no such movement will appear in the near future."[11] In his first editorial, Coser ruminated, "The least a radical can do in these years of the locusts is to try not to be a dupe. We may be unable to affect the course of history, but we can still control our thinking; we should at least avoid the double-talk and word-magic that is so popular today."[12] Appropriately, the first issue of *Dissent* contained an article by Mills, "The Conservative Mood," castigating that inclination in American thought and politics.[13]

Dissent never replaced *politics,* and its posture became less radical over time, edging toward a social-democratic liberalism. Yet as Maurice Isserman has argued, the magazine provided one of the few institutional bridges between the Old Left and the New.[14] For Mills, *Dissent* offered at least the modest hope that others might join him in practicing a politics of truth. Though Mills declined to serve on its editorial board, he defended the magazine against Nathan Glazer's attack in *Commentary* that alleged *Dissent* lacked a consistent political program. Mills argued that Glazer asked too much of a magazine in its infancy: "There comes a time . . . when to think freshly, to define reality again, to try to find a way out of a trap, the prevailing mood has got to be debunked and transcended." *Dissent,* then, was valuable as an attempt at "the joining of intelligence and politics."[15]

It was in the pages of *Dissent* in 1954 that Mills published "On Knowledge and Power," his most definitive statement on the responsibility of intellectuals since "The Powerless People," published in 1944. "On Knowledge and Power" began with Mills's familiar lament that American intellectuals had abandoned the "the grand role of reason in civilization" and "the old ideal of the public relevance of knowledge."[16] The collapse of liberal ideology was a central part of Mills's story. He argued that the New Deal had left behind no powerful organization to continue to push for reforms and had transformed liberalism into a banal rhetoric, a set of administrative routines rather than a fighting political faith. Dismissing McCarthyism as a passing movement of the status-frustrated, Mills was more disturbed by liberal intellectuals "so busy defending civil liberties that they have had neither the time nor the inclination to *use* them."[17] It is remarkable that Mills so easily dismissed the postwar red scare, given its significant role in repressing radical ideas and politics. Several of the postwar liberals whom Mills attacked defended civil liberties from the McCarthyist threat more vigorously than did Mills.

Mills's foremost theme in "On Knowledge and Power" was the "absence of mind as any sort of a public force," and his key insight was that truth itself was political, "officially defined by those who have power."[18] Practicing the politics of truth held out the promise that truth might become political in another sense, that is, that it could become open to democratic debate. Mills assigned intellectuals a special task in developing the politics of truth, for though they were powerless to make political decisions, they remained politically relevant "in connection with the legitimations and the representations of power and decision."[19] Mills fully elaborated his notion of the intellectual's responsibility:

> As a type of social man, the intellectual does not have any one political direction, but the work of any man of knowledge, if he is the genuine article, does have a distinct kind of political relevance: his politics, in the first instance, are the politics of truth, for his job is the maintenance of an adequate definition of reality. In so far as he is politically adroit, the main tenet of this politics is to find out as much of the truth as he can, and to tell it to the right people, at the right time, and in the right way. Or, stated negatively: to deny publicly what he knows to be false, whenever it appears in the assertions of no matter whom. . . . The intellectual ought to be the moral conscience of his society, at least with reference to the value of truth, for in the defining instance, that *is* his politics. And he ought also to be a man absorbed in the attempt to know what is real and unreal.[20]

The focus on intellectuals' political duty in "On Knowledge and Power" was remarkably consistent with that of "The Powerless People," published a decade earlier. Both essays recognized the extent to which elites bypassed democratic debate and postulated the intellectual's responsibility to counteract that development by practicing a politics of truth. Mills's honest despair about the potential for left-wing movements in each essay caused him to emphasize his certainty in the special duties of the intellectual at a time when he was very uncertain about what, if anything, could be done politically. Both essays shared similar problems. Neither, for example, resolved the epistemological tension between pragmatism and rationalism. Mills viewed truth as inherently contextual and political, yet his call for a politics of truth rested on the notion that if one could see through the obfuscation of official shams, one could uncover *the* truth about American society. Though Mills thought that beliefs were fixed *socially,* an idea ingrained in his mind-set from his early engagement with pragmatism and the sociology of knowledge, his politics of truth placed its faith in the efforts of coura-geous *individuals.* Moreover, in claiming that the independent radical intellectual could obtain a privileged access to the truth, Mills employed a circular logic: the intellectual could find out the truth because he was radical, and yet he was radical because he told the truth.

Nevertheless, there was a small but perceptible difference in tone between "The Powerless People" and "On Knowledge and Power." In "On Knowledge and Power," Mills appeared more optimistic about the potential for knowledge to have "liberating public relevance."[21] Mills moved ever so slightly away from the dark disillusionment of the late 1940s and early 1950s toward a more hopeful outlook. The appearance of *Dissent* suggested to Mills a thawing in the postwar political atmo-sphere. In the magazine's first issue, Mills presented the retreat of intel-lectuals into a "conservative mood" not as structurally determined, but as a potentially reversible trend. No longer hoping for a union of power and intellect, Mills began to believe in the political potential of autonomous intellect, a development that would eventually culminate with his embrace of the "cultural apparatus" as a New Left agency. Yet, as Mills still saw no significant agency for left-wing change, "On Knowledge and Power" concluded with the negative judgment that "knowledge does not now have democratic relevance in America."[22]

Mills incorporated much of "On Knowledge and Power" into *The Power Elite.* Even though the book remained a work of disillusioned radicalism, offering a pessimistic portrait of American democracy, Mills wrote it with the modest hope of making some difference by advanc-ing the type of understanding needed as a precondition of change. The interest many of his friends took in the book, a number of whom were connected to *Dissent,* encouraged Mills. As he wrote to Harvey Swados, "I think I want to say that many people want to help make it less open to criticism because they so want this said. They are tired of the bullshit you know, and it may just be that the book will become a little pivot on which the tide will turn."[23] *The Power Elite* offered the clearest expression of Mills's politics of truth. As Mills explained in "Why I Wrote *The Power Elite,*" after the book had been adopted as a selection by the Book Find News book club, "Today, as readers and writers, we must make an effort to avoid being taken in, for this is an age of the myth and the distraction. In such an age, the task of any serious book is to unmask illusion in order truly to define important features of social reality. The task cannot be accomplished merely through providing information, although information on the high and mighty is badly needed, we must also try to grind a lens through which we can perhaps see a little more clearly the world in which we live."[24]

'THE POWER ELITE'

Shortly after finishing *White Collar*, Mills began work on a book he tentatively titled *The High and the Mighty*. This book on the upper classes would complete his "trilogy" on American social stratification that had begun with a book on the labor movement and continued with his investigation of white-collar workers. In these three books, Mills explained, he would cover the bottom, middle, and top of the American social order.[25] Research for the new book proved challenging, since locating definitive information on the elite was difficult. As Mills reflected in the book's acknowledgments, "Were we to select our field of study according to the ready availability of much unworked material, we should never choose the elite. And yet, if we are trying to understand something of the true nature of the society in which we live, we cannot allow the impossibility of rigorous proof to keep us from studying whatever we believe important."[26] Mills drew on a variety of sources to construct career-line biographies of the nation's top economic, military, and political leaders, sketching their social and economic backgrounds and tracing their paths to obtaining important posts. Yet, as Mills himself realized, this evidence hardly proved his far-reaching claims about the domination of the power elite and the weakness of American democracy. To compensate for the general lack of research on the elite, Mills brilliantly developed his own interpretation of mainstream media stories, drawing particularly from the *New York Times* and the business press. "The magazine is being cut up, literally issue by issue, for the purposes of this study," he wrote in an unsuccessful attempt to persuade Columbia to reimburse his 1953 subscription to *Fortune* magazine as a research expense.[27] Mills's wife, Ruth Harper Mills, an experienced statistical researcher, proved indispensable as the book's "chief researcher and editorial adviser."[28]

For the most part, *The Power Elite* reads as the gradual development of a single thesis, making it more coherent than *White Collar*. After an initial chapter outlining his argument, Mills began slowly, describing the historical shift of power in the United States from the local to the national level. He then devoted multiple chapters to examining each portion of the power elite in turn: the "corporate rich," the "warlords," and the "political directorate." Distinguishing his theory of the power elite from the "theory of balance" promulgated by liberal pluralists, Mills then described the interlocking nature of what he described as a "triangle of power."[29] A thirteenth chapter discussed the "mass society," reprising the analysis of *White Collar,* but also introducing Mills's normative notion of a democracy based on widespread public discussion and participation. The final two chapters, based on earlier articles condemning the conservative mood among American intellectuals, denounced an irresponsible "higher immorality" among the elites.

Mills's "power elite" concept perplexed many of the book's commentators, yet some of this confusion can be cleared up if we recall the pragmatist, historicist, and contextualist methodology Mills had espoused since his student years. As a theoretical concept, Mills's "power elite" was deceptively straightforward: it referred to a minority of leaders who, though not omnipotent, held enough power to be demarcated sharply from the mass of citizens. Mills rejected the idea, which he attributed to the classic sociological theorists of elites—Vilfredo Pareto, Gaetano Mosca, and Robert Michels—that an elite always functioned as the operating force in history. According to Mosca, for instance, "In all societies . . . two classes of people appear—a class that rules and a class that is ruled. The first class, always the less numerous, performs all political functions, monopolizes power and enjoys the advantages that power brings."[30] In contrast, Mills dismissed any such generalizations, contending that the existence of a power elite was open to empirical inquiry. Simply because he used the term "elite," many commentators incorrectly assumed that elite theorists had significantly influenced Mills.[31]

The concept of a "power elite" can be applied to any society in which a minority holds a disproportionate amount of power. One could speak of "power elites" in nineteenth-century France, for example, or of "power elites" in earlier epochs of U.S. history, as Mills did. Mills, however, invited confusion by using the term both as a theoretical concept and as an empirical description. Primarily, he used it to refer to *the* power elite of the mid-twentieth-century United States. After all, Mills's book was valuable not for any general theoretical contribution, but for his account of who ruled America at that time. As an empirical description of contemporary American society, "power elite" specified "those political, economic, and military circles which as an intricate set of overlapping cliques share decisions having at least national consequences."[32] By locating power in the political, economic, and military realms (three of the five social orders identified by Mills and Gerth in *Character and Social Structure*), Mills denied significant autonomous power to institutions of religion and kinship. Moreover, Mills argued that because of the enlargement and centralization of large-scale bureaucracies and the development of nuclear technology, American leaders possessed greater power than any previous set of leaders; thus, in historical terms, they could be considered *the* power elite.

The Power Elite expressed Mills's fundamentally institutional understanding of power as located in the control of pivotal organizations, a perspective he had developed through his earlier engagement with thinkers such as Weber and Veblen. Mills thus identified power in the "major hierarchies and organizations of modern society" and the "strategic command posts of the social structure."[33] Making a semantic choice that provoked a great deal of commentary from left-wing critics, Mills stated in a much-scrutinized footnote that he preferred the term "power elite" to the Marxist "ruling class" because he felt the Marxist term implied a "short-cut theory," prejudging the issue of whether an economic class ruled politically.[34] Mills confused many of his readers by defining "class" as strictly economic, a definition not always shared by either fellow social scientists or left-wing critics. Many Marxists employed more subtle theories of a ruling class that did not reduce everything to economics; in fact, Frankfurt School Marxist Franz Neumann influenced Mills's own theory of the power elite. Even so, Mills distinguished himself from vulgar Marxists by emphasizing the real or potential autonomy of political and military power. Following Weber, Mills rejected the rigid economic determinism he attributed to Marxists and stressed the autonomy of different social spheres. In his rejection of the term "ruling class," Mills used language similar to that employed in the introduction to Gerth and Mills's *From Max Weber:* "We hold that such a simple view of 'economic determinism' must be elaborated by 'political determinism' and 'military determinism'; that the higher agents of each of these three domains now often have a noticeable degree of autonomy; and that only in the often intricate ways of coalition do they make up and carry through the most important decisions."[35]

In the first chapters of *The Power Elite*, Mills argued that power in the United States was no longer dispersed locally or regionally but was now concentrated nationally. Though the book contained chapters on "local society" and the "metropolitan 400," Mills demonstrated that "during the past century, local society has become part of a national economy; its status and power hierarchies have come to be subordinate parts of the larger hierarchies of the nation. Even as early as the decades after the Civil War, persons of local eminence were becoming—merely local."[36] Eventually, even those who wanted to retain local prominence had to connect themselves to national institutions. Mills argued that not only power but also prestige had become nationalized, through the emergence of an American celebrity system. In these early chapters, Mills continued his attack on localized "milieu" approaches to sociology, criticizing figures such as W. Lloyd Warner, who sought to extrapolate the American system of power from studies of local communities.[37]

Following his discussion of local and metropolitan leaders, Mills proceeded to discuss the nationally important economic, military, and political elites. Mills's career-line data established that wealth in America tended to perpetuate itself and undermined the myth that the post–New Deal United States no longer had a class of the "very rich." Seven out of ten members of the very rich in the contemporary United States, Mills explained, came from upper-class backgrounds. Moreover, they constituted a "uniform social type": white, Protestant, urban, and well educated. Mills maintained that Americans accumulated wealth through neither entrepreneurial ingenuity nor a bureaucratic crawl to the top of an organization, but through financial, speculative, and legal manipulations of the market. There was more than a little muckraking in these chapters, which unmasked the inherited privileges of the American rich, as Mills drew upon the work of earlier American critics such as Matthew Josephson, Gustavus Myers, and Thorstein Veblen.[38]

Mills updated the standard progressive critique by taking into account the rise of "the corporate rich." Mills stressed the power that corporations, which as "political institutions . . . are of course totalitarian and dictatorial," held over the economic lives of all Americans.[39] "Their private decisions," Mills wrote, "responsibly made in the interests of their feudal-like world of private property and income, determine the size and shape of the national economy, the level of employment, the purchasing power of the consumer, the prices that are advertised, the investments that are channeled."[40] Mills argued that the wealth of very rich individuals increasingly depended on their institutional role in corporations. For instance, Mills pointed to the growth of "higher emoluments," his phrase for the tax-free benefits enjoyed by top corporate executives, such as expense accounts, free travel, and luxurious entertainment facilities. And, as Mills pointed out, a mere 0.2 to 0.3 percent of the population owned the bulk of corporate stock. Though he admitted some divisions and conflicts, Mills portrayed a highly unified rich that possessed the class consciousness lacking among American workers, be their collars blue or white. In social terms, the rich participated in the same institutions, such as elite boarding schools, private universities, and clubs. In structural terms, Mills even claimed that some top corporate leaders were completing the "move from the industrial point of interest and outlook to the interests and outlook of the class of all big corporate property as a whole," because their wealth and position increasingly relied on corporations.[41]

Mills argued that the "military ascendancy" since World War II justified his inclusion of top military leaders in the power elite. Their rise was evident in the vast percentage of the federal budget—ranging from 30 to 50 percent since the start of World War II—devoted to military expenses at the time.[42] Drawing on his career-line data, Mills argued that military leaders achieved their position through the most bureaucratic route of any of the elites. The symbol of the military bureaucracy was the newly constructed Pentagon, which represented "the scale and shape of the new military edifice" and "the organized brain of the American means of violence."[43] According to Mills, the military ascendancy had overturned the longtime American tradition of civilian control, upsetting the optimistic assumptions of nineteenth-century liberals that the military would come to play a diminishing role in industrial societies. Mills claimed that military leaders filled a power vacuum left by political leaders, and in many cases conducted diplomacy and made foreign policy on their own initiative. In addition to acquiring new political power, the military also played an increasingly important role in the economy. Mills further showed that retired military leaders served on the boards of many corporations that profited from increased military expenditure.

The third group forming Mills's power elite was the "political directorate." Mills believed that political institutions were now central to the American power structure, yet a fundamental element of Mills's critique of American politics was the decline of the autonomy of elected political leaders. At one point, Mills remarked, "It is the professional politician that has lost the most [since World War II], so much that in examining the events and decisions, one is tempted to speak of a political vacuum in which the corporate rich and the high warlord, in their coinciding interests, rule."[44] Mills's career-line data indicated that top political leaders in the executive branch were increasingly "political outsiders" from the corporate or military sector rather than professional politicians. Because the United States lacked an independent civil service, industry insiders had captured government regulation agencies and used them for their own ends. Mills contrasted the postwar era with the "political decade" of the 1930s, when "the power of business was not replaced, but it was contested and supplemented: it became one major power within a structure of power that was chiefly run by political men, and not by economic or military men turned political."[45]

Though Mills saw the economic, political, and military institutional orders as distinct, he made a strong case for the power elite's cohesiveness. "Nowhere in America is there as great a 'class consciousness' as among the elite; nowhere is it organized as effectively as among the power elite."[46] Mills cited instances of elite circulation through these three spheres, examples that were numerous in the Eisenhower administration. Of the approximately fifty top executive posts in that administration, three-quarters were filled by political outsiders with little professional experience in politics. The majority had close ties to the corporate world, such as Charles Erwin Wilson, Eisenhower's secretary of defense and the former CEO of General Motors, who famously said in his confirmation hearing that "what was good for the country was good for General Motors, and vice versa."[47] Of course, Eisenhower himself had no experience as an elected official, but had moved from general to president, with a short stint in between as Mills's boss as president of Columbia University. Hence, Mills concluded, "This administration . . . is largely an inner circle of political outsiders who have taken over the key executive posts of administrative command; it is composed of members and agents of the corporate rich and of the high military in an uneasy alliance with selected professional party politicians seated primarily in the Congress."[48]

In part, Mills's argument about elite cohesiveness rested on "psychological and social bases for their unity."[49] Referring to corporate leaders who obtained top government posts, Mills speculated, "The interesting point is how impossible it is for such men to divest themselves of their engagement with the corporate world in general and with their own corporations in particular. Not only their money, but their friends, their interests, their training—their lives in short—are deeply involved in this world."[50]

Mills argued that elite unity relied primarily on the integration of political, military, and corporate institutions since World War II. "The increased personnel traffic that goes on between the military and the corporate realms," he claimed, "is more important as one clue to a structural fact about the United States than as an expeditious way of handling war contracts. Back of this shift at the top, and behind the increased military budget upon which it rests, there lies the great structural shift of modern American capitalism toward a permanent war economy."[51] The postwar debate over the reconversion of the wartime economy, he claimed, constituted a crucial moment in prolonging the military-corporate cooperation that had emerged during World War II: "The military might lose power; the corporations would no longer produce under the prime contracts they held; reconversion, if not handled carefully, could easily disturb the patterns of monopoly prevailing before war production began. The generals and the dollar-a-year executives saw to it that this did not happen."[52] Those familiar with his earlier work could recognize Mills's heavy borrowing from his own analysis of sophisticated conservatism, which he developed during the 1940s. Yet surprisingly, since a considerable part of Mills's thesis rested on proving the existence of a permanent war economy coordinated by economic, military, and political elites, Mills only referred to this in passing. Mills did not provide a detailed analysis of the collusion of different groups of the power elite in the construction of a permanent military economy, even though he contended that such a conjunction of institutional interests provided the most conclusive proof of the existence of a power elite.

The Power Elite undermined the prevailing pluralist understanding of American democracy that had had pervaded American social science since the interwar period and was particularly influential after World War II. To pluralists, the state was a neutral arena in which various interest groups competed, rather than a significant force in its own right. According to this theory, the American political system was dominated by competing "interest groups" (David Truman), "veto groups" (David Riesman), or "countervailing powers" (John Kenneth Galbraith), which provided balance and stability by checking one another's power.[53] In the view of influential pluralist Robert Dahl, the United States operated as a "polyarchal democracy" in which "minorities" of powerful interest groups ruled. It was a system in which "non-leaders exercise a high degree of control over governmental leaders" but which did not entail the informed participation of most ordinary citizens.[54] Generally wary of mass political participation, liberal social scientists like Dahl placed their faith in the leadership of responsible elites.[55]

Mills's critique of pluralists, whom he mocked as the "balancing boys" because of their belief that interest group conflict created a harmonious order, was both empirical and normative. His institutional approach to American politics challenged the widespread statistical approach. As he argued, the political scientist neglected crucial structural features of American politics, often becoming merely a "systematic student of elections, of who voted for whom."[56] To a large degree, Mills accepted the pluralist claim that competing interest groups heavily influenced the legislative branch of government, but he argued that Congress was merely at the "middle levels of power," with congressmen representing local interests and pressure groups "concerned merely with their particular cut."[57] Many crucial "big decisions," Mills pointed out, were not presented for legislative or public debate and were unaffected by the input of interest groups. Countering the pluralists, Mills demonstrated that political and military institutions increasingly empowered those who controlled them and were often insulated from interest group pressure.

Mills's most convincing point was that the decisions made by a few leaders in the powerful and often secretive national security state could not be understood in pluralist terms. "Exactly *what,*" he asked sarcastically, "directly or indirectly, did 'small retailers' or 'brick masons' have to do with the sequence of decision and event that led to World War II? What did 'insurance agents,' or, for that matter, the Congress, have to do with the decision to make or not to make, to drop or not to drop, the early model of the new weapon?"[58] The power to decide foreign and military policy, Mills pointed out, was not dispersed among competing interest groups. Rather, such power was concentrated in the hands of a few top leaders. No decision was as important as that to make war, particularly in the nuclear age. For this reason, Mills's argument that the American and Soviet elites were the most powerful in history was persuasive: "The men of either circle," Mills grimly observed, "can cause great cities to be wiped out in a single night, and in a few weeks turn continents into thermonuclear wastelands."[59] Furthermore, Mills argued that with the rise of a permanent war economy, even domestic policy could no longer be understood in terms of struggles among competing interest groups, as "international issues are truly at the center of the most important national decisions and increasingly relevant to virtually all decisions of consequence."[60]

Because Mills correctly perceived that power had become increasingly concentrated in crucial national institutions, the attempts by some pluralists over the next decade to disprove *The Power Elite* through community studies missed their mark.[61] Yet Mills's institutional critique of the pluralist understanding of the American political system was vulnerable to some criticism, suffering from his tendency toward overstatement. Even if domestic politics were increasingly bound up with foreign policy, it was difficult to understand these dynamics without looking more closely at what Mills called the "middle levels of power." Mills's suggestion that "Between [the power elite] . . . and the family and the small community . . . we find no intermediate associations in which men feel secure and with which they feel powerful" overlooked a host of political associations in which Americans participated.[62] Moreover, significant political power in the United States remained on the local, state, and regional levels, as well as in the legislative and judicial branches of the national government. Accordingly, *The Power Elite* failed as a model for understanding racism in American society, an issue to which Mills turned a blind eye in any case. The framework of *The Power Elite* could hardly imagine the emergence to national prominence of the African-American civil rights movement, rooted in community and religious networks, even though the book was published after the Montgomery bus boycott of 1955 to 1956. Thus, even though *The Power Elite* succeeded in refuting the prevailing pluralist descriptions of American democracy, it offered an incomplete account of American democracy.

Mills's most basic challenge to the pluralists rested not on his different empirical description of American politics but on his competing value judgments. Insisting that values were necessarily implicated in any social analysis, Mills exposed pluralism as an ideology justifying the status quo. For pluralists to praise the American political system for achieving harmony among interests, Mills argued, was to accept the present balance of interests: "But . . . the goals for which interests struggle are not merely given; they reflect the current state of expectation and acceptance. Accordingly, to say that various interests are 'balanced' is generally to evaluate the *status quo* as satisfactory or even good; the hopeful ideal of balance often masquerades as a description of fact."[63] Dahl, for example, praised the American political structure as "a relatively efficient system for reinforcing agreement, encouraging moderation, and maintaining social peace in a restless and immoderate people operating a gigantic, powerful, diversified, and incredibly complex society."[64]

Mills argued that the pluralist understanding of democracy was impoverished. In its stead, he advanced a more expansive definition of democracy, suggesting that only when ordinary citizens employed substantive reasoning to shape government policy directly could a society be considered truly democratic. Mills's ideal society was one "in which men at large are presented with genuine alternatives, the moral meanings of which are clearly open to public debate."[65] Mills never used the phrase "participatory democracy," coined by the political theorist Arnold Kaufman and popularized by the New Left organization Students for a Democratic Society, but it accurately captured Mills's perspective.[66] Mills called for the reinvigoration of "publics" that offered competing definitions of reality and participated in widespread substantive debates of pressing social and political issues. Democratic participation, in this sense, not only achieved collective rational social control, but it also relieved individual alienation through participation in meaningful activity. As Mills wrote, "To belong in this [political] way is to make the human association a psychological center of one's self, to take into our conscience, deliberately and freely, its rules of conduct and its purposes, which we thus shape and which in turn shape us."[67]

Ultimately the contributions and limitations of *The Power Elite* as a work of social analysis can be attributed to Mills's disillusioned radicalism and his signature strategy, the politics of truth. One of the book's enduring strengths was Mills's recognition of the power of elites in the age of mass communication to define the terms by which citizens understand social and political reality. In contrast with the pluralist stress on government as responding to the concerns of organized interest groups, Mills emphasized the power of the state to shape, suppress, and distort public debate. In *The Power Elite,* this insight allowed Mills to challenge the pervasive cold war rhetoric that had emerged over the past decade. For Mills, the "crackpot realism" of cold war doctrine relied on the threat of "mutually assured destruction" as a means of peace. The military ascendancy, Mills argued, emerged from the prevailing "military definition of reality."[68] Indeed, the military itself, Mills noted, was involved in a public relations campaign to "define the reality of international relations in a military way, to portray the armed forces in a manner attractive to civilians, and thus to emphasize the need for the expansion of military facilities."[69] In an age when elites relied upon official secrecy and public relations, it was easy to see why Mills turned to truth-telling as an oppositional political strategy.

Mills's insight into the tremendous power of elites to shape the public's perception of reality was limited, however, by his disillusioned radicalism. Some of the general weaknesses of his perspective evident in *White Collar* were equally present in *The Power Elite*. Deeply frustrated with the contemporary prospects for left-wing movements, Mills presented an exaggerated picture of an American mass society. If the elites were as powerful as Mills portrayed them in *The Power Elite,* then the reader could easily conclude that resistance was hopeless. Mills's portrait of American society did not convey any sense of countertendencies or dialectical contradictions that might provide hope for future change. His acceptance of a strong version of the "mass society" thesis, which depicted most Americans as so passive and apathetic as to be considered "cheerful robots," prevented Mills from fully understanding the particular dynamics by which elites convinced ordinary citizens of the correctness of elite definitions of reality. So concerned with debunking the rhetoric of elites from a radical standpoint, Mills never truly fulfilled his promise to relate character to social structure by investigating the complex ways in which ordinary men and women made political sense of their lives. Remarkably, he asserted, "contemporary men of power . . . are able to command without any ideological cloak."[70] Mills saw the masses not only as falsely conscious of their best interests, but also lacking any ideology whatsoever.

Though the politics of truth gave *The Power Elite* its rhetorical force, it occasionally led Mills from social analysis toward moralistic condemnation. This dynamic was particularly evident in the final two chapters. Mills accused the power elite of a "higher immorality," without specifying exactly what he meant by the phrase.[71] He also advanced the problematic claim, which he originally made in his essay "On Knowledge and Power," that the contemporary power elite was "mindless."[72] He noted, for example, that George Washington had read Locke and Voltaire, whereas President Eisenhower relaxed with cowboy and detective stories. Yet the question of whether political and cultural elites now overlapped, as Mills argued they had during the age of the founding fathers, was not relevant to his concern for whether or not American society was democratic. Moreover, Mills's depiction of the power elite as mindless and mediocre did not square with his prevailing image of them as sophisticated manipulators of public images of reality who had coordinated the creation of a permanent war economy to retain their hold on power. Mills's overriding desire to make *The Power Elite* "a good loud blast at the bastards" compromised the coherence and strength of his analysis.[73] Even so, the politics of truth also provided the enduring appeal of *The Power Elite*. The strength of Mills's analysis came from his powerful, though not fully elaborated, notion that the politics of truth could invigorate democratic public discourse through the collective use of substantive reasoning. This commitment to a radical notion of democracy underlay Mills's most persuasive arguments against postwar pluralists and his most convincing criticisms of American society. It distinguished Mills from his liberal critics, with whom he nonetheless shared important, unacknowledged similarities.

THE END OF IDEOLOGY?
'THE POWER ELITE' AND ITS CRITICS

His later works *Listen, Yankee* and *The Causes of World War Three* would receive more attention in the newspapers, but *The Power Elite* was Mills's most influential book and the one most widely and extensively engaged by intellectuals. The book's explosive conclusions about American democracy made it one of the most controversial works of social analysis of its era, provoking a furious response in social scientific journals, Marxist magazines, and the popular press.[74] Even Mills's sharpest critics were forced to address the neglected issue of who ruled America, rather than simply assuming that the United States was a fully formed democratic society, the polar opposite of Soviet totalitarianism. Thus, Mills succeeded in his goal of "invit[ing] the reader to become a member of our dialogue about the higher circles in America."[75]

Reaction to the book in scholarly journals was more positive than one would expect from the now-pervasive image of Mills as an academic outsider. Virtually all reviewers welcomed the book's publication as a major event, even when disputing its conclusions. *Public Opinion Quarterly* declared it "one of the most incisive books dealing with America in a generation."[76] A more typical response in the *Journal of Economic History* concluded that Mills "has overstated his case" but that "no serious student of contemporary society can afford to ignore his book."[77] Reviewers for other journals similarly hailed the book's publication as a major event, though they quibbled with Mills's arguments and the way in which he presented them. Only the *American Journal of Sociology* ran a wholly negative review.[78] This treatment of Mills's work as of major significance suggests that his contributions were still accepted as a legitimate part of the discourse of academic social science, even as he reached a large audience outside of it. That many of the more positive reviews were written by scholars outside elite social scientific departments suggests that while disciplinary leaders sought to distance themselves from Mills's work, he retained many admirers among the larger mass of social scientists. Few sociologists, however, followed Mills's lead in investigating the American power structure, at least not immediately. Beginning in the 1960s, however, one notable sociologist, G. William Domhoff, devoted his career to modifying yet essentially substantiating the arguments of *The Power Elite*.[79] Reviewers for the nonacademic press approached the book as did those writing for professional journals, valuing the introduction of a new viewpoint into the discussion but challenging key aspects of Mills's thesis. A. A. Berle's review in the *New York Times* was typical: though he vigorously disputed many of the book's main arguments, he nonetheless concluded, "The book is so carefully documented, it deals with such real problems, it hits so many sore spots that it deserves to be read—also to be supplemented."[80]

For the small group of active leftists, the publication of *The Power Elite* was a major event, as could be seen in Paul Sweezy's review in *Monthly Review*. Established by Sweezy and Paul Baran in 1949, *Monthly Review* was the foremost American Marxist journal of the immediate postwar era.[81] In his review, "Power Elite or Ruling Class?" Sweezy praised Mills for "boldly break[ing] the tabu which respectable society has imposed on any serious discussion of how and by whom America is ruled."[82] Yet Sweezy faulted Mills for not taking his analysis in more of a Marxist direction by emphasizing the primacy of economic class conflict. (Robert Lynd's review in *The Nation*, though muddled, boiled down to a similar concern, as he claimed that Mills did not go far enough in identifying the power of a single corporate economic "class" at the heart of the American power structure.)[83] Sweezy questioned whether political or military elites really held any significant autonomous political power and contended that the notion of a corporate ruling class made more sense than Mills's interlocking directorate of a power elite. He criticized Mills for not devoting enough analysis to the "system of monopoly capitalism," yet he concluded, "His work is strongly influenced by a straightforward class theory which, if he had stuck to it and consistently explored its implications, would have enabled him to avoid completely the superficialities and pitfalls of elitist thinking."[84] At the same time, Sweezy asserted that it was precisely because the book broke with Marxist analysis and contained no explicit commitment to socialist ideals that it could reach a large audience. To Sweezy's ears, Mills spoke with the "authentic voice of

American radicalism."[85] Despite their differences, Sweezy and Mills respected each other as intellectual allies; in 1958, Mills published an excerpt of *The Sociological Imagination* in *Monthly Review* upon Sweezy's solicitation.[86]

Liberal intellectuals formulated the most important and influential criticisms of *The Power Elite*, including three long considerations of the book from leading liberal social scientists Daniel Bell, Robert Dahl, and Talcott Parsons. Collectively, liberal critics exposed a number of the weaknesses in Mills's arguments. Liberals pointed out that Mills significantly overstated the cohesiveness of the power elite group and thus came perilously close to the conspiracy theory that he explicitly disavowed. As Dahl observed, it was possible for top leaders to have "a high potential for control and a *low potential for unity*."[87] "To the superficial observer," Dahl contended, "it would scarcely appear that the military itself is a homogenous group, to say nothing of their supposed coalition with corporate and political executives."[88] Bell took this critique to an untenable extreme when he concluded, "I can think of only one issue on which top corporations are united: tax policy."[89] However, the critics were correct that Mills failed to recognize crucial divisions within the power elite.

Many reviewers wanted more analysis of how the "big decisions" Mills discussed were actually made.[90] What did the power elite actually do with its power? Responding to this charge, Mills claimed with some justice that critics were unrealistically demanding "a full-scale American history of our times, military, economic, and political."[91] Nevertheless, without a detailed analysis of how the power elite decided on a course of action, it was difficult to ascertain whether interlocking economic, political, and military leaders really were responsible for the "big decisions." Lacking such an analysis, *The Power Elite* was provocative and suggestive, but it could hardly be considered definitive. Moreover, by focusing primarily on decisions that were military in nature, Mills neglected domestic matters. As Bell pointed out, Mills had almost nothing to say about "the issues which divide men and create the interest conflicts that involve people in a sense of ongoing reality: labor issues, race problems, tax policy, and the like."[92]

Ultimately, the liberals' critique of *The Power Elite* rested on an appraisal of the postwar social order that was fundamentally different from Mills's. *The Power Elite* offered a sustained argument against liberal notions of political pluralism and in favor of a more direct, participatory democracy. Yet political pluralism itself rested on a more basic liberal assessment of postwar American society. While Mills described the dominance of a power elite, liberals perceived an "end of ideology in the West." This well-known postwar liberal concept, whose most significant exponents were sociologists, first came into use in 1955. Though the idea owed much to French intellectual Raymond Aron, the American sociologist Edward Shils coined the phrase. Shils celebrated a postwar consensus built on the consolidation of the welfare state, which rendered obsolete traditional distinctions between liberals and socialists. Utilizing notions of a postcapitalist society, liberal analysts of the end of ideology argued that postwar Western societies had solved, insofar as was possible, the traditional problems of industrial capitalism without a socialist revolution. Shils, for instance, pointed to the example of Scandinavian welfare states, created "in a matter-of-fact way which recognized no general principles and treated each emerging situation on its own merits" and which reflected the "growing hollowness of the conventional distinctions between socialism and capitalism."[93] Probably the most famous proponent of the concept was Mills's former friend Daniel Bell, who adopted it for his influential 1960 collection of essays, *The End of Ideology.* When Bell wrote that "for the radical intelligentsia, the old ideologies have lost their 'truth' and their power to persuade," he referred in part to his own journey from socialist to liberal.[94] Like Shils and Seymour Martin Lipset, Bell described "a rough consensus among intellectuals on political issues," which brought about "an end to chiliastic hopes, to millenarianism, to apocalyptic thinking—and to ideology."[95] Though Bell largely applauded this development, he complained that politics now offered little excitement. Indeed, the subtitle of Bell's collection of essays was "On the Exhaustion of Political Ideas in the Fifties."

End-of-ideology liberals viewed any position to the left of their moderate social-democratic stance as a misguided attempt to resurrect old, discredited radical ideas. Shils first introduced the term "end of ideology" in the European American left-liberal magazine *Encounter* while reflecting on an international conference held by the Congress for Cultural Freedom in Milan in 1955. Both the congress and *Encounter* were efforts by American and European intellectuals to build a cultural alliance of moderate leftists to counter the far left. The "end of ideology" notion neatly labeled as "ideological" any view that fundamentally challenged the postwar social order. Opponents of the postwar consensus were seen as motivated not by reason, but by passion or even by pathology. Liberals viewed Mills, a sharp critic of the postwar order, in precisely these terms and attempted to marginalize his viewpoint. For Bell, *The Power Elite* was a "book whose loose texture and powerful rhetoric have allowed different people to read their own emotions into it."[96] Rather than a work of social analysis with a valid perspective, it reflected Mills's "enormous [personal] anger at the growing bureaucratization of life."[97] And Talcott Parsons complained about *The Power Elite* that "There is no pretense of even trying to maintain a scientific neutrality; the book is a fiery and sarcastic attack on the pretensions of the 'higher circles' in America."[98]

Indeed, much of the force of *The Power Elite* came from its left-wing attack on the American power structure. Mills's disillusioned radicalism allowed him to debunk many of the hopeful illusions propagated by "end of ideology" liberals. If nothing else, his critique revealed the "end of ideology" as itself an ideology. One of the central contributions of *The Power Elite* was to identify a crucial postwar development for which liberals failed to account: the growth of a permanently militarized state in a nation that had no tradition of peacetime military buildup. It is true that Mills mistakenly accorded military leaders a role equal to that of corporate and political leaders in the power elite, as virtually every reviewer of *The Power Elite* noted. He also overstated the trend toward the appointment as political leaders of "outsiders" from both the military and corporate sectors. Mills relied too much on an analysis of the Eisenhower administration, which operated in a postwar political arena in which a former general was president and the ruling party had been out of political power for two decades, and thus had diminished political talent to draw upon for top posts. Nevertheless, Mills was right to raise serious questions about the massive growth of the military and its effects on American democracy. The decade after World War II saw the permanent militarization of American society and politics and the establishment of unprecedented legal and political foundations for a large and expensive military buildup. At the high point of defense spending, during the Korean War, nearly 14 percent of the American gross domestic product went toward defense. Foreign policy decisions were also made by an increasingly powerful executive branch, often operating in secrecy with little public input until after a course of action was already chosen.

Even if the power elite's decisions were not as closely coordinated as Mills suggested, his complaint that the "big decisions" were made by a tiny group of powerful men rang true for foreign policy decisions, as did his argument that such decisions were increasingly viewed in military terms. Mills's insistence that domestic policies were increasingly tied to these foreign policy decisions was also justified. Not only did "military Keynesianism" help foster economic growth, but it created a defense industry with a powerful interest in the continued buildup of arms.[99] This development liberals generally ignored, minimized, or ascribed solely to the need to combat the spread of Soviet Communism.[100] Ironically, Dwight Eisenhower, who seemed to personify Mills's power elite, brought larger public attention to the issue in his 1961 presidential farewell address that warned of a growing "military-industrial complex."[101]

Mills's critique of the militarization of the American state both influenced and anticipated a more widespread challenge to postwar liberalism by New Leftists in the coming decade. Yet if one looks more closely, the American society that Mills pictured in *The Power Elite* appears less as the antithesis of liberal ideas and more as an inversion of their "end of ideology" thesis. Liberals perceived a fundamental agreement on social and political issues. Mills observed a similar consensus in postwar America, only he condemned it as a false one. In the "mass society" depicted by Mills, significant ideological debate had indeed come to an end. Mills even seemed to agree with liberals that class conflict had been effectively ameliorated through the welfare state. Most important, he subscribed to their curiously static depiction of American society, viewing the United States as if it had come to a final stage of historical development. The weaknesses of Mills's viewpoint were much the same as those of his liberal opponents: a neglect of significant pockets of poverty within the affluent society, a failure to recognize hierarchies of race and gender as significant sources of social power, and an overestimation of the political and cultural stability of the United States. As a result, neither Mills nor his liberal interlocutors foresaw the emergence of powerful groups that would soon challenge the postwar consensus from both the left and the right. Of course, an inability to identify sources of opposition was a hallmark of Mills's disillusioned radicalism, constructed at a time when left-wing social movements were weak. *The Power Elite* was a book with a clear "they" (the leaders atop key institutional hierarchies) but no "we" (a movement that might challenge their power). His identification of a "they" most sharply distinguished Mills from postwar liberals, but both sides underrated how dynamic the postwar order really was.

Not only did Mills's picture of modern American society read like a dystopian version of the liberals' "end of ideology" thesis, but the values that Mills embraced in *The Power Elite* had more in common with those of his liberal critics than either side acknowledged. For instance, Parsons misinterpreted Mills when he claimed *The Power Elite* represented a thoroughly unrealistic protest against "social organization" as such.[102] Granted, Parsons correctly identified an anarchist element to Mills's book that could plausibly be interpreted as a "utopian conception of an ideal society in which power does not play a part at all."[103] Yet Mills's desire for a politics based on rational democratic social control formed a more dominant theme of *The Power Elite*. Mills would not have rejected Parsons's suggestion that power be used as a "resource" for the betterment of society. Indeed, Mills suggested that "war and peace and slump and prosperity are, precisely now, no longer matters of 'fortune' or 'fate,' . . . now more than ever, they are controllable."[104] In this desire for rational democratic social control, Mills placed himself in a long liberal and radical tradition stretching back to John Dewey and beyond, a tradition to which Parsons and other liberals were also indebted. Whereas "end of ideology" liberals such as Parsons perceived postwar American society as closely approximating that ideal of rational social control, Mills saw the opposite. Mills held important theoretical differences with Parsons, as he would soon make clear in the publication of his next major book, *The Sociological Imagination*. However, the dispute between Mills and Parsons over *The Power Elite* was based less on differing theoretical understandings of power than on competing evaluations of a postwar political and social order that they understood in surprisingly similar terms.

THE COMMON DENOMINATOR OF OUR CULTURAL PERIOD: 'THE SOCIOLOGICAL IMAGINATION'

Mills published *The Sociological Imagination* in 1959, at the height of his New Left phase and a year after his anti–cold war book *The Causes of World War Three*. He drafted the manuscript while a Fulbright fellow at the University of Copenhagen during the 1956–1957 academic year, a watershed period for Mills as he assumed a new role as analyst of and spokesperson for emerging global protest movements. Elements of *The Sociological Imagination* were indebted to Mills's engagement with the New Left; notably, parts of the book struck a decidedly more optimistic tone than *White Collar* or *The Power Elite*, revealing the softening of his disillusioned radicalism. Yet *The Sociological Imagination* owed more to Mills's sociological engagements over the past two decades than it did to the particular circumstances of when and where he wrote it. The book expressed Mills's estrangement from professional sociology, a process that was complete by the early 1950s. Its major themes were evident in two articles he published in the early 1950s: "Two Styles of Research in Current Social Studies" (1953) and "IBM Plus Reality Plus Humanism = Sociology" (1954).[105] Though the last of Mills's major works, *The Sociological Imagination* came closest to the themes and ideas that Mills first articulated as a student. Mills's vision of the sociological imagination rested on substantially the same principles he formulated in his student years: social scientific inquiry should address specific substantive social problems; ideas should be located in their social and historical contexts; theory and practice should coexist in the same inquiry; and all social scientific disciplines shared a common approach. In calling for a sociology endowed with a "sense of real problems, as they arise out of history," Mills sounded much like Dewey, who had wanted to make philosophy a "device for dealing with the problems of men."[106] Mills also drew on his early encounters with German sociologists such as Mannheim and Weber when he argued that sociological work should be comparative, historical, concerned with power and stratification, and seek to grasp total social structures.

While Mills voiced many of these ideas in his earliest essays, he wrote *The Sociological Imagination* with an appealing economy, clarity, and grace of style that those previous works lacked. In terms of style, *The Sociological Imagination* is Mills's best book. Slightly over half the length of *The New Men of Power, White Collar,* and *The Power Elite, The Sociological Imagination* unfolded concisely and logically. Mills used sharp critique and biting wit to polemical advantage against contemporary social science while at the same time providing an inspiring vision of what social science could be. After laying out "The Promise" of the sociological imagination in the first chapter, Mills devoted the next five chapters to an assault on prevailing trends in sociology. The final four chapters were devoted to "more positive—even programmatic—ideas of the promise of social science."[107] The book concluded with an appendix, "On Intellectual Craftsmanship," originally written in the early 1950s for Columbia students, which described Mills's method of work, thereby demonstrating what the sociological imagination looked like in practice.

As early as 1951, Mills anticipated the book's thesis, writing in a letter that the sociological discipline "is now split into statistical stuff and heavy duty theoretical bullshit."[108] Sociologists best remember *The Sociological Imagination* for its broadsides against two of the most influential sociologists of the period, Parsons and Lazarsfeld. Mills's critique of Parsons was in part political, as one might expect given the ideological differences between the two that had already emerged in their differing interpretations of Weber and in the debate over *The Power Elite*. In *The Sociological Imagination*, Mills argued that Parsons's theoretical exploration of modern society, in its emphasis on integration and harmony and its avoidance of issues of power and conflict, supported the American status quo. Yet the heart of Mills's critique of Parsonian grand theory emerged from his long-standing pragmatist-inspired attacks on formalism in social science. Mills argued that Parsons's generalized theoretical analysis was too abstract to provide an understanding of concrete historical developments: "The basic cause of grand theory is the initial choice of a level of thinking so general that its practitioners cannot logically get down to observation. They never, as grand theorists, get down from the higher generalities to problems in their historical and structural contexts."[109] "What is 'systematic' about this particular grand theory," Mills concluded, "is the way it outruns any specific and empirical problem."[110] To Mills, theory should be one part of the process of inquiry, not the "formalist withdrawal" Parsons's work represented. According to Mills, Parsons's pretentious and verbose style revealed the inadequacy of his ideas. In a memorable section of the book, Mills offered hilarious "translations" into plain English of several passages of Parsons's influential yet notoriously abstruse *The Social System*. Drawing on his pragmatist understanding of social science, Mills's polemic against grand theory produced a devastating, if not entirely fair, critique of Parsons's work.[111]

Mills devoted multiple chapters to his critique of Lazarsfeld, whom he saw as a greater threat to the sociological imagination than was Parsons. The critique of Lazarsfeldian abstracted empiricism built on Mills's long-held methodological principles, as well as his earlier experience at the Bureau of Applied Social Research. Because it generated detailed statistical analyses, bureau research appeared to be more empirical than grand theory. Yet Mills argued that it, too, was an abstract approach to the study of society. Survey statistics correlated variables, but they provided little specific structural or historical context helpful for understanding the data. No doubt influenced by his frustrating experience with the Decatur study, Mills criticized abstracted empiricism for its "methodological inhibition." Abstracted empiricists made methodological rigor an end in itself, not a means to understand substantive social problems. Though Mills remarked that no student of society could fault the particular methods of social research employed by bureau researchers, he concluded, "an empiricism as cautious and rigid as abstracted empiricism eliminates the great social problems and human issues of our time from inquiry."[112]

Mills was also troubled by the bureaucratic ethos fostered by the new organizations of social research, which encouraged social scientists to concern themselves solely with technique and to ignore questions of values. Mills claimed that this "new liberal practicality" of bureau research performed for outside clients in the corporate and government sectors was replacing the reformist mentality he had examined in his 1943 article "The Professional Ideology of Social Pathologists." In this transition from the old to the new practicalities, "[Sociologists'] positions change—from the academic to the bureaucratic, their publics change—from movements of reformers to circles of decision-makers; and their problems change—from those of their own choice to those of their new clients."[113] Bureau-driven sociologists, Mills contended, put their skills to work for corporations and government without questioning what ends their work served. In the process, they not only served established political powers, but they also helped spread "the ethos of bureaucracy into other spheres of cultural, moral, and intellectual life."[114]

In *The Sociological Imagination,* Mills promoted the version of reflexive sociology evident in his early sociology of knowledge, urging sociologists to locate their work in society. Rather than maintaining a neutral scientific pose, sociologists should accept that values were inevitable in sociological inquiry. Whether they liked it or not, sociologists played a political role, and "their political meanings might better be made explicit than left hidden."[115] As Mills stated in his first chapter, "My biases are of course no more or no less biases than those I am going to examine. Let those who do not care for mine use their rejections of them to make their own as explicit and as acknowledged as I am going to try to make mine! Then the moral problems of social study—the problem of social science as a public issue—will be recognized, and discussion will become possible. Then there will be greater self-awareness all around."[116] Mills's reflexive sociology underlay his critique of grand theory and abstracted empiricism, just as it had bol-

stered his attack on the "end of ideology" concept by faulting liberals
for failing to acknowledge the ideological content of their own ideas.

The book's critique of two leading styles of social research was
persuasive and compelling, but it was also tendentious. An incisive
polemic, *The Sociological Imagination* cannot be read as an accurate
account of postwar sociology. For one thing, it offered an incomplete
survey of dominant tendencies in the field. Though Mills criticized
two of the three acknowledged disciplinary leaders of the period, he
neglected to mention the third, Robert Merton. In one passage, Mills
referred to a "statesman" who sought to reconcile grand theory with
abstracted empiricism, denying the differences between the two. This
"statesman" achieved a prominent position not through substantive
study but through vacuous promises of the need to reconcile theory
and research. "The role the statesman comes to play," Mills concluded,
"keeps him from his actual work. The prestige he has accumulated
is . . . disproportionate to what he has actually accomplished."[117] This
passage could be taken as a critique of Merton and his advocacy of
"theories of the middle range," which sought to merge the best aspects
of Parsonian-style theory and Lazarsfeldian bureau research. In fact,
Lazarsfeld read this passage as a "vicious attack" on Merton, though
he was virtually alone in doing so.[118] Even if this passage did contain a
veiled attack on Merton, it is interesting that Mills chose not to criticize Merton by name, something he had no scruples about with regard
to his Columbia colleague Lazarsfeld. It may be that Mills had fond
memories of his earlier friendship with Merton or still felt gratitude
toward him for his key role in advancing Mills's career. Or perhaps
Mills still saw some virtue in Merton's work. In any case, no critique
of postwar sociology could be complete without taking Merton explicitly into account.

More important, by reducing the discipline to abstracted empiricism and grand theory, *The Sociological Imagination* failed to consider other prominent trends in postwar sociology. Mills contrasted
grand theory and abstracted empiricism with the tradition of "classic
sociology," evident in the work of past thinkers such as Durkheim,
Mannheim, Marx, Weber, and even Herbert Spencer. In doing so, Mills
implied that contemporary social science as a whole had defaulted on
the promise of its classic heritage. Mills's neglect of alternative trends
in contemporary social science disturbed several social scientists otherwise sympathetic to his account. As Barrington Moore complained,
"The contrast of 'grand theory' and 'abstract empiricism' is dramatic,

but too stark to give a precise and just picture of present-day social science. . . . Mills does not convey much of a notion of the richness and diversity in present-day work in sociology."[119]

Mills's omission of alternative trends to those he critiqued was curious. In the 1954 article that anticipated the arguments of the book, Mills divided sociologists into three groups. Along with the grand theorists and abstracted empiricists (then referred to as "the Scientists"), Mills identified a "third camp" who continued the tradition of classic sociology. This "third camp" included an ideologically diverse group of scholars such as Robert Dahl, John Galbraith, Harold Lasswell, Charles Lindblom, Gunnar Myrdal, David Riesman, Joseph Schumpeter, and the thinkers of the Frankfurt School.[120] Moreover, Mills shared drafts of *The Sociological Imagination* with several social scientists, many of whom responded favorably to Mills's critique of disciplinary trends and to his positive vision of the sociological imagination. Among those who expressed considerable agreement with either the manuscript version of *The Sociological Imagination* or the 1954 article were Herbert Blumer, Lewis Coser, Andrew Hacker, Richard Hofstadter, H. Stuart Hughes, Floyd Hunter, Charles Lindblom, Ralph Miliband, Barrington Moore, Howard Odum, and David Riesman.[121] This favorable response indicates that Mills was hardly alone in his antipathy to grand theory and abstract empiricism. By the late 1950s, many of Mills's criticisms were echoed by prominent sociologists such as Alvin Gouldner and Barrington Moore, who transformed the social sciences in the 1960s.[122]

The Sociological Imagination suffered for not including a discussion of sociology's "third camp." Without it, the book played out as the critique of an outsider against an entire profession, a motif that Mills intentionally created and which ensured a less sympathetic response from his sociological peers than it might otherwise have enjoyed. Mills had written his friend William Miller regarding the first draft of the book, "I must ask that you *not* mention any of this to our friends, especially on Morningside Heights. I want it to be just one big, dandy surprise: as from a prophet who comes in from the desert."[123] While the sense of a conflict between Mills and the profession at large (and his Columbia colleagues such as Lazarsfeld in particular) contributed to the dramatic tension of the book, it did so at the expense of providing a more complete overview of American social science. Thus, although it was not Mills's intention, readers were apt to identify the "sociological imagination" with Mills's own particular type of sociology.

The reviews of *The Sociological Imagination* suggested that Mills's perspective had some support, even within the discipline he disparaged. Certain leading sociologists were predictably hostile. After the book's publication, some sought to write Mills out of the discipline altogether. Edward Shils voiced the most vitriolic attack, labeling Mills "a sort of Joe McCarthy of sociology, full of wild accusations and gross inaccuracies, bullying manners, harsh words, and shifting grounds."[124] In the *British Journal of Sociology*, Seymour Martin Lipset and Neil Smelser warned their British readers from engaging with Mills's work, asserting that it "has little importance for contemporary American sociology."[125] And, in an ironic instance of cooperation among the leaders of the two divergent trends criticized in *The Sociological Imagination*, Talcott Parsons persuaded Paul Lazarsfeld to exclude Mills from speaking at the Sixth World Congress of Sociology in 1962, despite the desire of sociologists in other nations to hear him talk.[126] But reviews of the book in the major sociological journals were not entirely dismissive. Writing in the *American Journal of Sociology*, Harvard's George Homans suggested that he agreed with some of Mills's critique, though he disliked the intemperate manner in which Mills voiced it.[127] William Kolb, in *American Sociological Review*, loved Mills's exposition of the "sociological imagination," though he differed with Mills's "inflexible" and "dogmatic" application of it.[128] While Lewis Feuer disagreed with Mills on several points, his review was surprisingly positive, concluding that the book was "of great importance" and that every graduate student should read the book's appendix, "On Intellectual Craftsmanship."[129]

On one level, *The Sociological Imagination* can be read as a frontal assault on the academic sociology of its period, albeit one that garnered some sympathy from within the discipline. Yet even when presenting a gloomy view of contemporary sociology divided between abstracted empiricism and grand theory, with few alternatives in sight, the very vehemence of Mills's attack reflected his continued faith in a particular sociological worldview. In 1958, after reading Mills's original draft of the book, which bore the despairing title *Autopsy of Social Science*, David Riesman expressed surprise at how deeply Mills cared about the state of the social sciences. Riesman saw Mills's analysis of the present state of the social sciences as a diversion from the more important task of analyzing the society itself: "It seems to me that you are allowing yourself to be too much distracted by these men—it is as if Marx had gone on the rest of his life attacking Feuerbach," he wrote. "Surely you would agree that sociology is not *that* important," Riesman concluded,

claiming that Mills had "launched elephant gun criticisms of the mos-
quitoes who ride on the back of American intellectual life."[130] But sociology still *was* that important to Mills. Along with a polemic against
contemporary trends in the discipline, *The Sociological Imagination*
articulated Mills's ambitious vision of the "promise" of social science.
Though Mills believed that disciplinary leaders had defaulted on this
promise, he hoped it might have better success in the culture at large.
Mills's decision to change the title of the book from *Autopsy of Social
Science* to *The Sociological Imagination* reflected his belief in social
science's potential. Perhaps encouraged by the many favorable letters
he had received about the manuscript, Mills declared that the social
sciences were not dead, merely "sick," and that "recognition of this fact
can and should be taken as a call for diagnosis and perhaps even a sign
of coming health."[131]

The name Mills gave to this promise was *the sociological imagination*, defined as that "quality of mind essential to comprehend the interplay of man and society, of biography and history, of self and world."[132]
The sociological imagination offered the ability to comprehend the
significant interrelations between different parts of society. As Mills
wrote, "What is specifically 'sociological' in the study of any particular
feature of a total society is the continual effort to relate that feature to
others, in order to gain a conception of the whole."[133] The sociological imagination connected individual biography with larger historical
and structural forces; or, to use the terms that Mills employed earlier
in his career, character and social structure. In concentrating on total
social structures, the sociological imagination would not lose sight of
the individual, as it contained "the capacity to range from the most
impersonal and remote transformations to the most intimate features
of the human self—and to see the relations between the two."[134] Mills's
definition of the sociological imagination was capacious, explaining
the remarkable appeal of the phrase to sociologists at the time and ever
since. The sociological imagination as defined by Mills, however, was
not identical to the particular style of radical sociology as practiced by
Mills. Indeed, critics often identified ways in which Mills's own work
failed to live up to the demanding standards set by the sociological
imagination.[135]

Though Mills did see an important political role for the sociological
imagination, he did not limit it to a single ideological position. Some
of Mills's political allies were frustrated by this. The British socialist
Ralph Miliband, for example, complained to Mills, "The social scien-

tist's role must inevitably, and on your definitions, be critical, unorthodox, attacking, subversive of existing concentrations of power. What
you are saying right through is that the good social scientist must in
fact be a socialist and seek the renovation in a socialist-democratic
direction of social structures. That's what it really means, doesn't it?
But you don't quite say it, you imply."[136] Miliband's remark pinpointed
a key tension in the book between Mills's contention that sociological
knowledge necessarily served radical ends and his insistence that the
sociological imagination was available to all who addressed substantive issues and linked individual biography to wider social and historical trends. But it was precisely because of this ambiguity that *The
Sociological Imagination* appealed beyond its left-wing readership.
Indeed, Mills's book found an unexpected source of support among
conservative reviewers who praised his embrace of the "classical tradition" and his critique of the "bureaucratic ethos"; Russell Kirk, for
instance, though he had already lampooned Mills's leftist politics in
print, endorsed Mills's view of sociology.[137]

Though Mills painted a bleak portrait of contemporary social science, he was more optimistic regarding the cultural promise of the sociological imagination. "The social sciences," he argued, "are becoming
the common denominator of our cultural period."[138] The sociological
imagination could fill a void left by the decline of scientific authority in
the atomic age. Mills asserted that already "journalist and scholars, artists and publics, scientists and editors" were turning to the sociological
imagination to "help them to use information and to develop reason in
order to achieve lucid summations of what is going on in the world and
of what may be happening within themselves."[139] Mills was encouraged
by the growing success enjoyed by social critics with a sociological
mind-set in the 1950s, such as Vance Packard, A. C. Spectorsky, and
William H. Whyte.[140] In fact, in 1955 Mills had written a glowing
review of Spectorsky's *The Exurbanites*, praising the book in terms
very similar to those he used to define the sociological imagination,
that "by enabling the reader to locate himself as part of a social phenomena . . . it invites him to understand his very individuality as . . .
profoundly related to the external trends of his time."[141] Ironically, the
very disciplinary leaders Mills attacked shared his expectation that
sociological ways of thinking would become increasingly prevalent in
the United States. In the same year that *The Sociological Imagination*
was published, Parsons declared that "a 'sociological' era had begun to
emerge."[142]

Mills believed that the diffusion of the sociological imagination within American culture contained the political promise of helping individuals better understand and control the larger structural forces that shaped their lives. Many people, he claimed, failed to comprehend the impact of large-scale social institutions in their lives. They either understood their lives in terms of a local milieu of private troubles or were falsely conscious of their place in society. The sociological imagination would enable them to link their personal biographies to larger historical and structural trends and, in doing so, allow them to translate their seemingly private "troubles" into public "issues."[143] By using the sociological imagination, they could fully participate in making America a more democratic society. Thus, for Mills, the "intellectual promise of social science" was fundamentally related to "the political promise of the role of reason in human affairs."[144]

The Sociological Imagination ended with the most compelling of Mills's persistent calls to bring intellect to bear on issues of power. As in *The Power Elite,* Mills demanded that social scientists practice a politics of truth: "In a world of widely communicated nonsense, any statement of fact is of political and moral significance. . . . All social scientists, by the fact of their existence, are involved in the struggle between enlightenment and obscurantism. In such a world as ours, to practice social science is, first of all, to practice the politics of truth."[145] Social scientists could contribute to the creation of a democratic society in which substantive reason would play a fundamental role, for the values of freedom and reason could only be realized in a participatory democracy in which public reasoning and debate were central. Here, Mills continued to define democracy as "some kind of collective self-control over the structural mechanics of history itself."[146] By translating private troubles into public issues, sociologists could contribute to democratic participation by helping to "build and to strengthen self-cultivating publics."[147] Mills imagined that such a role was automatically radical: "When many policies—debated and undebated—are based on inadequate and misleading definitions of reality, then those who are out to define reality more adequately are bound to be upsetting influences. That is why publics of the sort I have described . . . are, by their very existence in such a society, radical."[148] Even as he described this inspirational vision, Mills struck a characteristically pessimistic note: "What are the chances of success?" he asked. "Given the political structure within which we must now act, I do not believe it is very likely that social scientists will become effective carriers of reason."[149] Nevertheless, as international protest movements began to emerge in the late 1950s and early 1960s, Mills came to see his sociologically grounded politics of truth as not just a desperate holding act but as a potential strategy for a radical movement of the "young intelligentsia." Practiced on a mass level, the politics of truth could challenge the elite concentration of political power by helping to build a New Left.

CHAPTER 6

Worldly Ambitions

The Emergence of a Global New Left

For American left student activists of the early 1960s aiming to practice their own politics of truth, Mills's "Letter to the New Left" of
1960 provided inspiration. Attacking the liberal notion of an "end
of ideology," Mills suggested that radical ideals could once again
affect the course of history by stirring the masses out of their apathy.
Defending "utopian" thinking, he showed the necessity of a New Left
that would break through the limits of the cold war consensus politics
of the 1950s. Most important, Mills proclaimed to the emerging white
student movement that "new generations of intellectuals" could be
"real live agencies of social change."[1] To readers who already revered
Mills for his trenchant social analysis, "Letter to the New Left" legiti-
mated the notion that relatively privileged university students could be
pivotal agents of social transformation. Shortly after its publication,
Mills's "Letter" was reprinted in the foremost intellectual journal of
the American New Left, *Studies on the Left*. It was also published in
pamphlet form by its most prominent organization, the Students for
a Democratic Society (SDS), whose 1962 manifesto "The Port Huron
Statement" heralded a New Left social movement of those "bred in at
least modest comfort, housed now in the universities, looking uncom-
fortably to the world we inherit."[2]

Though "Letter to the New Left" is best known for its influence on
the American student movement, Mills conceived of the New Left in
international terms. In fact, his "Letter" was originally published in the

British journal *New Left Review*. It was the product of the final phase of Mills's career, from the publication of *The Power Elite* in 1956 to his untimely death in 1962, which was marked by the internationalization of his thought and his discovery of a New Left. In 1956, Mills traveled to Europe for the first time, earning a Fulbright teaching fellowship in Denmark that allowed him to tour the continent. It proved to be, as Mills remarked at the time, a "pivotal year" for him, during which he expanded the horizons of his political activity and social analysis. Intellectuals, he now argued, must "become international again" when thinking about radical social change and "attempt to get in touch with our opposite numbers in all countries of the world."[3] Encountering a diverse range of intellectual networks and political movements abroad, Mills reconceived the possibilities for radical social protest in the post–World War II world. No longer looking to the working class as the most promising agent for social change, as he had during the 1940s, he theorized the galvanizing effects of middle-class intellectual and cultural dissent in the United States and Europe in his unpublished book-length manuscript *The Cultural Apparatus*. No longer focusing primarily on American society, Mills enlightened U.S. and world audiences on issues of international significance by publishing two influential books, *The Causes of World War Three*, which grew out of his engagement with the peace movement in the United States and abroad, and *Listen, Yankee*, a defense of the Cuban Revolution.

In his "Letter to the New Left," Mills asked, "Who is it that is getting fed up with what Marx called 'all the old crap'? Who is it that is thinking and acting in radical ways? All over the world . . . the answer's the same: it is the young intelligentsia."[4] To illustrate his point, Mills cited the revolution in Cuba, the antinuclear march at Aldermaston in Britain, the civil rights movement in the American South, and protests in Turkey, South Korea, Taiwan, and Japan, all of which involved a younger generation taking a leading role. Mills's identification of the "young intelligentsia" as the New Left agent of change actually conflated two different groups. The term suggested a broad-based middle-class movement of cultural producers. As he explained in a 1960 interview, "I am using this word 'intelligentsia' in the East European sense to mean the whole white-collar pyramid, as well as artists, scientists, and intellectuals in our sense."[5] But if Mills's use of the term *intelligentsia* reminded readers of the Bolshevik Revolution, it is because it also encompassed another distinct group. In an unpublished 1959 note, Mills wrote, "the historic lever has been and is now the political intelligentsia of pre-industrial countries," adding in the margins, "Lenin is correct."[6] To this end, Mills hoped that global change could emerge from revolutionary yet non-Communist socialist movements in the third world.

Mills's New Left engagements opened up new opportunities for intellectual and political development and revealed much that was of value in his radicalism. Neither dogmatic nor sectarian, Mills looked for sources of left-wing social change from whatever corners of society they might arise. Yet his new role as herald of the global New Left was fraught with difficulties. Though Mills never became a political activist as such, neither building organizations nor organizing protests, he was drawn into commenting more directly on timely political issues. While this enhanced Mills's influence, it also proved perilous, for he now took public positions without the benefit of time for sociological reflection. As a result, Mills's later work lacked the subtlety and sophistication of his earlier works of social criticism. Unlike Mills's major sociological works, *The Causes of World War Three* and *Listen, Yankee* hold only historical interest today. What was to be Mills's primary theoretical contribution to the New Left, *The Cultural Apparatus*, remained unfinished, largely because of his pressing political engagements. At times, Mills seemed to be abandoning sociology and crafting a new role for himself as an unofficial spokesman for the left. In 1961, he concluded, "I have a big responsibility to thousands of people all over the world to tell the truth as I see it and to tell it exactly and with drama and quit horsing around with sociological bullshit."[7] Yet sociology was too deeply ingrained in Mills for him to truly abandon it; consequently, he juggled his newfound role as prominent radical spokesperson with the demands of more sustained intellectual work.

The wide-ranging intellectual and political engagements of Mills's later career cast light on the emergence of an international New Left. To interpret Mills's relationship with the New Left primarily in terms of his seminal influence on the student leaders of SDS, as prior scholars have done, is to miss much of what is most interesting and important about this phase of his career.[8] Mills's case enables us, as very few others do, to map the reemergence of international left-wing dissent at the end of the 1950s and the start of the 1960s. His example points to the significance of an international dimension of the American New Left that historians have generally ignored.[9] Indeed, the very origin of the term *New Left* reveals the movement's international interconnections. British Marxists associated with *New Left Review* borrowed the term from non-Communist French intellectuals of the *nouvelle gauche,* a group identified with the search for socialist alternatives beyond Soviet-style Communism and American capitalism.[10] Mills's use of the phrase in his "Letter" played a crucial role in its adoption in the United States. Examining what he meant by the term and how he came to use it not only helps us to understand this fascinating last period of his career, but also suggests new historical understandings of the New Left.

BECOMING INTERNATIONAL AGAIN

From 1956 to 1962, Mills's writings and activities took place in an international context. Though he had been influenced by European thinkers throughout his career, Mills's work had focused almost exclusively on American society until the mid-1950s. In 1952, Mills wrote Max Horkheimer of his desire to travel: "I have all my life lived in a country that is only some six or seven generations old, and the longer I work here and the older I get, the more provincial and limited I feel. I want to live in Europe for a while, to put it positively, in order to establish points of comparisons."[11] Mills first visited Europe in January 1956, when he took a short course on motorcycle mechanics at a BMW factory in Munich. He returned in the fall on a Fulbright fellowship to lecture on social psychology at the University of Copenhagen, which he used as a base to explore the rest of Europe.

As a result of his frequent travels, Mills spent less time at Columbia University in his later years. He was promoted to full professor in 1956, achieving the position at a young age, shortly before he turned forty years old. Unfortunately, his relationships with his colleagues continued to deteriorate, especially after the publication of *The Sociological Imagination.* When Mills suffered a severe heart attack in 1960, only one member of the sociology department (Robert Lynd) wrote a letter of condolence.[12] In addition, Mills grew increasingly frustrated with the lack of institutional support Columbia provided for his research. In a sarcastic letter to Dean Jacques Barzun in 1959, Mills complained, "Does it not seem curious that a full professor at a leading university who has produced 8 books in the last dozen years hasn't got a girl to type his mail?"[13] Even so, Mills remained a member of the Columbia faculty until the end of his life, although he continued to express ambivalence about his position. "Why, then, do men stay in such [academic] jobs?" Mills reflected at one point. "Here I need answer only for myself. . . . Because despite everything—which you must agree is quite a lot—it is still the only job in which you are considerably free to teach and study and write social science."[14]

The first several months of Mills's Fulbright year were uneventful. He found Copenhagen itself a bit dull. He began to make progress on a draft of *The Sociological Imagination,* but, as argued in chapter 5, that book was more a settling of old accounts than a new direction. At first, Mills felt even more intellectually isolated than he had in the United States. At one low point, Mills wrote to Gerth, "As you see, I've no will just now for writing at all. . . . I've lost any notion of a public for whom I might once have thought I was writing."[15] Yet the timing of Mills's visit fortuitously coincided with the first stirrings of the European New Left. As Alan Hooper has argued, if one has to select a single year that the development of those European social movements associated with the 1960s began, 1956 is the best choice.[16] Out of the events of 1956 emerged groups that advocated democratic socialism as an alternative to both Eastern bloc Communism and Western capitalist democracy. Soviet premier Nikita Khrushchev's revelations of Stalinist atrocities at the Twentieth Party Congress in February and his violent suppression of the Hungarian revolution in November discredited the Soviet model. Meanwhile the Suez crisis, beginning in October, sparked renewed anti-imperialist protest in Western Europe.

Mills traveled to England in March 1957 to lecture at the London School of Economics (LSE). There he discovered the community of left-wing intellectuals that had eluded him in the United States, connecting with radical social scientists Norman Birnbaum, T. B. Bottomore, and Ralph Miliband. Writing to the director of the school following the event, Mills gushed, "I haven't yet seen all of the western world, but, from what I have seen, I cannot believe that there is in it any intellectual center more stimulating than the London School of Economics. To be there was especially gratifying to me because in recent years, quite frankly, I have often felt the lack of an audience with which I could believe I was truly in communication. Last weekend I came to realize what such an audience looks like."[17] Mills reported to Lewis Coser, "My God, it is nice to know it makes a difference somewhere. Well, it damned well does there. Naturally, I'm nuts about the place and everyone I met there." "It's becoming quite a year," he continued, "a pivotal year, I think, for me. . . . Suddenly there's the need to make a big sum-up. Suddenly there's a lot of ideas to do it with. They write themselves."[18]

Mills's trip to London put him in touch with the emerging British

New Left, which would prove the most significant intellectual connection of his later life. Mills traveled frequently to Britain after 1957. Indeed, he felt so at home in the British intellectual milieu that in 1961 he seriously considered permanently relocating to take a chair in sociology at the newly created University of Sussex.[19] In the British New Left Mills found not only intellectual interlocutors, but also an exciting attempt to reconstruct left-wing politics. Consisting of two separate strands, the British New Left emerged in reaction to the events of 1956. The first group centered around a set of longtime Communist intellectuals who, in the wake of Khrushchev's speech and the Soviet suppression of the Hungarian revolution, broke with the party under the banner of socialist humanism. This group, based in Yorkshire, coalesced around the journal *New Reasoner,* edited by E. P. Thompson and John Saville. In contrast, the second group was younger, without a prior connection to Communism, and based in Oxford and London. Consisting largely of current students or recent graduates, it published the journal *Universities and Left Review* and founded a series of New Left clubs to promote political discussion. Though of different origins, the two groups worked closely together, and in 1960, *New Reasoner* and *Universities and Left Review* merged to form *New Left Review.*

Mills found that he shared a common perspective with British New Leftists. Together they sought a socialist alternative to Communism—a new left. An eclectic intellectual and cultural movement, the British New Left rejected the bureaucratic political organization of the Communist-based Old Left. Its strategy was to counter public apathy by reinvigorating a left-wing public sphere of journals and clubs. Mills and British New Leftists shared the hope that, by constructing alternative ideas that were "utopian" in the sense that they could not be politically implemented in the short term, intellectuals could clear the ground for the reemergence of a popular left-wing movement.[20] As Stuart Hall wrote Mills regarding his "Letter to the New Left," "The point about our thinking being explicitly 'utopian' is what we all feel; and it has a pretty decisive effect, too, with presenting these ideas to younger people."[21]

Mills was not the only American to interact with the British New Left. Michael Walzer, for instance, who became closely associated with *Dissent,* was decisively influenced by a year he spent at Oxford in 1956– 1957, when he fell in with the *Universities and Left Review* crowd.[22] The influential left-wing sociologist Norman Birnbaum, an American teaching at the LSE whom Mills befriended, was on the editorial board of *Universities and Left Review* and later a founding editor of *New Left Review*.[23] Another American, Norm Fruchter, was Stuart Hall's assistant editor at *New Left Review* from 1960 to 1962, before he returned to the United States to help edit *Studies on the Left;* he later helped found the internationalist U.S. film collective Newsreel.[24] Yet it was Mills who became the iconic American radical for British leftists. He influenced them with his ideas about the cultural apparatus and the nature of the New Left. But perhaps more important, British leftists took hope from Mills's example that they might find compatriots in a nation that, since World War II, had increasingly come to be seen by Europeans as a bastion of conservatism. A writer for the *London Tribune* hailed Mills as "the true voice of American radicalism."[25] Leading left-wing Labour Party MP Michael Foot praised Mills's work as "the strongest blast of fresh air which has come across the Atlantic for years."[26]

Nevertheless, there was a key difference between Mills and his new British friends, who were more rooted in the Marxist tradition than he was. In his "Letter to the New Left," Mills expressed puzzlement that his British counterparts "cling so mightily to 'the working class' of the advanced capitalist societies as *the* historic agency, or even as the most important agency, in the face of the really impressive historical evidence that now stands against this expectation."[27] Even though it was primarily a middle-class movement committed to finding new agents for social change, the British New Left remained committed to a tradition of working-class radicalism that was stronger in Britain than in the United States, and which had some political expression in the left wing of a major political group, the Labour Party. As a result, they disagreed with Mills's sharp rejection of the "labor metaphysic." Stuart Hall protested to Mills, "I don't think that it is just a Marxist hangover which made me question some of the assumptions you made in your LSE lectures last year." Because of the stronger labor tradition in Britain, Hall argued, "we cannot write off the working class in the same way."[28] E. P. Thompson similarly complained, "You say that 'labor alone' can't do the job of transforming our society, and then suggest that intellectuals ought to try and realize their goals by themselves. Aren't you tipping the balance too far the other way?"[29]

Mills's closest relationship with British New Leftists was with Ralph Miliband, a Marxist scholar at the LSE whom Mills met during his trip in 1957. In fact, the first draft of Mills's "Letter to the New Left," was written as a letter addressed to Miliband.[30] A Belgian Jew, Miliband emigrated to Britain in 1940 at the age of seventeen and went on to study at the LSE under the prominent British leftist Harold Laski.[31] A lifelong independent socialist, Miliband was the only member of the editorial board of *New Reasoner* who had never joined the Communist Party. Of all the intellectuals of the early British New Left, Miliband's interests ran toward political and social science rather than cultural studies or history, which perhaps explains why he became closest to Mills. Eight years younger than Mills, Miliband looked up to him as if he were an older brother. As he later recalled, "I got to feel closer to Mills than I have ever felt to any man, or should feel again, I should think."[32] *The Power Elite* was a major influence on Miliband's major work, *The State in Capitalist Society,* which he published in 1969 and dedicated to Mills's memory.[33]

In the summer of 1957, Mills persuaded Miliband to meet him in Austria and to travel with him through Eastern Europe. Though Mills at first had hoped to journey by motorcycle, they drove an automobile instead. Although they stopped in Yugoslavia, it was Poland that made the greatest impression upon Mills. As in Hungary, political dissent in Poland emerged in 1956, following Khrushchev's speech denouncing the crimes of the Stalin era at the Twentieth Party Congress. Unlike Hungary, however, where the Soviet invasion quashed all political opposition, Poland saw a degree of cultural liberalization in the late 1950s. During his sixteen-day visit to Warsaw, Mills interviewed a variety of Polish intellectuals for his planned book *The Cultural Apparatus.* Mills was particularly impressed with the dissident Polish philosopher Leszek Kołakowski, one of the more radical critics of the Stalinist legacy and one of the strongest advocates for democratization. In the late 1960s, Kołakowski fled Poland after being sanctioned for his outspokenness, and he eventually rejected Marxism altogether. Yet when Mills visited in 1957, Kołakowski was a leading international exponent of Marxist humanist philosophy. In 1958, Mills declared, "I can no longer write with moral surety unless I know that Leszek Kolakowski will understand where I stand."[34] Kołakowski offered Mills a model of how intellectual dissent could be politically explosive. Kołakowski believed that only the "socialist consciousness of the intelligentsia" could rescue socialism from a repressive Communist bureaucracy.[35] The emphasis Kołakowski and other Eastern bloc socialist dissidents placed on the potential political power of the "intelligentsia" was a crucial influence on Mills's conception of the "young intelligentsia" as the key New Left agency.

Mills's "pivotal year" forced him to think internationally as he began to conceptualize what a new left might look like. After 1957, Mills traveled frequently. In early 1959, he not only traveled to Britain to deliver a series of lectures titled "Culture and Politics," but he also returned to Europe in September to attend an international sociology conference in Italy, and he visited Austria, Germany, and London in October before traveling to Brazil. In early 1960, Mills went to Mexico City to teach a seminar on Marxism at the University of Mexico. In April 1960, Mills toured the Soviet Union for a month, conducting thirty intensive interviews with Soviet intellectuals and officials.[36] In August 1960, he traveled to Cuba, and he spent the better part of 1961 in Europe, visiting the Soviet Union once again. It was in 1961 that Mills considered permanently moving to England, but ultimately he still felt rooted in the American environment. Explaining to his parents why he refused the offer from the University of Sussex, he wrote, "The decision has less to do with the many attractions of England than with the fact that my argument lies in America and has to be worked out there."[37]

Mills's international turn was evident in three projects he embarked upon during the late 1950s. Mills believed that to be truly international, American intellectuals needed to contact their counterparts in the Soviet bloc. This was the idea behind "Contacting the Enemy: Letters to Tovarich," a series of letters that Mills wrote to an imaginary Soviet intellectual from 1956 to 1960. Hoping that connections across the divide could help transcend the alignments and conflicts of cold war nation-states, Mills proposed that intellectuals make their own separate peace. Disappointed with the Soviet intellectuals he met during his visit, because most of them parroted the party line, Mills addressed his letters to an imaginary Soviet counterpart, Tovarich. Often autobiographical in nature, these letters were the most personal form of writing that Mills had ever written for publication, though "Contacting the Enemy" was never in fact published.[38]

During his travels Mills continued to think in grand sociological terms. In 1958 he embarked upon an elaborate project on comparative world sociology that was truly Weberian in scope. Mills planned "to undertake a fully comparative study of the world range of present-day structures and of the variety of their economic and intellectual elites." As Mills explained in a request for funding, "This project is going to be my major work for my next period of work. Having written several books about the United States, and having worked in the social sciences

for nearly twenty years, I feel the need to settle down now to a long-
term endeavor. . . . I feel that I am at a pivotal juncture in my work
as a whole."[39] Mills was frustrated in his attempts to secure research
funding for the project, although he did receive a small grant from the
California-based Fund for the Republic. He used this money to hire
research assistants, but by the time of his death Mills had made progress only on the first step of the project, the construction of a master file
listing basic information about all existing nations. Mills had planned
to then narrow his study to approximately ten "representative" nations.
In 1960, he began to reconceptualize the project: "This year I've learned
so god damned much about 'freedom,' about 'democracy'—in Brazil,
Mexico, Russia—and now reading on Cuba, that I'll have to rethink
the whole question."[40] Mills's project was absurdly ambitious given
his previous focus on the United States and the several other writing
projects and activities that he frantically pursued during the late 1950s
and early 1960s. His attempt, however, reveals that, in spite of his
increasingly prominent role as a public voice for left-wing causes, there
remained virtually no limit to Mills's sociological imagination.

Mills's posthumously published *The Marxists* also grew out of his
international turn, and in particular out of his desire to reach a new
international audience that was steeped in the Marxist intellectual
tradition. In 1959, Mills explained that he needed to have "a real confrontation with 'Marxism.'" "You see," he continued, "I have always
written with reference to liberalism, because that is a kind of common
denominator of the public for which I write."[41] *The Marxists* was an
oddly structured work, a hybrid between introductory reader and
critical commentary that combined a series of selections from Marxist
writers with Mills's own reflections. Mills's declaration that he was a
"plain Marxist" proclaimed his solidarity with non-Communist leftists
around the globe. For Mills, being a "plain Marxist" meant accepting
Marx as one of the great classical sociologists and political theorists
while refusing to dogmatically follow his ideas. Mills aligned himself
with other "plain Marxists" such as G.D.H. Cole, Antonio Gramsci,
Kołakowski, Rosa Luxemburg, John-Paul Sartre, Paul Sweezy, and
William Appleman Williams.

Nevertheless, *The Marxists* showed very little engagement with the
intellectual traditions Perry Anderson termed "Western Marxism,"
a movement of primarily Western European left-wing thinkers who
rejected Soviet Communism and sought to reinvigorate twentieth-
century Marxism by combining it with other fields of intellectual

discourse.[42] In spite of his substantial prior engagement with the unorthodox Marxism of the Frankfurt School, Mills interpreted Marx in an orthodox fashion. His selection of Marxist texts emphasized the writings of Communist political leaders, and his commentary stressed a critique of conventional Marxist notions, such as the ultimate primacy of economics in social analysis, which Western Marxists had challenged for decades. As a result, Mills failed to seriously grapple with the writings of Marx himself, which were far more complex than Mills allowed for. Thus, *The Marxists,* while clarifying Mills's opposition to the official Marxism of the Soviet bloc, was less rewarding as a serious engagement with more sophisticated varieties of Marxism. As such, it reveals the limitation of Mills's international turn in his final years. Even as Mills's "pivotal year" opened up new possibilities for social analysis and political engagement, it tempted him to pursue too many projects at once; he often sacrificed depth of thought to his newfound breadth. As Mills wrote Gerth in June 1960, "I know it is ridiculous but I am actually at work on six books, all of them at least halfway written. . . . One pays a price for this sort of moral and psychic energy; I am sure I am not aware of the full price, intellectually I mean."[43]

'THE CULTURAL APPARATUS'

In his "Letter to the New Left," Mills wrote, "It is with this problem of agency in mind, that I have been studying, for several years, the cultural apparatus, the intellectuals—as a possible, immediate, radical agency of change."[44] Of all of Mills's late unfinished projects, the most important one was *The Cultural Apparatus.* Begun in 1955, the project started out as an attempt to delineate the degeneration of public debate into mass apathy, expanding on themes from Mills's earlier work.[45] Yet during his "pivotal year" abroad, Mills transformed what was originally to be a book about American intellectuals into a large-scale comparative study that would examine the contemporary politics of culture in all regions of the world, including Western Europe, the Soviet Bloc, and the underdeveloped world. In particular, as he encountered an emerging New Left, Mills became more optimistic that the "cultural apparatus" possessed an autonomy that might allow it to reenergize oppositional publics. Mills thus widened his past emphasis on the "intellectual" to encompass a larger stratum of "cultural workmen." He now suggested that intellectuals were not "powerless people." Acting as a group, they

could serve as a significant agency for left-wing change. Even though
the manuscript was never completed, the idea of the cultural apparatus
animated much of Mills's later thought, particularly his conception of
the New Left. In 1960, Mills even considered changing the title of the
manuscript to *The New Left.*

In a 1960 draft preface explaining the origins of *The Cultural
Apparatus,* Mills stressed that the project emerged from his lifelong
concern with "the role of ideas in politics and society, the power of
intellect." Although he did not know it at the time, Mills indicated,
the project had begun with his writing of "The Powerless People" for
Dwight Macdonald's *politics* in 1944. "Coming upon an earlier draft
of it early one morning last year," he wrote, "I was both depressed
and pleased to see how many themes it contained which, during the
last sixteen years, in later books, I have been working out. It may be
that I have had no really new themes since then, although I have of
course had many topics."[46] *The Cultural Apparatus,* Mills continued,
would build on the "Brains, Inc." chapter of *White Collar* and on two
chapters about the "cultural elite" excised from *The Power Elite.* In his
original proposals, Mills indicated that the roots of the project went
back even further, to the articles he had published on the sociology of
knowledge, beginning with "Language, Logic, and Culture" in 1939.
Here lay much of the promise of *The Cultural Apparatus.* Ever since
"The Powerless People," Mills had clearly articulated the special duties
of intellectuals, and his attack on the deficiencies of liberal intellectuals
remained a constant refrain in his later work. But by returning to his
roots in the sociology of knowledge, *The Cultural Apparatus* suggested
a real development in Mills's social analysis, matching his earlier analysis of class, stratification, and power with a more sophisticated and
nuanced understanding of ideas and culture. Mills's new approach was
reflected in his shift in vocabulary from *intellectuals* to *cultural apparatus,* defined as "all those organizations and *milieux* in which artistic,
intellectual and scientific work goes on" and "all the means by which
such work is made available to small circles, wider publics, and to great
masses."[47] Hence, he encompassed a much larger social group than he
had in his earlier work on *intellectuals,* which had referred primarily
to fellow social scientists and writers centered around little magazines
such as *politics* and *Partisan Review.* When Mills first publicly used
the term *cultural apparatus,* he did so in a 1958 speech to industrial
designers.

The Cultural Apparatus contained an unresolved tension between

Mills's newfound optimism that the "cultural apparatus" could serve as a possible new agency for left-wing change and the bleak pessimism of his disillusioned radicalism, which he never fully set aside. Mills's use of the term "cultural *apparatus*" suggested a formidable mechanism that smoothly functioned to uphold the established political and social order. In this sense, Mills's new project simply expanded upon his earlier analysis that responsible "publics" were being replaced by apathetic "masses." Mills argued that, in the West, cultural institutions and workmen were becoming increasingly absorbed into the larger economy and polity.[48] For instance, Mills claimed that in the United States, "Cultural activities, on the one hand, tend to become a commercial part of an overdeveloped capitalist economy, or, on the other, an official part of the Science Machine of the Garrison State."[49]

In capitalist societies, Mills contended, the cultural apparatus was dominated by a marketing mentality that manipulated consumer demand and restrained cultural workmen from producing quality work for a discriminating public. Cultural workmen could be "hacks" or "stars," but not genuine craftsmen. Here Mills tied his analysis of the cultural apparatus to a wider critique of what he now called the "overdeveloped society." Sharing the assumption of many postwar liberals that material deprivation was no longer a serious problem in the industrialized West, Mills defined the overdeveloped society as one in which "the standard of living dominates the styles of life; its inhabitants are possessed, as it were, by its industrial and commercial apparatus; individually, by the frenzied pursuit and maintenance of commodities . . . the struggle for status supplements the struggle for survival; a panic for status replaces the proddings of poverty."[50] The cultural apparatus played an integral role in corporate capitalism, generating consumer desire for new goods. Here Mills continued his left-wing critique of mass culture, which, he claimed, produced "the kind of human being who really is, psychologically and socially, in his sensibilities and in his reasoning, like mass culture itself . . . distracted, shallow, banalized."[51]

In the overdeveloped societies, Mills contended, the cultural apparatus was subordinated not only to the economy, but also to the nation-state: "the cultural apparatus is officially established and the cultural workman altogether established as a politically qualified man."[52] The cultural apparatus performed a necessary function for power elites: "The prestige of culture transforms mere power into spell-binding authority. That is why the cultural apparatus, no mater how internally free, tends in every nation to become a close adjunct of national authority and a leading agency of nationalist propaganda."[53] The purest example of established culture was in the Soviet Union, where "the source of money is the one-party state; masses of people are the managed public for culture; cultural activities are official activities. Opposition is traitorous and exists mainly as a more or less hidden literary mood."[54] Yet also in the West there was the "tendency and the strain for quite unofficial cultural workmen voluntarily to coordinate themselves and their work in conformity with officially defined needs as well as in anticipation of needs not yet officially proclaimed."[55] This pattern was most apparent, Mills claimed, in the support most American intellectuals gave to the cold war.

What Mills was trying to pinpoint in *The Cultural Apparatus* was nothing less than what Jürgen Habermas referred to in the title of his book *The Structural Transformation of the Public Sphere*. Had Mills remained in good health, he might have published *The Cultural Apparatus* in 1962, the same year that the German thinker published his important work, in which he cited at length Mills's distinction between "public" and "mass" from *The Power Elite*.[56] With the term *cultural apparatus*, Mills identified a social phenomenon similar to Habermas's "public sphere." Mills's project focused primarily on cultural producers rather than the public sphere as such, but, like Habermas, he defined a social arena that mediated between citizens and state authority. If functioning properly, it would provide the mechanism by which private individuals could bring critical reason to bear on state policy. Through it, informed citizens could build a society based on democratic deliberation, where the best argument would win out through reasoned discussion.

Both Habermas and Mills regarded the eighteenth century as a period in which the public sphere, whatever its faults, fulfilled its ideal function. Mills's unfinished analysis of what he called the "bourgeois public" is less sophisticated and less historically rich than Habermas's now classic account. Unlike Mills, Habermas had a clear sense of the contradictions of the Enlightenment-era public sphere that arose from the dual identity of its bourgeois participants both as citizens committed to the use of reason and the ideal of common humanity, as well as property owners with a specific class interest. Nevertheless, it is worth quoting an unpublished passage by Mills that parallels Habermas's account:

Then emerges the bourgeois public, and the cultural workman is liberated
from dependence upon patrons, royal or otherwise. As entrepreneur, the
cultural workman is supported by money received for his products bought
by anonymous publics. In this stage, for a brief liberal period in Western
history, many intellectuals were in a somewhat unique historical situation, even as the situation of the small entrepreneur of classic liberalism
was unique: one historic phase sandwiched between two more organized
phases. The eighteenth-century intellectual stood on common ground
with the bourgeois entrepreneur: both were fighting, each in his own
way, against the remnants of feudal control . . . a new kind of freedom,
the writer for an anonymous public, the businessman for an anonymous
and unbounded market.[57]

Mills's account of the absorption of the cultural apparatus into the
polity and economy during the modern period also resembled Habermas's
analysis of the structural transformation of the public sphere in the
twentieth century from a "culture-debating" to a "culture-consuming"
public.[58] In Habermas's account, as the public sphere lost its autonomy
to corporate capitalism and the expanded power of the nation-state,
it could no longer mediate between state and society. Both Mills and
Habermas argued that mass culture created manipulated and falsely
privatized individuals incapable of contributing to reasoned debate
about public policies. Neither open nor democratic, public opinion was
manipulated from above by public relations rather than shaped by citizens employing substantive reason. Conceived by a second-generation
member of the Frankfurt School, Habermas's account of the structural
transformation of the public sphere emerged from the same type of
disillusioned radicalism as did Mills's.

As he continued to write *The Cultural Apparatus,* however, Mills
combined his account of the structural transformation of the cultural
apparatus with a more optimistic and intriguing analysis of the cultural
apparatus as a potential agent of New Left social change. If, on the
one hand, the concept of a cultural *apparatus* suggested that cultural
institutions were becoming seamlessly integrated with the political
status quo, on the other hand, it also implied that cultural activity possessed a significant power of its own. In his 1959 London lecture "The
Cultural Apparatus," Mills drew on a pragmatist tradition emphasizing the constitutive power of language in order to stress the autonomy
of the cultural apparatus. "Men live in second-hand worlds," he noted.
"They are aware of much more than they have personally experienced,
and their own experience is always indirect."[59] As that social realm
mediating between consciousness and existence, the cultural apparatus

defined "our standards of credibility, our definitions of reality, our modes of sensibility."[60] "The consciousness of men does not determine their material existence; nor does their material existence determine their consciousness," Mills continued. "Between consciousness and existence stand meanings and communications which other men have passed on—first, in human speech itself, and later, by the management of symbols."[61] In one sense, Mills explained, everybody was part of the cultural apparatus, "for everyone to some extent uses symbols, exercises skills, and manipulates things." But Mills focused his attention on cultural workmen, who were particularly powerful in shaping images of reality in "an elaborate set of institutions: of schools and theaters, newspapers and census bureau, studios, laboratories, museums, little magazines, radio networks."[62] If autonomous, cultural workmen could question established institutions and spark a wider challenge to them.

In asserting the potential power of cultural institutions, Mills was strongly influenced by his British interlocutors. As Stuart Hall has observed, a central belief of British New Leftists was that the "cultural and ideological domain" was "not a secondary, but a constitutive dimension of society."[63] By conceiving of culture as a key ground of political conflict, *The Cultural Apparatus* bore a strong resemblance to the ideas of British New Left critic Raymond Williams, who saw cultural struggle as an essential part of what he called the "long revolution."[64] Similarly, British New Left historians such as E. P. Thompson conceived of class in terms of cultural identity rather than mere economic position.[65] Appropriately, the major public expression of Mills's "cultural apparatus" thesis was a series of three lectures he delivered at the LSE in early 1959 titled "Culture and Politics." Enthusiastically received by British New Leftists, the lectures were broadcast on BBC radio and created a stir in the British press. The *London Observer,* for example, described "a huge, alarming Texan [who] has just been lecturing to the London School of Economics, to an excited audience of sweaters, black stockings and duffel coats."[66]

In Mills's final LSE lecture, "The Decline of the Left," he attributed the waning of radical power to the nationalization of Communism and the disastrous effects of identifying socialism with the Soviet Union. A second and less obvious reason for the left's decline, however, was "the expropriation from cultural workmen of their means of cultural distribution, and, increasingly, of cultural production as well."[67] Mills suggested a program of workers' control for cultural producers: "What we ought now to do," he proposed, "is repossess our cultural apparatus, and use it for our own purposes."[68] Intellectuals need no longer rely on other agents, such as the moribund labor movement, to effect social transformation. "Intellectuals have created standards and pointed out goals," Mills said. "And then, always, they have looked around for other groups, other circles, other strata who might realize them. Is it not now time for us to try to realize them ourselves?"[69] Calling for a repossession of the cultural apparatus by cultural workmen, Mills also articulated a more nuanced view of cultural consumers, seeing in them potentially active agents of a public, rather than simply passive dupes of mass culture. Mills claimed that only if cultural workmen attempted to repossess the cultural apparatus could we know "whether the general political apathy that now prevails so generally is endemic in modern society or whether it is in considerable part due to the default of cultural workmen and their withdrawal from politics."[70]

In the unpublished manuscript *The Cultural Apparatus*, Mills pursued "utopian" thinking, calling for the "release [of] the human imagination, in order to explore all the alternatives now open to the human community."[71] Mills envisioned a society distinguished from both the "overdeveloped" industrialized world and the "underdeveloped" third world. In this "properly developing society," an "ethos of craftsmanship was pervasive": workers would produce neither for material incentives nor to achieve social status, but for the pleasure of creating.[72] In his exploration of the "properly developing society," Mills set forth ideals that were nearly identical to those he had articulated in earlier works, such as in the section on craftsmanship in *White Collar*. The difference here, however, was that instead of locating these ideals in a romanticized past or articulating them to lay bare the standpoint of his social critique, Mills now presented them as guidelines for a possible future. Mills posited his utopia on the material abundance that modern technology had made possible. In imagining the possibilities presented by a post-scarcity economy, Mills aligned himself not only with contemporary radicals such as Paul Goodman and Herbert Marcuse, but also with liberal social thinkers such as John Kenneth Galbraith, Eric Larrabee, and David Riesman.[73] Mills looked to cultural workmen, who most valued craftsmanship and were most aware of how current social structures frustrated that value, as the key agent for moving society closer to this utopian ideal.

By asserting a power within culture that was potentially autonomous from the prevailing political establishment, and by expanding "intellectual" to include journalists, clergy, scientists, industrial designers, screenwriters, and others, Mills suggested that the cultural apparatus could be an agent of the New Left. His conception of the global New Left in terms of the oppositional potential of a cultural apparatus, evident in the British New Left and among dissident intellectuals in Eastern Europe, bore important insights. It also undermined Mills's own tendency, still very much present in his later career, to present that now-familiar image of himself as a lone rebel against 1950s-era complacency. Instead, the notion of a cultural apparatus allowed him to focus on what intellectuals, broadly defined, could do as a group. Mills's view of the intelligentsia as a new source of political agency offered needed inspiration to New Leftists across the globe, reassuring them that intellectual and cultural activity could be politically significant, that ideas can and do matter. Finally, by urging intellectuals to conceive of their movement in international terms, Mills challenged attempts to nationalize thought and culture by enlisting them in the cold war struggle. Mills's notion of the power of oppositional ideas left its mark on 1960s-era radicalism. Operating largely outside new or established political parties and institutions in both the United States and Western Europe, the New Left revealed that a mass movement based on "speaking truth to power" (to borrow a popular phrase from the period) could have an explosive effect by exposing state actions to public scrutiny.

Nevertheless, Mills's conception of the cultural apparatus as an agent for social change left many questions unanswered. As E. P. Thompson pointed out in a letter to Mills, "You argue intellectual workers must repossess their own cultural apparatus and use it for their own purposes. In what sense have they ever possessed it?"[74] Moreover, Mills never specified exactly what cultural workmen should do once they repossessed the apparatus. In addition, although Mills expanded his notion of "cultural workmen" to include a much larger group than traditional intellectuals, he was nevertheless open to charges of elitism. Even ordinary cultural workmen were relatively privileged members of society, and Mills failed to consider the political agency of others who lacked cultural capital and whose participation would presumably be essential for any significant left-wing social transformation. Finally, Mills never explained how reenergizing public debate would lead to radical social and political change. How could the activity of the cultural apparatus spark a larger mass political movement with the capacity to directly alter state policy? In other words, how could cultural opposition translate into institutional political change? In the United

States and Europe, the New Left ultimately had to confront the limits of a political opposition using predominantly intellectual and cultural means. Nevertheless, Mills's conception of the potential agency of the cultural apparatus proved fruitful in a period when left-wing movements were just reemerging. Mills's ability to reach a mass audience with *The Causes of World War Three* and *Listen, Yankee* suggested that there was indeed a new receptiveness to radical ideas within the cultural apparatus. Mills's interaction with the peace movement in the United States and abroad demonstrated the merit of his notion of intellectual and cultural activity as a key spark for political activism.

A PROGRAM FOR PEACE

Even as he encountered an emerging New Left in Europe, Mills sensed a shift in the public mood back in the United States. As he wrote Harvey Swados in 1957, "I've not read American publications for over a year now . . . but isn't it true that there's something of a swing away from conservative silliness and incapacity for moral discernment that's paralyzed the postwar imagination? Aren't there signs I wouldn't have seen? I've the vague feeling that 'we' may be coming into our own in the next five or ten years."[75] Back in the United States, Mills sought to spread his new internationalism by drawing attention to developments abroad. Tellingly, Mills associated himself with the segment of the U.S. left most focused on international events and most closely linked to compatriots overseas: the peace movement. It was to this movement that he contributed his 1958 book, *The Causes of World War Three,* which found a receptive audience that Mills had failed to reach with his earlier books.

The reemergence of the U.S. peace movement in the late 1950s was part of a worldwide increase in antinuclear protests across the industrialized world, in North America, Europe, Japan, and Australia. Because peace could only be achieved through international cooperation, peace activists formed global networks and thought of their movement in international terms. The international "ban the bomb" movement used immediate demands, such as an end to nuclear testing, to launch a more basic challenge to the buildup of nuclear weapons and cold war policies. The antinuclear movement was strongest in Japan, where public opinion was overwhelmingly against nuclear testing: a massive series of rallies led by university students attracted an estimated 350,000 participants in May 1957. In Britain, the New Left was closely

linked with the formation of the Campaign for Nuclear Disarmament
(CND) in 1958. Popular antinuclear sentiment was evident in Britain
in the well-attended and widely publicized annual marches, beginning
in April 1958, from London to the Aldermaston nuclear facility fifty
miles away.[76]

In the United States, key activists kept radical pacifism alive after
World War II and provided an experienced leadership that could mobilize the growing dissent of the late 1950s. Energized by civil rights
protests in the South that utilized nonviolent direct action and sens-
ing changing public attitudes toward the cold war, A. J. Muste, David
Dellinger, and Bayard Rustin founded *Liberation* magazine in 1956.
Over the next several years, *Liberation* provided a valuable forum for
the revival of pacifist and radical thought. Readers of *Liberation* were
keenly aware of developments throughout the world and took heart
from the growth of the peace movement in other nations. In 1957, the
Committee for a Sane Nuclear Policy (SANE) formed around opposition to nuclear testing, quickly and unexpectedly tapping into a mass
base of opposition to American nuclear policies. SANE resembled the
CND in terms of its middle-class composition and modeled itself in
part on the British organization. By the summer of 1958, SANE had
grown to 130 chapters, with an estimated membership of 25,000. And
in 1958, a small group of American pacifists connected to the more
radical Committee for Nonviolent Action (CNVA) garnered international attention by sailing into a nuclear test zone site in the Pacific
Ocean to disrupt the implosion of a hydrogen bomb.[77]

Beginning in the late 1950s, Mills developed close ties with radical
pacifist organizations. Though most closely linked to the peace movement in the United States, Mills had connections to the British peace
movement as well, and he cited antinuclear protests throughout the
world as a key element of the global New Left in his "Letter to the
New Left." Mills's principal contribution to this revitalized international peace movement was his 1958 book *The Causes of World War
Three,* which developed from two popular articles that he published in
The Nation and from the Sidney Hillman lectures he had delivered in
April 1958 to a standing-room-only crowd at Howard University.[78] A
slightly revised 1960 edition of the book, priced at only fifty cents, was
printed as a mass paperback and released in time for the presidential
election. Unlike his earlier works, which were based on painstaking
sociological research and sophisticated theoretical analysis, *Causes*
was a short book, written quickly to address a pressing contemporary

topic and reach a mass audience. Indeed, Mills referred to *Causes* and *Listen, Yankee* as "pamphlets" to distinguish them from his earlier books. While of little enduring intellectual significance, these books did have an important cultural and political impact. Addressed "neither to power elites nor to people in general, but to those who are generally aware of what is going on, who have thought about the preparation of World War III and who are becoming uneasy about it," *Causes* connected Mills with the educated readers he hoped would form a public for a left-wing revival.[79]

In *Causes,* Mills used his notoriety as a social critic to focus public attention on the dangers of nuclear war. At the heart of the book was his passionate attack on the "insanity" and "idiocy" of escalating nuclear diplomacy between the superpowers. By the late 1950s, an expanding arms race held out the nightmare of a massive nuclear confrontation. In identifying a "drift and thrust" toward World War III, Mills relied on his earlier arguments about the irresponsibility of power elites. Indeed, *Causes* can be viewed as a kind of sequel to *The Power Elite.* Much of the first section of the book summarized Mills's "power elite" argument that the American government was run by a small group of interconnected political, corporate, and military leaders. When Mills described the "causes" of World War III, he blamed the acceptance of a "military metaphysic" among both Soviet and American policy makers seeking to solve political problems through military means, and he noted the expanded political power of both militaries. Focusing on the United States in particular, Mills detailed the wasteful military expenditures of the permanent war economy, which reinforced a nuclear arms buildup. He also pointed to a "capitalist brinksmanship" in American foreign policy, which involved taking risks to protect American economic interests abroad. Though his analysis concentrated primarily on the American government, Mills observed the vicious circle created by the arms race, and in particular how military buildup in one superpower strengthened the hands of hard-liners in the other. Thus, Mills argued, "The immediate cause of World War III is the preparation for it."[80]

Though Mills provided a convincing enough critique of the nuclear arms race, he failed to explain why an arms buildup would necessarily result in World War III, only imagining a scenario in which nuclear war would arise accidentally from a failure of mechanical equipment. This nuclear nightmare was the stuff of popular novels and films of the era, and readers might have expected more analysis from Mills. Indeed, considering the title of the book, Mills was strangely weak on the issue of causation. In particular, Mills did not analyze at any length the history and geopolitical causes of cold war confrontation. When Mills did analyze specific situations, he was often insightful, as when he noted the growing prominence of oil politics in the Middle East. Presciently suggesting the possibility of war in Iraq, Mills remarked, "Western civilization began in the Middle East; the beginnings of its end could also occur there."[81] For the most part, though, Mills failed to suggest what scenario would actually result in World War III. In what instance would either power elite actually initiate nuclear war?

In many ways, *Causes* was even bleaker than *The Power Elite*. Not only would the domination of the power elite erode American democracy, but it might also spell the end of human society. Yet in addressing the growing peace movement, *Causes* had a decidedly more optimistic tone than anything Mills had written in a decade. Intellectually isolated for so long, Mills felt heartened that he had finally reached a public for his work. The very fact that Mills would propose a "program"—something he had refused to do since his days as a labor intellectual—suggested that he sensed an audience for his ideas about the cold war. Mills's analysis of modern society remained dark, and suggested seemingly insurmountable structural obstacles to left-wing political action, yet Mills insisted that he and his readers could take steps to alter the course of history. Nevertheless, an undercurrent of desperation remained even behind Mills's most impassioned calls to action.

Initially published in *The Nation,* Mills's "Program for Peace" was revised for *Causes,* but it remained basically unchanged. Mills's theme was that the coexistence of superpowers was a necessity in the nuclear age: "We must demand that the coexistence of these two world-established models of industrialization be fully recognized and that the competition between them be conducted in economic and cultural and political ways."[82] Mills's proposals were of mixed utility. At points, his program was vague, as when he urged the abolition of "the military metaphysic and the doctrinaire idea of capitalism."[83] Some of his demands were more imaginative, as when he proposed that the U.N. should take charge of oil resources in the Middle East and that 20 percent of the U.S. military budget be devoted to aid for underdeveloped nations. Characteristically, Mills emphasized intellectual and cultural proposals, as in his suggestion that, using U.S. funds, the U.N. should establish first-class educational programs in the third world emphasizing the humanities and social studies. He also included a number of suggestions central to the mainstream peace movement (and that were, in fact, implemented in the next two decades, largely due to public agitation). These included an end to nuclear testing, negotiations with the Soviet Union to reduce nuclear stockpiles, and recognition of Communist China. Mills's boldest and most controversial proposals called for unilateral nuclear disarmament by the United States, the abolition of NATO, and the closing of all overseas U.S. bases. Such proposals were of use in the frankly utopian sense of imagining a long-term alternative to the cold war, and they pushed the peace movement to go beyond reforms such as an end to nuclear testing toward a more fundamental critique of American foreign policy.

The peace movement that Mills addressed in his proposals differed in important respects from the labor movement he had enthusiastically supported in the 1940s. Based in churches and universities, it consisted primarily of members of the educated middle classes. With a strong moralistic edge, the peace movement represented the emergence of a community of conscience that would help shape the politics of liberalism and radicalism over the coming decades. Mills indicated that he grasped the peace movement's base in liberal Protestantism in "A Pagan Sermon to the Christian Clergy." Originally delivered as a lecture to the United Church of Canada in Toronto in February 1958, the piece was also published in *The Nation* and incorporated into *Causes*. "A Pagan Sermon" sharply condemned American Christians for failing to live up to their ostensible pacifist ideals by speaking out against the cold war: "Total war ought indeed to be difficult for the Christian conscience to confront, but the current Christian way out makes it easy; war is defended morally and Christians easily fall into line."[84]

Like "A Program for Peace," "Pagan Sermon" received an enthusiastic response from readers, particularly liberal clergy, who protested Mills's neglect of a pacifist Christian minority yet nevertheless found in Mills's article an affirmation of their own views. Mills's essay was mentioned in sermons throughout the nation and caused a stir in the liberal Christian press. For example, the editors of *Christian Century* applauded Mills's "Pagan Sermon," though they objected to Mills's one-sided view of organized Christianity. "Take time to look at the churches in action, visit the front where the ministers you address are busy," they told Mills, and "you will see a great deal of action on the correct side from your viewpoint."[85] Mills took the advice, addressing the First Midwest Conference of the Unitarian Church in April 1958 and a number of church meetings following that. In December 1958, Mills wrote to Ralph Miliband, "Tomorrow I go lecture in Atlantic

City to another group of big shot clergymen. Amazing, but they are, in truth, apart from university groups, the only real audience I have, and some of them are very good indeed. I am learning how to get to them and shake them up."[86]

The positive reception Mills received from liberal Protestants was a response to a heightened moralistic emphasis in his work on the necessity of acting on the basis of individual conscience. Mills had always stressed the special responsibility of intellectuals to tell the truth and confront unjust power, but he now widened his plea to appeal to a larger stratum of society. Thus, in his "Pagan Sermon," he confronted ministers with the question, "Why do you not make of yourself the pivot, and of your congregation the forum, of a public that is morally directed and that is morally standing up?"[87] Mills remained decidedly secular, yet his moralistic rhetoric appealed to Christian radicals. Indeed, the venerable Christian radical pacifist A. J. Muste valued *Causes* primarily for its argument that national policy needed to be held to higher moral standards. In a review published in *Dissent,* Muste claimed that the book implied a stance of "revolutionary pacifism" based on the protest of conscientious individuals. In fact, as his endorsement of the Cuban revolution would soon underline, Mills never became a pacifist, but he must have been heartened by Muste's praise of *Causes* as "an event in the world struggle against war" and possibly "a major turning point."[88]

Though *Causes* received mixed reviews in the press, the enthusiastic response of some readers confirmed Mills's tentative hopes about the growth of a New Left. Mills received dozens of letters from readers, many of whom claimed to be galvanized to action after reading it. A Presbyterian minister in Detroit told Mills that "much of what you write appears to be a searing shaft of light illuminating the darkness of an otherwise insane public apathy."[89] "We have been pacifists for generations, but now, we feel, we can no longer be passive," wrote a dentist and his wife from Sheboygan, Wisconsin.[90] "Your book made me angry, and I am looking for an outlet for my anger," concluded a New York art critic, who also confessed that the book left her confused about what sort of action to take. Some readers took it upon themselves to promote the book as a form of political action. Jesse Gordon, a New York public relations executive, forwarded a copy of Mills's 1960 *Nation* article, which then became part of the revised book, to Senator Mike Mansfield. After Mansfield wrote a paragraph of qualified endorsement (noting that "We need very much the kind of bold analysis he advances, whether we agree with it in whole or part or not at all"), Gordon forwarded the comments to President Eisenhower.[91] And a doctor from Tampa, Florida, wrote the publisher to purchase hundreds of copies of the book, which he distributed in packets of twenty-five to university presidents across the country.[92]

That the reaction to *Causes* was not limited to Americans testified both to Mills's new status as an international intellectual and to the emergence of middle-class opposition to the cold war throughout the world. Some British readers treasured the book not only for its anti-nuclear critique, but also as evidence that American society was not monolithically supportive of the cold war policies of its government. As one reader wrote, "You cheer my heart to hear that something different is coming out of the USA. I have read your most interesting book, and now I hear your broadcasts, and feel that you have to muster some courage to put this over."[93] *Causes* was also reviewed in important newspapers outside the United States and Britain, including in the *Johannesburg Star,* the *Montreal Star,* and *Die Welt.* A German student praised the book to Mills, as did a doctor in western Australia who told him, "The sanity of it appeals—the more so as to thoughtful people the World over the foreign policy of the United States since Hiroshima appears increasingly psychopathic."[94] An Italian informed Mills that "many intellectuals in Europe think in the frank and non conformist spirit you affirm in your work."[95]

If *Causes* won Mills many new political allies, it also cost him an old one. Along with Muste's positive review, *Dissent* published a harsh response by Irving Howe, who offered trenchant criticism of the book: As a work of social analysis, *Causes* did not live up to Mills's earlier books, nor did it provide a theory of the causes of World War III. But Howe's primary objection was to Mills's treatment of Communism in the Soviet bloc. The nature of Soviet Communism was not central to *Causes.* Indeed, Howe was probably reacting less to the book itself than to a meeting he had shortly after Mills's return from Europe in which they discussed developments in the Communist world.[96] From his 1957 trip to Eastern Europe until his death, Mills hoped that Eastern-bloc Communism might transform itself into a more humane and democratic type of socialism. Mills was influenced by the analysis of Marxist scholar Isaac Deutscher, who argued that, in the wake of Stalin's death, one could expect a series of democratizing reforms that would go far beyond the current measures of the Khrushchev government.[97] Mills stopped short of making such bold predictions, but he left it as an open question whether such reforms might occur. For instance, in an interview in early 1960 Mills referred to "trends toward democratization" in the Soviet bloc and claimed that "maybe the secular and humanist values of Marxism may still be available—despite everything—in the future of the Soviet Union."[98]

Reviewing *Causes,* Howe charged Mills with endorsing not only "political coexistence" with the Soviet Union, but "also a kind of 'moral coexistence,' by which I mean an accommodation not merely with Russia as a power but with Communist dictatorship as a form of society."[99] Such a stance, Howe concluded, was "unacceptable for the democratic left."[100] Howe must have known that the sharp tone of his review would cost him a friend and *Dissent* an ally. The next issue of *Dissent* contained a nasty exchange between Howe and Mills, "Intellectuals and Russia," which revealed much about the changing politics of anti-Communism on the American left.

Howe's critique was correct in a number of particulars but mistaken in its general implication that Mills was an apologist for Soviet dictatorship. In his reply to Howe, Mills adequately summed up their differences: "You do not take as seriously as I do the new beginnings in the Soviet Bloc since the death of Stalin. You no longer take as seriously as I do the lack of new beginnings and the disuse of formal freedom in the USA since World War Two."[101] Howe correctly argued that Mills's hope for "new beginnings" in the Soviet bloc was overly optimistic, particularly when juxtaposed with Mills's often static and monolithic view of the potential for change within American society. Mills's optimistic perspective on the Soviet bloc also alarmed some members of the British New Left, such as Dorothy Thompson, who remained suspicious of Communism because of their prior experiences in the party.[102]

Nevertheless, to the extent that Mills implied any moral equivalence between the United States and the USSR in *Causes,* it was a wholly negative one. Throughout the book, Mills described both Soviet and American societies as controlled by power elites whose views of the world were colored by a "military metaphysic" and who benefited from the apathy of their peoples. The problem with Mills's equivalence argument was not that he was soft on Communist dictatorships, but that he underrated democratic elements of American society. Even so, with some justification, Mills defended his argument as a rhetorical strategy: "I do not 'assimilate' the U.S. and the USSR 'into one category.' One writes in a context in which the two are regularly presented as polar opposites, one good, the other evil. Therefore, I state differences, but I stress parallels."[103] Overall, Howe misunderstood the purpose of Mills's discussion of the Soviet Union in *Causes*. Mills aimed to prove that Soviet elites would be willing to negotiate nuclear disarmament and the de-escalation of the cold war, a judgment that proved correct. However, Mills neither excused nor defended Communist governments. Indeed he explicitly criticized them.[104] In his unpublished "The Cultural Apparatus," Mills stated quite clearly, "Yes, I am an anti-communist and have been ever since the late 'thirties when I came to some sort of political awareness."[105]

Ultimately, the exchange revealed more about Howe's obsessive anti-Communism than it did about the limits of Mills's analysis of the Communist bloc. Mills wondered why Howe had not taken "due note of differences and then gone on to build a new left."[106] Why did the exchange not remain a friendly debate instead of a bitter exchange that led to a parting of ways? For Howe, democratic leftists could not differ on the issue of Communism. Mills suspected that Howe was more interested in fighting old battles than in engaging with the emerging New Left. In 1957, Howe and Lewis Coser published a history of the U.S. Communist Party, a vitriolic book that seemed to belong to an earlier era, when the Communist Party was actually a significant influence on the American left and not the institution that had been decimated by the postwar red scare and was now practically irrelevant.[107] As with other Old Leftists such as Michael Harrington, the sectarian baggage that Howe carried with him from his days as a Trotskyist would lead him to rashly attack the early New Left student movement for being insufficiently anti-Communist, costing himself the opportunity to exert a valuable influence upon student activists. Indeed, Mills predicted this fate when he cruelly labeled Howe and his circle "Old Futilitarians of the dead American left."[108] In this instance, the fact that Mills had become a radical in the early 1940s and had never belonged to any political party placed him in a better position to influence the New Left. However, in an important respect, Mills's position was more consistent with 1940s anti-Stalinism than was Howe's. Unlike Howe, who clearly preferred the American side in the cold war, Mills clung to the position he had advanced in the unpublished manifesto he coauthored with Lewis Coser and Irving Sanes in 1948. Mills was still searching for a "third camp" in a two-power world, and he now believed he might have found it in the activities of the cultural apparatus and Cuban revolutionaries.

In contrast to Howe and other intellectual holdovers from the Old Left, Mills was willing to look for radical sources of change from wherever they might come. For that reason, it is particularly curious that even as Mills developed strong connections to the reemerging peace movement, he generally ignored the African-American civil rights movement, which was irrefutably the central force reenergizing American radicalism and liberalism in the late 1950s and early 1960s and was based on the kind of public appeal to morality and reason that Mills advocated. To be sure, Mills supported racial equality. In a rare comment on the movement, in a 1959 speech, Mills hailed the civil rights movement for reopening the question of "whether or not a democratic making of history is possible." Approving the demand for legal rights as a legitimate goal for the movement, Mills praised civil rights activists for their "moral urge to act" that inherently challenged "the psychology of political apathy and political spectatorship."[109] It is possible to imagine that if Mills had lived longer, he would have recognized the serious limitation that his blind spot to racial issues was for his social analysis and political radicalism. Indeed, in 1960, in a passage he intended for future publication, Mills declared the United States a "racial tyranny" and admitted, "I have never been interested in what is called 'the Negro problem.' Perhaps I should have been and should be now."[110] Even so, Mills's references to race remained few and far between. Instead of joining the growing civil rights movement in the United States, he looked to developing events in a small island off the coast of Florida.

CUBA AND THE HUNGRY-NATION BLOC

Before 1960, Mills's international engagements had oriented him primarily toward Europe. His trip to Mexico and subsequent involvement with the Cuban Revolution introduced him to a different kind of internationalism focused on what he called the "hungry-nation bloc."[111] New Leftists, he now argued, would have to confront the global imbalance of power between the industrialized and underdeveloped worlds. In his best-selling 1960 book *Listen, Yankee,* Mills championed the Cuban Revolution as a model for left-wing anti-imperialist movements in Latin America, Asia, and Africa. Support for the Cuban Revolution also confirmed Mills's belief in the potential emergence of protest within an international cultural apparatus. Playing a significant role in a wider Cuban solidarity movement, *Listen, Yankee* demonstrated the significance of international events and networks for the development of national New Left movements in the United States, Europe, and Latin America.

A year before he published *Listen, Yankee,* Mills knew little about Cuba, but discussions with Latin American intellectuals in Brazil in the fall of 1959 and in Mexico in early 1960 compelled him to confront the issue. In particular, during his three-month stay in Mexico City, Mills became close to leading left-wing Mexican writers, including the prominent novelist Carlos Fuentes. This set of intellectuals proved to be crucial contacts for Mills, allowing him first to discover and then to reach a wider Latin American left. Fuentes, in particular, became for Mills a model of the engaged Latin American intellectual and a key representative of what Mills, in a 1961 letter to Fuentes, referred to as "our New Left."[112] Mills was strongly influenced by Fuentes's belief that "after the assassination in Spain of the ideal internationalism of the first few decades of the twentieth century, we are now witnessing the emergence of a concrete internationalism: that of the underdeveloped nations."[113]

After speaking with Fuentes and other Latin American leftists in Brazil and Mexico, Mills came to share their hope that the Cuban Revolution would provide the impetus for this new internationalism. Fuentes—like many Latin American leftists, drawn to socialism but disenchanted with the Soviet example—looked to developments in Cuba as a new model for radical social change.[114] In an early 1960 interview in Mexico with Fuentes and other Mexican intellectuals, Mills tentatively voiced the appeal of the Cuban Revolution as a New Left force: "It is not within advanced capitalism or within the Soviet bloc, but within the underdeveloped countries perilously outside both blocs that I see the best possibilities for an independent Left. As for the *probabilities* of it, quite frankly I don't estimate them very high. . . . I don't know of any country which has yet displayed for us a really new beginning—a third model of industrialization which, of course, would be the basis for any international New Left. Maybe Cuba will turn out that way; I haven't been there."[115] When Mills returned to the United States from Mexico, he arranged to visit Cuba in August 1960. No doubt Mills was flattered and intrigued to hear a report that Castro had read *The Power Elite* while leading the guerrilla campaign in the Sierra Maestra, but the primary purpose of his trip was to see for himself whether Cuba really did represent a possible New Left "third model."[116]

Mills's visit came at a time of rapidly deteriorating relations between Cuba and the United States. In June, at the request of the U.S. government, American oil refineries in Cuba refused to process Soviet crude oil, leading to their nationalization by the Cuban government. In retaliation, the United States cancelled Cuba's guaranteed quota of sugar sales. Although Castro had previously received positive U.S. press coverage, by 1960 he was generally portrayed as a dangerous Communist dictator, even though he was not yet a Communist. Mills's trip also occurred against the backdrop of the development of a Cuban solidarity movement in the United States led by the Fair Play for Cuba Committee (FPCC), founded in 1960. By opposing the conduct of American foreign policy and expressing solidarity with revolutionary movements in third world nations, the FPCC was a crucial early organization in 1960s-era radicalism. Seeking a "fair hearing" for the Cuban Revolution, the FPCC was led by former CBS journalist Robert Taber. It countered negative and inaccurate portrayals of the Cuban Revolution in the mass media and urged the American government not to support counterrevolutionary activities. Beginning as a tiny ad hoc group that published an advertisement in the *New York Times,* by the end of 1960 it had seven thousand members in twenty-seven adult chapters and forty student councils. Presenting itself as "a group of distinguished writers, artists, journalists, and professionals," the FPCC seemed to fulfill Mills's calls for the repossession of the cultural apparatus.[117] Taber helped Mills arrange his trip to Cuba. When he arrived in Cuba, Mills met another prominent FPCC activist, Saul Landau, a graduate student from the University of Wisconsin and an editor and cofounder of *Studies on the Left,* who would subsequently become Mills's research assistant, traveling with him to Europe in 1961.[118]

Mills spent barely more than two weeks in Cuba, but he made the most of his time. With the assistance of a translator, he conducted interviews with members of the revolutionary movement at all levels. He spent "three and a half eighteen-hour days" with Castro himself.[119] Because he did not speak Spanish, because his time was short, and because his activities were largely arranged by Cuban government officials, there were very clear limits to what Mills was able to learn during his trip. Though he sometimes worried he might not be properly prepared to comment on Cuba, Mills was swept up in the excitement of the revolutionary situation. He also calculated that no other figure was willing and capable of offering a sympathetic perspective on the revolution for a mass American audience. As one of the only prominent American leftists with no history of association with the Communist Party or Popular Front organizations, Mills believed he was ideally suited to argue the case of the Cuban revolutionaries in the United States. One Cuban with whom Mills talked during his trip asked Mills whether he'd be "considered a Communist" if he criticized U.S. policy toward Cuba. "On the contrary," Mills replied, "it is known that I'm not. This is the most worrisome thing about me."[120]

When Mills returned from Cuba, he wrote *Listen, Yankee* within a matter of weeks. It was published in November 1960 as a mass-market paperback. Though it contained an introduction and conclusion in Mills's own voice, the body of *Listen, Yankee* was written as a series of letters addressed to the American public by a fictional Cuban revolutionary. This stylistic device expressed one of Mills's central concerns, emphasized by the FPCC, that the Cuban Revolution deserved a fair hearing, which was not provided by the biased mainstream media. Readers today are likely to be struck by the audacity of Mills's effort to portray a Cuban revolutionary, but many Latin American intellectuals at the time were unconcerned by his use of this technique. Mills himself worried about feigning a Cuban voice, but he was reassured by his Cuban translator.[121] For Mills, speaking in the voice of a Cuban revolutionary was a way of expressing solidarity. Even when writing in his own voice, Mills privileged the need to identify with the revolutionaries. "I do not worry about the Cuban Revolution," he wrote, "I worry with it."[122] Even so, one should certainly be skeptical of Mills's claim that "the facts and interpretations presented in these letters from Cuba accurately reflect . . . the views of the Cuban revolutionary. . . . I have merely organized them—in the most direct and immediate fashion of which I am capable."[123]

The most convincing aspect of *Listen, Yankee* was its sharp challenge to American foreign policy. Mills detailed the long history of American intervention in Cuba, highlighting U.S. government support of the corrupt and brutal dictator Fulgencio Batista, who was overthrown by the 26th of July Movement led by Castro. Mills also explored the larger context of U.S. imperialism in Latin America, pointing to U.S. policies driven by the search for profit and power rather than the nation's professed commitment to democratic ideals. As Mills correctly predicted, American economic sanctions against Cuba escalated into military support for a counterrevolution. "Isn't your Government really left with only one way to act against our Government and against us, military violence against Cuba?" asked Mills's fictional Cuban.[124] Already by 1960 the U.S. government was gearing up for the Bay of Pigs debacle of April 1961, when CIA-backed exiles launched a surprise invasion of the island and were easily repelled. American hostility to Cuba, Mills perceived, was a major force pushing Castro's government into the Soviet orbit. One of the most effective rhetorical strategies of *Listen, Yankee* was the direct appeal of the fictional Cuban revolutionary to the American public to scrutinize and change their government's policies: "Because Cuba—listen, Yankee—Cuba is your big chance. It's your chance to establish once again what the United States perhaps once did mean to the world. It's your chance to make it clear how you're going to respond to all the chaos and tumult and glory, all the revolution and bloody mess and enormous hopes that are coming about among all the impoverished, disease-ridden, illiterate, hungry peoples of the world in which you, Yankee, are getting so fat and so drowsy."[125]

Like the influential historian and critic of American imperialism William Appleman Williams, Mills used the Cuban example to argue that the United States needed to reevaluate its foreign policy toward third world revolutions.[126] From the very first page, Mills made it clear that his concern was not just with Cuba itself, but with the exploited peoples of the underdeveloped world and their struggles against their imperial or neo-imperial masters. "Cuba's voice today is a voice of the hungry-nation bloc," he proclaimed, "and the Cuban revolutionary is now speaking—most effectively—in the name of that bloc." "In Africa, in Asia, as well as in Latin America," he continued, "the people behind this voice are becoming strong in a kind of fury they've never known before."[127] Not surprisingly, Mills failed to grasp the crucial racial dimension of the Cuban Revolution, and of the anticolonial struggle more generally. This omission proved an important distinction between *Listen, Yankee* and the enthusiastic accounts of the Cuban Revolution offered by African-American radicals such as LeRoi Jones and Robert F. Williams.[128]

Listen, Yankee left little doubt that Mills believed the Cuban Revolution was the "third model" he had hoped for in world politics. "The Cuban revolutionary *is* a new and distinct type of left-wing thinker and actor," Mills declared. "He is neither capitalist nor Communist. He is socialist in manner, I believe, both practical and humane."[129] The Cuban Revolution, Mills believed, had freed itself from the Communist baggage of the Old Left. Though he noted that the Cuban government received aid from the Soviet Union, Mills insisted on the non-Communist nature of the revolution. Through the voice of his fictional Cuban, Mills hailed the Cuban Revolution as a new beginning for the international left: "We are revolutionaries of the post-Stalin

era. . . . We've never had any 'God That Failed.' . . . We are new radicals. We really are, we think, a new left in the world. A left that has
never suffered from all that Stalinism has meant to the old left all over
the world."[130]

In describing the Cuban Revolution as a nondogmatic yet radical
social transformation that portended a left-wing revival centered in the
third world, Mills found himself in agreement with many U.S. and
European leftists. The editors of *Monthly Review,* Leo Huberman and
Paul Sweezy, traveled to Cuba a few months before Mills; their book,
Cuba: Anatomy of a Revolution, appeared shortly before *Listen,
Yankee.* Huberman and Sweezy enthused that "this is the first time—
ever, anywhere—that a genuine socialist revolution has been made by
non-Communists!"[131] *Studies on the Left* similarly viewed the Cuban
Revolution as a "refreshing combination of humanism and rationalism."[132] *Studies on the Left* published an article by the French intellectual John-Paul Sartre, who traveled to Cuba shortly after the revolution
and hailed it as a new beginning for the international left.[133] Mills's
portrayal of Cuban revolutionaries as a radical "third force" beyond
Soviet communism and American capitalism also rested in large part
on Cuban leaders' self-portrayals at the time. For instance, Mills quoted
Fidel Castro's statement "Capitalism sacrifices man; the Communist
state, by its totalitarian concept, sacrifices the rights of man."[134]

Mills's interpretation of the Cuban Revolution was oversimplified
and in many ways naïve. In his zeal to identify with the revolution,
Mills overlooked the faults of the Cuban government. This was particularly evident in the book's letter on the political system, titled
"Revolutionary Euphoria." Though Mills was right to emphasize the
popularity of the government (the failure of the Bay of Pigs invasion
to attract any local support would prove that), he overlooked the dangers of revolutionary dictatorship and failed to acknowledge the vested
interest of the government in staying in power. Mills's fictional letter
writer emphasized the necessity of dictatorship for the current phase
of the revolution. "If we had an organized political system," he wrote,
"we could not have done the things we have done in such a short time.
Any system would lower the velocity of the revolution."[135] He praised
Fidel Castro for his "anti-bureaucratic personality" and called him
"the most directly radical and democratic force in Cuba."[136] "Above
all," he claimed, "we believe neither Fidel Castro nor any other of our
revolutionary leaders will use force to maintain himself in power."[137]

In his concluding note to the reader, Mills adopted a more sober

tone, admitting, "My worries for Cuba—like those of knowledgeable
Cuban revolutionaries—have to do, first, with problems of politics."[138]
He added, "I do not like such dependence upon one man as exists
in Cuba today, nor the virtually absolute power that one man pos-
sesses."[139] Despite the revolutionary euphoria in the letters, there was
an undercurrent of characteristic Millsian pessimism in *Listen, Yankee*.
For Cuba to remain neutral in the cold war conflict and thus have
a good chance to continue to represent a "third force," Mills argued
that the U.S. government would have to commit to a policy of nonin-
tervention. Given its material interests in Latin America, this meant
that the U.S. government would have to "transform its own imperialist
economy." This would require a truly "deep transformation," to say the
least.[140] Having made this assessment, Mills might have predicted that
American hostility to the revolution would have helped force Castro
into the Soviet bloc, thus undermining the status of Cuba as a possible third force in world affairs. By instead emphasizing "revolutionary euphoria" and closely identifying with the revolutionaries, Mills
perhaps set himself up for future disappointment. Mills's uncritical
embrace of the Cuban Revolution may have been the inevitable result
of his desperate search for New Left agents after suffering through long
years of left-wing defeat.

Mills's embrace of the Cuban Revolution complicated his analysis of
the global New Left in terms of the agency of the "cultural apparatus."
Mills saw the Cuban revolution as the work of a "young intelligentsia
in contact with the poorer people."[141] Indeed, the leaders of the Cuban
revolution were educated and relatively young. But Mills failed to
recognize that, as revolutionaries who had seized state power, Cuban
leaders were a very different type of political agent than the cultural
apparatus of the United States and Britain, or even Poland or Mexico.
Mills helped to bring about an alliance between the revolutionary intelligentsia of Cuba and the cultural apparatus in other nations, but his
lumping them together as a single international New Left obscured
crucial differences among them.

At times, Mills worried that he had rushed to judgment about Cuba.
As he wrote to E. P. Thompson in late 1960, "I've been running since
last February, when I went first to Mexico, then Russia, then Cuba. Too
much fast writing, too many decisions of moral and intellectual types,
made too fast, on too little evidence."[142] In one sense, Mills's willingness to uncritically embrace the Cuban Revolution foreshadowed the
unfortunate identification of later New Leftists with undemocratic

Communist movements in the third world. But Castro was hardly Mao Zedong or Ho Chi Minh. In 1960, Mills's analysis of the Cuban Revolution as popular, non-Communist, and radical, if oversimplified and overly optimistic, was at least plausible.[143] Rather than seeing Mills's championing of the Cuban Revolution as evidence of an attraction to "totalitarian" socialism, as his friend Harvey Swados once suggested, it is more accurately viewed as a rare departure for a critical intellectual who had once pledged "not to sink my life and my mind within *any* organization, much less one nation or another."[144]

As Cuba edged closer to the Soviet bloc in 1961 and 1962, Mills began to have second thoughts about Castro. At first, Mills defended the revolution. In his last piece of writing on the revolution, the afterword to the Spanish translation of *Listen, Yankee,* Mills stated that nothing had happened to alter his earlier views.[145] And, at a June 1961 meeting with John-Paul Sartre and Simone de Beauvoir in a Paris restaurant, Mills defended Castro to his French counterparts, who were becoming disenchanted with the revolution's direction.[146] However, there is strong evidence that indicates that Mills became sharply critical after Castro signaled his conversion to Communism in a December 1961 speech in which he declared himself a Marxist-Leninist. The evidence suggests that Mills felt personally betrayed by Castro.[147] It is impossible to know what Mills would have written about these developments had he lived longer, but it is difficult to imagine that he would have supported Cuba as a model for New Left change after it became Communist. After all, Mills's hope for the Cuban Revolution was always that it represented a non-Communist "third model" for left-wing political change.

Positive responses to *Listen, Yankee* demonstrated the importance of the Cuban revolution—and Mills's advocacy of it—for the growth of an international New Left. Mills never proposed that the Cuban Revolution could serve as a model for political change within the industrialized West. However, he did hope that its example could help foster an internationalist New Left consciousness in the United States and in the world as a whole. "Whether they know it or not," Mills wrote in a blurb for Sartre's *On Cuba,* "for the generation just coming to maturity, the revolution in Cuba is their 'Spanish Civil War.'"[148]

Mills's book, of course, was primarily addressed to its "yankee" audience. Mills aimed to "get the United States . . . out of its present status as the provincial zone of the Americas."[149] Cuba was a test case for how Americans would respond to third world liberation movements, and Mills hoped the American people could be galvanized to

alter the policies of their government. Indeed, *Listen, Yankee* injected
new debate about American foreign policy toward Cuba into the public
sphere, and in the process helped to focus American public opinion on
the justness of American policies toward the underdeveloped world as a
whole. Released in October 1960, the book sold a remarkable 370,000
copies by January 1961. Many other readers were exposed to it through
an excerpt published in *Harper's* magazine.[150] The book was reviewed
in countless magazines and newspapers throughout the nation. Like
Mills's earlier books, it was reviewed in major urban newspapers,
but it was also reviewed in countless smaller publications, such as the
*Crawfordsville (Indiana) Journal and Review, The Virginian-Pilot and
the Plymouth Star,* the *Lafayette (Louisiana) Observer,* and the *Bristol
(Connecticut) Press.* Though the book was denounced more often than
praised, the response suggested that there was indeed an opening in
the cultural apparatus to the views of a radical. No less a figure than
Eleanor Roosevelt praised Mills's "most controversial but interesting
book."[151]

The impact of *Listen, Yankee* was hardly limited to the United
States. British New Leftists also followed events in Cuba closely.
Emphasizing the need for critical support of the revolution, the editors of the *New Left Review* declared, "Cuba's example will be of
the very greatest importance to countries—in Latin America, Africa,
Asia—where a similar combination of circumstances could lead on to
a similar understanding." Noting that none of its British contributors
had yet been to Cuba, the editors indicated that they "must rely on
second-hand accounts" from "some of our most-trusted fellow socialists" abroad, including Huberman and Sweezy, Sartre, and, of course,
Mills.[152] Subsequently, the *New Left Review* published an interview
with Saul Landau, conducted when Landau was traveling in Europe
with Mills.[153] Mills sought to create ties between the British New Left
and the Cuban Revolution. For instance, he tried (unsuccessfully) to
convince the Cuban government to hire E. P. Thompson as a visiting
professor at the University of Oriente.[154] Before his death, Mills had
also agreed to collaborate with British New Leftist Robin Blackburn
on a project about Cuba.[155]

Listen, Yankee also had a significant impact in Latin America. Shortly
after the book was published in the United States, a Spanish translation
appeared. The publisher was the influential left-wing Mexican publishing
house Fondo de Cultura Económica, headed by the Argentinean radical
Arnaldo Orfila Reynal.[156] Fuentes played a key role in helping Mills

find this publisher, one that Mills hoped would distribute the book not only in bookstores, but also in railroad stations.[157] When Mills's book was criticized by the U.S. press, left-wing Latin American intellectuals were quick to defend it. To such Latin American intellectuals, just as to British New Leftists before, Mills became a symbol of a reawakened American radicalism. His example suggested that there were elements within American society that supported greater democracy and social justice in the hemisphere rather than U.S. dominance. Fuentes, for instance, looked for allies among "those nuclei of democratic opinion in the US that are in a position to support our liberation movements."[158] He later dedicated his novel *The Death of Artemio Cruz* to Mills as a "true representative of the American people."[159] Within Cuba itself, Mills's book was hailed for its accurate depiction of the revolution.

Because of the book's impact, in December 1960 Mills was invited to appear on the NBC television show *The Nation's Future* to debate Kennedy administration spokesperson A. A. Berle. Unfortunately, Mills suffered a heart attack on the eve of the program and had to cancel the engagement.[160] After that, he never fully recovered his former energy, though he was able to travel in 1961 and complete *The Marxists* while also making progress on several other projects. He died of a subsequent heart attack in the spring of 1962. As a result, Mills never lived to see the development of the international New Left, to which he had so prominently contributed. Nevertheless, Mills's writings and his example influenced New Leftists, especially in the United States but also in Europe and Latin America, who did much to spread his legacy.

EPILOGUE

The Legacy of C. Wright Mills

On March 20, 1962, at the age of forty-five, Mills died of a heart attack in his home in West Nyack, New York. Observances of his death marked the distance that he had traveled in the two-and-a-half decades of his intellectual career. Hans Gerth traveled from Wisconsin to speak at the memorial service held at Columbia University, along with Daniel Bell, once a key influence on Mills's radicalism, but by then one of Mills's leading liberal targets. Other prominent Columbia sociologists, Merton and Lazarsfeld included, were conspicuously absent.[1] A Quaker service for friends and family, held at the interfaith pacifist Fellowship of Reconciliation in Nyack, reflected Mills's newfound connections with the international peace movement. Fidel Castro sent a wreath of flowers to the service.[2]

Mills's early death was a great loss both for American social thought and for the left. Ironically, the timing may have enhanced his influence during the 1960s, and not only because his early death added to his romantic image. Since Mills died in 1962, his neglect of issues of gender and race was more excusable. Mills had just begun to voice his support for African-American equality near the end of his life. Would he have addressed racial inequality more seriously had he lived longer? Likewise, how would he have responded to the growth of the second-wave feminist movement, which would likely have challenged Mills's neglect of gender hierarchies and his masculine persona as a tough, independent intellectual?[3] And how would he have reacted to later

New Left trends, particularly its adoption of countercultural styles and militant tactics? How would Mills, who conceived of power in wholly institutional terms, have responded to the notion that "the personal is political"? Or how would he have judged the student occupation of Columbia University in 1968: a laudable assault on university bureaucracy or a tactic that undermined reasoned democratic deliberation? Any answers to such questions would be purely speculative. Yet it is precisely because Mills was no longer around to take sides on such divisive issues that he remained an appealing icon for advocates of different visions of radical politics in the 1960s.

Despite his untimely death, it is virtually impossible to imagine the development of American sociology or the left without Mills. In the original draft of *The Sociological Imagination,* he wrote, "I should like to see the tasks and methods that I understand to be proper and urgent taken up by others, especially of course by younger men who are just now beginning independent work. It is, in fact, mainly for them that I write."[4] As Mills hoped, *The Sociological Imagination* and his other works had an important effect on academic social science, even though he had created no school and had no disciples. Many scholars trained during the 1960s were inspired by Mills's vision of the sociological imagination to rebel against Parsonian social theory and bureau-driven social research and to expand their sense of what social science could be. The result was a sociological discipline more divided and confused about its identity, but one far more open to the questions and concerns that Mills had pursued throughout his career. In the 1960s and 1970s, sociologists posthumously reintegrated Mills into the academic milieu out of which he had originally emerged. Beginning in 1964, and continuing to the present day, the Society for the Study of Social Problems has offered the C. Wright Mills Award to books that exemplify Mills's sociological vision.

Mills's enduring impact on academic social science was evident in a 1964 collection edited by Irving Louis Horowitz, *The New Sociology: Essays in Social Science and Social Theory in Honor of C. Wright Mills.* Horowitz had proposed the book to Mills in 1960. As Mills explained to his literary agent, though he thought he was "much too young for this sort of thing," he was interested because "I'm in a fight of course with the profession of sociology: *The Sociological Imagination* . . . made a lot of them mad, but the young ones it made glad; and maybe it's a good idea to firm them up."[5] Dedicated to "American graduate students of Social Science," *The New Sociology* contained twenty-eight essays by social

scientists from the United States, Britain, and Latin America, including
T. B. Bottomore, Erich Fromm, Alvin Gouldner, Andrew Hacker, and
Ralph Miliband.[6] Collectively, the essays critically appraised Mills's
legacy and represented a new effort to create a public sociology that
directly confronted the significant moral and political issues of the day.
In his introductory essay, Horowitz reclaimed Mills for the social sciences and hinted that a transformation toward a new sociology was
already under way. "The ceaseless barrage of criticism caused Mills to
think himself a 'lone wolf,'" Horowitz wrote. "He was mistaken in his
romantic notion of being one and isolated. Any authentic movement or
authentic sociological method invites many people; and since the new
turn in sociology is intrinsically broad in scope, many scholars (from
all over the human sciences and humanities) have been attracted to it."[7]
Horowitz concluded, "When social science is tied to social responsibility, the legacy of Mills will be realized."[8]

Another 1964 publication, "Radical Nomad: Essays on C. Wright
Mills and His Times," revealed a different aspect of Mills's legacy. A
master's thesis written by a principal leader of the young New Left, Tom
Hayden, "Radical Nomad" demonstrated the resonance of Mills's radical politics of truth for a new generation. Mills became best known for
his influence on radicals of the 1960s. "If any one person was the intellectual father of The Movement," wrote Paul Jacobs and Saul Landau
in 1966, "it was C. Wright Mills," noting that "several Movement
babies have been named C. Wright."[9] A leader of the Students for a
Democratic Society (SDS), Hayden drafted its influential 1962 manifesto, the "Port Huron Statement." For Hayden, Mills's willingness
to tell truths that others ignored made him a worthy progenitor. He
saw Mills as one of the few postwar thinkers able to see "through the
hypocrisy, fraud, obfuscation, privilege, irrationality, and totalitarianism."[10] Hayden found Mills's work compelling for its commitment to
a "participatory democracy where men together make the decisions
which order and direct their lives."[11] His depiction of Mills as a "radical nomad" contributed to the pervasive mythology of Mills as the lone
rebel who spoke out against the political complacency and conformity
of the postwar era.

As this book has shown, Mills's ideas were far more embedded in
his time than Hayden recognized. Yet just as new sociologists criticized
Mills's eagerness to play the maverick, certain aspects of Mills's thinking struck the new generation of leftists as inadequate. Particularly
problematic were Mills's failures to address issues of race, poverty, and

gender, as well as the bleak pessimism of his disillusioned radicalism, which to Hayden seemed to allow "no chance for protest or revolt."[12] Mills's influence on 1960s-era radicalism extended beyond the white student New Left represented by Hayden. For example, one of the greatest admirers of Mills's work was the African-American intellectual and leading theorist of Black Power, Harold Cruse. In *The Crisis of the Negro Intellectual*, Cruse argued that even though Mills was "an Anglo-Saxon and a Southerner at that," he was a significant New Left theorist who introduced "a new method for a new radical criticism of American society."[13] Cruse praised Mills's analysis of the "structural question of the American cultural apparatus," and applied it by arguing that African-American intellectuals needed to develop their own autonomous ideas and institutions.[14]

Today, Mills's legacy endures, even though his radical ambitions for left-wing social change and the widespread public relevance of sociology remain unfulfilled. His best works are still worth reading today. *The New Men of Power* identifies key causes of organized labor's decline, while *White Collar* still speaks to anyone who has ever worked in an office. *The Sociological Imagination* remains an inspiring account of the possibilities of social science, and *The Power Elite* has acquired new relevance during the period of the so-called war on terror, in which it is difficult to ignore the close connections between political, corporate, and military leaders or the ways in which government officials use their power to distort the truth. Clearly, Mills is a figure whose legacy deserves serious acknowledgment. Yet we should not make Mills larger than life by portraying him as a maverick intellectual hero. Mills's sociological and political imagination had significant flaws as well as considerable merits. His neglect of the issues of race and gender alone make him a problematic model for contemporary radicals. Moreover, while his work remains relevant, Mills sought to understand a society that has changed in important respects since his death over half a century ago. Mills once observed that "we must accuse" Karl Marx of having written in the nineteenth century.[15] So must we accuse Mills of having written in the twentieth century. One lesson of any intellectual history is that, as Quentin Skinner once put it, "we must learn to do our thinking for ourselves."[16] The best way to continue Mills's legacy is to critically apply his insights to think for ourselves about the contemporary prospects for American sociology and the left in our own time.

Notes

INTRODUCTION: MAVERICK ON A MOTORCYCLE?

1. Russell Jacoby, afterword to C. Wright Mills, *White Collar* (New York: Oxford University Press, 2001), 365.

2. Tom Hayden, "Radical Nomad: Essays on C. Wright Mills and His Times" (Ann Arbor: Center for Conflict Resolution, University of Michigan, 1964). Originally Hayden's master's thesis, this work has been republished as *Radical Nomad: C. Wright Mills and His Times* (Boulder, CO: Paradigm Publishers, 2006).

3. James Miller, "Democracy and the Intellectual: C. Wright Mills Reconsidered," *Salmagundi* 70–71 (Spring–Summer 1986): 83.

4. Harvey Molotch, "Going Out," *Sociological Forum* 9 (June 1994): 231.

5. Todd Gitlin, afterword to C. Wright Mills, *The Sociological Imagination* (New York: Oxford University Press, 2000), 231. The best scholarship on Mills to date has been written by Richard Gillam. In his unpublished doctoral dissertation and in a series of articles, Gillam offers a careful and sophisticated account of Mills's intellectual and historical context. For all its merits, however, Gillam's work still emphasizes the ways in which the idiosyncratic personality of this "truculent renegade" shaped Mills's work. Accordingly, Gillam neither offers a detailed analysis of Mills's political development nor fully examines the decisive significance of Mills's sociological background. See Richard Gillam, "C. Wright Mills: An Intellectual Biography, 1916–1948" (Ph.D. diss., Stanford University, 1972); "*White Collar* from Start to Finish," *Theory and Society* 10 (1981): 1–30; "C. Wright Mills and the Politics of Truth: *The Power Elite* Revisited," *American Quarterly* 26 (Oct. 1975): 461–79; "Richard Hofstadter, C. Wright Mills, and the 'Critical Ideal,'" *American Scholar* 47 (Winter 1977–1978): 69–85; "C. Wright Mills and Lionel Trilling:

'Imagination' and the Fifties," *Gettysburg Review* 2 (Autumn 1989): 680–89. The quote is from Gillam, "C. Wright Mills: An Intellectual Biography," 4.

6. As quoted in James Miller, *Democracy Is in the Streets: From Port Huron to the Siege of Chicago* (New York: Simon and Schuster, 1987), 79.

7. On the particular appeal of Mills to male radicals, see Van Gosse, *Where the Boys Are: Cuba, Cold War America, and the Making of a New Left* (New York: Verso Books, 1993), 176–83, and Doug Rossinow, *The Politics of Authenticity: Liberalism, Christianity, and the New Left in America* (New York: Columbia University Press, 1998), 297–98.

8. Russell Jacoby, *The Last Intellectuals: American Culture in the Age of Academe* (New York: Basic Books, 1987). Hagiographic depictions of Mills have engendered opposing accounts of his life. For example, Guy Oakes and Arthur Vidich argue that Mills was an academic careerist whose fame rested on his ability to advance as his own the ideas of his sometime collaborator, Hans Gerth. Yet Oakes and Vidich merely invert the standard image of Mills, retaining the common focus on his personality over his ideas. Thus, they get us no closer to understanding him. See Guy Oakes and Arthur J. Vidich, *Collaboration, Reputation, and Ethics in American Academic Life: Hans H. Gerth and C. Wright Mills* (Urbana: University of Illinois Press, 1999).

9. Reliable information about Mills's life, and many important primary documents, can be found in a collection edited by his daughters: Kathryn Mills with Pamela Mills, eds., *C. Wright Mills: Letters and Autobiographical Writings* (Berkeley: University of California Press, 2000), hereafter cited as *Letters and Autobiographical Writings*. The best source on Mills's early life is Gillam, "C. Wright Mills: An Intellectual Biography."

10. Jacoby, *The Last Intellectuals*, 95.

11. Rick Tilman, *C. Wright Mills: A Native Radical and His American Intellectual Roots* (University Park: Pennsylvania State University Press, 1984); Irving Louis Horowitz, *C. Wright Mills: An American Utopian* (New York: Free Press, 1983). Tilman's book is a serious effort to discover the origins of Mills's ideas, though it neglects the particular historical context in which Mills's thought developed. The most commonly cited work on Mills, Horowitz's book usefully locates Mills and his ideas in different sociological contexts, but it is an unreliable source of information about him. Horowitz's biography is based in large part on documents that he acquired shortly after Mills's death and retained contrary to the wishes of the Mills family. Horowitz has recently donated his papers, including this material, to Pennsylvania State University, but they are not yet available to the public. It is hoped that future Mills scholars will have access to this material. For a sharply critical account of Horowitz's relationship to Mills, see John Summers, "The Epigone's Embrace: Irving Louis Horowitz on C. Wright Mills," *Minnesota Review* 68 (Spring 2007): 107–24.

12. Russell Jacoby makes the dubious claim that, in the postwar period, Jewish intellectuals with a recent family history of immigration more willingly abandoned their radicalism than did thinkers with a longer American heritage, such as Mills. See *The Last Intellectuals*, 72–111.

13. C. Wright Mills, "Letter to the New Left," *New Left Review* 1 (Sept.–Oct. 1960): 18–23.

14. Andrew Jamison and Ron Eyerman, *Seeds of the Sixties* (Berkeley: University of California Press, 1994), 30–46; Kevin Mattson, *Intellectuals in Action: The Origins of the New Left and Racial Liberalism, 1945–1970* (University Park: Pennsylvania State University Press, 1994), 43–96; Miller, *Democracy Is in the Streets*, 78–91.

15. Three works of intellectual history that do give proper attention to the 1940s are: Howard Brick, *Daniel Bell and the Decline of Intellectual Radicalism: Social Theory and Political Reconciliation in the 1940s* (Madison: University of Wisconsin Press, 1986); Daniel Horowitz, *Betty Friedan and the Making of* The Feminine Mystique (Amherst: University of Massachusetts Press, 1998); and Gregory Sumner, *Dwight Macdonald and the* politics *Circle* (Ithaca, NY: Cornell University Press, 1996).

16. C. Wright Mills, *The Sociological Imagination* (New York: Oxford University Press, 1959), 6.

17. C. Wright Mills, *The New Men of Power: America's Labor Leaders* (New York: Harcourt, Brace, 1948).

18. Mills, "Letter to the New Left."

19. C. Wright Mills, *The Power Elite* (New York: Oxford University Press, 1956), 8.

20. Hofstadter to Mills, July 3, 1958, Box 4B 400, C. Wright Mills Papers, Center for American History, University of Texas, Austin (henceforth referred to as "UT").

21. Mills, *The Sociological Imagination*, 166.

22. Ibid., 168.

23. Ibid., 174.

24. Reinhold Niebuhr, *The Children of Light and the Children of Darkness* (New York: Scribner's, 1944); Arthur Schlesinger Jr., *The Vital Center: The Politics of Freedom* (Boston: Houghton, Mifflin, 1949).

25. George Cotkin, *Existential America* (Baltimore, MD: Johns Hopkins University Press, 2003).

26. Mills to Lambert Davis, Oct. 30, 1948, UT 4B 339.

27. C. Wright Mills, "The Powerless People: The Role of the Intellectual in Society," *politics* 1 (Apr. 1944): 72.

28. Herbert Marcuse, *One-Dimensional Man: Studies in the Ideology of Advanced Industrial Society* (Boston: Beacon Press, 1964).

29. Richard Hofstadter, *The American Political Tradition* (New York: Knopf, 1948), 8; Louis Hartz, *The Liberal Tradition in America: An Interpretation of American Political Thought since the Revolution* (New York: Harcourt, Brace, 1955).

30. George Orwell, *Nineteen Eighty-Four: A Novel* (New York: Harcourt, Brace, 1949).

31. Thom Anderson, "Red Hollywood," in *Literature and the Visual Arts in Contemporary Society*, ed. Suzanne Ferguson and Barbara Groseclose (Columbus: Ohio State University Press, 1984), 141–96. Anderson identifies

a *film gris* genre of the 1940s consisting of films made by leftists who offered pessimistic critiques of American society.

32. Seymour Martin Lipset, *Political Man: The Social Bases of Politics* (New York: Doubleday, 1960), 442–43.

33. Ibid., 441.

34. Mills, "Letter to the New Left," 24.

35. Mills, *White Collar,* 110.

36. "Educator Hits 'Era of Public Immorality,'" *Washington Post and Times Herald,* Nov. 12, 1955.

37. On postwar liberalism see Howard Brick, *Transcending Capitalism: Visions of a New Society in Modern American Thought* (Ithaca, NY: Cornell University Press, 2006), 121–218; Daniel Horowitz, *Anxieties of Affluence: Critiques of American Consumer Culture, 1939–1979* (Amherst: University of Massachusetts Press, 2004); Nelson Lichtenstein, ed., *American Capitalism: Social Thought and Political Economy in the Twentieth Century* (Philadelphia: University of Pennsylvania Press, 2006); and Richard H. Pells, *The Liberal Mind in a Conservative Age: American Intellectuals in the 1940s and 1950s* (New York: Harper & Row, 1985).

38. I emphasize the particular importance of the discipline of sociology for Mills's thought. Yet Mills's ideas grew out of and had implications for other social scientific disciplines as well. Moreover, Mills himself rejected sharp disciplinary boundaries and saw all social scientific inquiry as part of a common endeavor. Accordingly, *Radical Ambition* concerns itself with the history of sociology in particular, but also the history of the social sciences as a whole.

39. Incidentally, Mills coined the term "public intellectual" when he used it in passing in his book *The Causes of World War Three* (New York: Oxford University Press, 1958), 135.

40. Stanley Aronowitz, "Introduction," in C. Wright Mills, ed. Aronowitz (London: Sage Publications, 2004), ix.

41. Mills, "Guggenheim Application," in *Letters and Autobiographical Writings,* 80.

42. Nathan Glazer, "The Study of Man," *Commentary* 1 (Nov. 1945): 84.

43. As quoted in Craig Calhoun and Jonathan VanAntwerpen, "Orthodoxy, Heterodoxy, and Hierarchy," in *Sociology in America,* ed. Calhoun (Chicago: University of Chicago Press, 2007), 381.

44. For recent accounts that stress the hegemony of a coherent paradigm led by Parsons, Lazarsfeld, and Merton in postwar sociology, see David Paul Haney, *The Americanization of Social Science: Intellectuals and Public Responsibility in the Postwar United States* (Philadelphia: Temple University Press, 2008), and George Steinmetz, "American Sociology Before and After World War II: The (Temporary) Settling of a Disciplinary Field," in *Sociology in America,* 314–66. For a persuasive challenge to this common account, see Calhoun and VanAntwerpen, "Orthodoxy, Heterodoxy, and Hierarchy."

45. Alvin W. Gouldner, *The Coming Crisis of Western Sociology* (New York: Basic Books, 1970), 15.

46. Michael Burawoy, "For Public Sociology," *American Sociological Review* 70 (Feb. 2005): 4–28.

47. Howard Brick, "The Reformist Dimension of Talcott Parsons' Early Social Theory," in *The Culture of the Market: Historical Essays*, ed. Thomas L. Haskell and Richard F. Teichgraeber III (New York: Cambridge University Press, 1993), 357–95; Howard Brick, "Talcott Parsons' 'Shift Away From Economics,' 1937–1946," *Journal of American History* 87 (Sept. 2000): 490–514; David Hollinger, "The Defense of Democracy and Robert K. Merton's Formulation of the Scientific Ethos," in *Science, Jews, and Secular Culture: Studies in Mid-Twentieth-Century American Intellectual History* (Princeton, NJ: Princeton University Press, 1996), 80–96.

48. As quoted in Mark C. Smith, "A Tale of Two Charlies: Political Science, History and Civil Reform, 1890–1940," in *Modern Political Science: Anglo-American Exchanges since 1880*, ed. Robert Adcock, Mark Bevir, and Shannon C. Stimson (Princeton, NJ: Princeton University Press, 2007), 130.

49. On "taking it big," see Dan Wakefield, "Taking It Big: A Memoir of C. Wright Mills," *Atlantic Monthly* 228 (Sept. 1971): 65–71.

CHAPTER 1. STUDENT AMBITIONS

1. Mattson, *Intellectuals in Action*, 48.

2. Mills, "Self-Images and Ambitions" (1960), in *Letters and Autobiographical Writings*, 304.

3. C. Wright Mills, "The Social Life of a Modern Community," *American Sociological Review* 7 (Apr. 1942): 271.

4. Read Bain to Mills, June 19, 1939, UT 4B 339.

5. Mills, Untitled manuscript (dated Jan. 30, 1939), UT 4B 362.

6. Joel Isaac, "Theories of Knowledge and the Human Sciences, 1920–1960" (Ph.D. diss., University of Cambridge, U.K., 2005).

7. Mills to parents, Oct. 21, 1936, UT 4B 353.

8. Gouldner, *The Coming Crisis*, 11.

9. C. Wright Mills, "The Professional Ideology of Social Pathologists," *American Journal of Sociology* 49 (Sept. 1943): 165–80.

10. As quoted in Gillam, "C. Wright Mills: An Intellectual Biography," 26–27. For information on Mills's youth, see also *Letters and Autobiographical Writings*, 21–34.

11. "A freshman" to the *Battalion*, Apr. 3, 1935, as quoted in *Letters and Autobiographical Writings*, 31.

12. Ibid., 32, 33.

13. Ibid., 33–34. It is likely that the textbook Mills referred to was Robert Park and Ernest Burgess's classic of Chicago School sociology, *Introduction to the Science of Sociology*. See Gillam, "C. Wright Mills: An Intellectual Biography," 41.

14. Mills, "The Value Situation and the Vocabulary of Morals," UT 4B 360.

15. George Herbert Mead, *The Philosophy of the Act*, edited with an introduction by Charles W. Morris with John M. Brewster, Albert M. Dunham,

and David L. Miller (Chicago: University of Chicago Press, 1938); "In Memoriam: David Louis Miller," www.utexas.edu/faculty/council/2000–2001/memorials/SCANNED/miller_d.pdf, accessed Aug. 4, 2008; "In Memoriam: George V. Gentry," www.utexas.edu/faculty/council/2000–2001/memorials/AMR/Gentry/gentry.pdf, accessed Aug. 4, 2008. Miller also collaborated with Gentry to produce a pragmatist critique of Alfred North Whitehead in David L. Miller and George V. Gentry, *The Philosophy of A.N. Whitehead* (Minneapolis, MN: Burgess, 1938).

16. Mills to "Sanders," Nov. 16, 1940, UT 4B 339. Henceforth, quotations from letters, drafts, and other informal documents will be reproduced as written without commenting on errors or variant spellings.

17. C. Wright Mills, "Reflection, Behavior, and Culture" (M.A. thesis, University of Texas at Austin, 1939), 21. For works that treat the general influence of pragmatism on Mills, see Tilman, *C. Wright Mills*, and Cornell West, *The American Evasion of Philosophy: A Genealogy of Pragmatism* (Madison: University of Wisconsin Press, 1989), 124–38.

18. Darnell Rucker, *The Chicago Pragmatists* (Minneapolis: University of Minnesota Press, 1969). On the professionalization of philosophy, see Bruce Kuklick, *The Rise of American Philosophy* (New Haven, CT: Yale University Press, 1977), 451–572.

19. On "the revolt against formalism," see Morton White, *Social Thought in America: The Revolt Against Formalism* (Boston: Beacon, 1947). See also James Kloppenberg, *Uncertain Victory: Social Democracy and Progressivism* (New York: Oxford University Press, 1986); and David Hollinger, "The Problem of Pragmatism in American History," in *In the American Province* (Baltimore, MD: Johns Hopkins University Press, 1985), 23–43. For a useful interpretation of Mills's social scientific methodology that stresses Mills's indebtedness to pragmatist notions of science, see Robert Paul Jones, "The Fixing of Social Belief: The Sociology of C. Wright Mills" (Ph.D. diss., University of Missouri, 1977). While Jones mistakenly argues that Mills displayed a consistent and coherent pragmatist approach to social science throughout his career, Jones's insightful investigation of Mills's methodology stresses important elements of his thought that few other commentators have noticed.

20. Mills, "Reflection, Behavior, and Culture," 13.

21. Mills, *The Sociological Imagination*, 25–49.

22. See Mills's attack on "Christian sociology" in "Science of Religion," a paper written for Miller's seminar "Sci. Method," UT 4B 336.

23. Mills, "The Value Situation and the Vocabulary of Morals."

24. Mills, "Concerning the So-Called Integration of the Self," paper dated Apr. 25, 1937, UT 4B 337.

25. Mills, "The Value Situation and the Vocabulary of Morals."

26. Mills, "Reflection, Behavior, and Culture," 21.

27. "In Memoriam: Warner Ensign Gettys," www.utexas.edu/faculty/council/2000–2001/memorials/SCANNED/gettys.pdf, accessed Aug. 4, 2006.

28. Mills to parents, Sept. 29, 1935, UT 4B 353; Mills to parents, undated (Friday noon), UT 4B 353; Mills to parents, Mar. 3, 1937, UT 4B 353.

29. Warner Gettys, review of *Structure of Social Action,* by Talcott Parsons, *Social Forces* 17 (Mar. 1939): 425.

30. Warner Gettys, "Human Ecology and Social Theory," *Social Forces* 18 (May 1940): 469–76.

31. Martin Bulmer, *The Chicago School: Institutionalization, Diversity, and the Rise of Sociological Research* (Chicago: University of Chicago Press, 1984).

32. Andrew Abbott, *Department and Discipline: Chicago Sociology at One Hundred* (Chicago: University of Chicago Press, 1999), 196–97.

33. Mills, "Reflection, Behavior, and Culture," 76. See W.I. Thomas and Florian Znaniecki, *The Polish Peasant in Europe and America* (Chicago: University of Chicago Press, 1918–1920).

34. Ayres to Charner Perry, Mar. 2, 1939, Box 3F 291, Clarence Ayres Papers, Center for American History, University of Texas at Austin.

35. William Breit and William Patton Culbertson Jr., "Clarence Edwin Ayres: An Intellectual's Portrait," in *Science and Ceremony: The Institutional Economics of C.E. Ayres,* ed. Breit and Culbertson (Austin: University of Texas Press, 1976), 3–22; www.utexas.edu/faculty/council/2000–2001/memorials/SCANNED/ayres.pdf, accessed June 26, 2006.

36. Michael A. Bernstein, *A Perilous Progress: Economists and Public Purpose in Twentieth-Century America* (Princeton, NJ: Princeton University Press, 2001), 44–48; Dorothy Ross, *The Origins of American Social Science* (New York: Cambridge University Press, 1991), 414–20.

37. Mills, "Science and Society," 1938, UT 4B 362. This paper was in part an attack on Miller, the professor who graded it. Mills objected to an article in the university newspaper in which Miller confidently asserted that "modern science . . . looks evil in the face and kicks it in the pants" ("The Professor Speaks," *Daily Texan,* July 11, 1937).

38. Mills, "Reflection, Behavior, and Culture," 114.

39. C. Wright Mills, "Language, Logic, and Culture," *American Sociological Review* 4 (Oct. 1939): 670.

40. Ibid., 675.

41. Ibid., 677.

42. Kenneth Burke, *Permanence and Change: An Anatomy of Purpose* (New York: New Republic, 1935); Grace de Laguna, *Speech: Its Function and Development* (New Haven, CT: Yale University Press, 1927); Charles W. Morris, *Foundations of the Theory of Signs* (Chicago: University of Chicago Press, 1938); Edward Sapir, *Language: An Introduction to the Study of Speech* (New York: Harcourt, Brace, 1921).

43. Mills, "Language, Logic, and Culture," 680 n.

44. Ibid., 671.

45. Ibid., 677.

46. *Letters and Autobiographical Writings,* 39.

47. Robert Bannister, *Sociology and Scientism: the American Quest for Objectivity, 1880–1940* (Chapel Hill: University of North Carolina Press, 1987), 255.

48. Ibid., 188–238; Norbert Wiley, "The Rise and Fall of Dominating

Theories in American Sociology," in *Contemporary Issues in Theory and Research*, ed. William E. Snizek, Ellsworth R. Fuhrman, and Michael K. Miller (Westport, CT: Greenwood, 1979), 57–63; Henrika Kuklick, "'A Scientific Revolution': Sociological Theory in the United States, 1930–1945," *Sociological Inquiry* 43 (1973): 3–22. Kuklick's argument that sociology underwent a Kuhnian "paradigm shift" in the late 1930 not only places the shift toward functionalist predominance too early, but it also illustrates the perils of applying a theory drawn from the study of physical science to the social sciences, in which disciplinary consensus is far more difficult to achieve.

49. Talcott Parsons, "The Role of Theory in Social Research," *American Sociological Review* 3 (Feb. 1938): 14.

50. Hans Gerth, "Howard Becker, 1899–1960," *American Sociological Review* 25 (Oct. 1960): 748–49.

51. As quoted in Bannister, *Sociology and Scientism*, 219–20.

52. Don Martindale, *The Monologue: Hans Gerth (1908–1976), a Memoir* (Ghaziabad, India: Intercontinental Press, 1982), 156.

53. "Bob" to Mills, undated letter (written Dec. 1940); Mills to "Bob," Monday noon, UT 4B 339.

54. Mills, "Sociological Methods and Philosophies of Science," UT 4B 362; Howard P. Becker, "The Limits of Sociological Positivism," *Journal of Social Philosophy* (July 1941): 362–69.

55. George Lundberg, *Foundations of Sociology* (New York: Macmillan, 1939).

56. Mills, "Sociological Methods and Philosophies of Science." Becker quoted this sentence in his article, the only reference he made to Mills's paper.

57. Ibid.

58. Blumer to Mills, Nov. 11, 1939, UT 4B 339; Blumer to Mills, Nov. 19, 1940, UT 4B 339.

59. Mills, "The Language and Ideas of Ancient China," unpublished graduate paper, 1940, reprinted in Irving Louis Horowitz, ed., *Power, Politics, and People: The Collected Essays of C. Wright Mills* (New York: Oxford University Press, 1963), 463.

60. Talcott Parsons, *The Structure of Social Action* (New York: McGraw-Hill, 1937); Charles Camic, "Structure After 50 Years: The Anatomy of a Charter," *American Journal of Sociology* 95 (July 1989): 38–107.

61. Brick, "The Reformist Dimension of Talcott Parsons' Early Social Theory."

62. As quoted in Camic, "Structure After 50 Years," 44.

63. Howard Brick, "Society," in *Encyclopedia of the United States in the Twentieth Century*, vol. 2, ed. Stanley Kutler, Robert Dallek, David Hollinger, and Thomas McGraw (New York: Charles Scribner's Sons, 1996), 917–39.

64. Howard Becker, "Introduction," in Leopold von Weise, *Systematic Sociology* (New York: John Wiley, 1932), viii.

65. Parsons, *The Structure of Social Action*, 774.

66. Camic, "Structure After 50 Years."

67. Mills, "A Note on the Classification of the Social-Psychological Sci-

ences," UT 4B 339. Mills's manuscript was rejected for publication by the *American Journal of Sociology* and *Social Forces*.

68. Ibid.

69. Mills to "My Dear Friend," Feb. 25, 1941, UT 4B 377.

70. On the American reception of Mannheim, I have relied on David Kettler and Volker Meja, *Karl Mannheim and the Crisis of Liberalism: The Secret of These New Times* (New Brunswick, NJ: Transaction, 1995), 193–245. Though an excellent account, it does not mention Mills's role in this debate. For more on the reception of *Ideologie and Utopie* by a particular group of German intellectuals, see Martin Jay, "The Frankfurt School's Critique of Karl Mannheim and the Sociology of Knowledge," in *Permanent Exiles: Essays on the Intellectual Migration from Germany to America* (New York: Oxford University Press, 1986), 62–78. In the United States, *Ideology and Utopia* did not provoke the same sort of wide-ranging discussion of the political implications of Mannheim's work as in Germany, where debate had centered on the relationship of the sociology of knowledge to Marxism.

71. Karl Mannheim, *Ideology and Utopia*, trans. Louis Wirth and Edward Shils (New York: Harcourt, Brace, 1936), 57.

72. Ibid., 80.

73. Ibid., 154.

74. See Volker Meja and Nico Stehr, "Introduction," in *The Sociology of Knowledge*, 1:xiv–xvi. On Mannheim's attempt to rehabilitate Enlightenment ideas, see H. Stuart Hughes, *Consciousness and Society: The Reconstruction of European Social Thought, 1890–1930* (New York: Knopf, 1958), 418–27.

75. Hans Speier, "The Social Determination of Ideas," *Social Research* 5 (May 1938): 182–205.

76. Alexander von Schelting, review of *Ideologie und Utopie*, by Karl Mannheim, *American Sociological Review* 1 (Aug. 1936): 674.

77. Talcott Parsons, review of *Max Webers Wissenschaftslehre*, by Alexander Von Schelting, *American Sociological Review* 1 (Aug. 1936): 680.

78. Ibid., 681.

79. Gerth would later exert a significant influence on Mills during his graduate studies. Gerth did not come to Wisconsin, however, until 1940, after Mills had already developed his own interpretation of Mannheim.

80. C. Wright Mills, "The Methodological Consequences of the Sociology of Knowledge," *American Journal of Sociology* 46 (Nov. 1940): 319.

81. Mills to Merton, Nov. 12, 1940, UT 4B 339.

82. Mills, "Methodological Consequences," 324.

83. Ibid., 318.

84. Thomas Kuhn, *The Structure of Scientific Revolutions* (Chicago: University of Chicago Press, 1962).

85. Mills, "Methodological Consequences," 320.

86. Robert K. Merton, "A Life of Learning," ACLS Occasional Paper No. 25 (New York, 1994).

87. Robert Merton, "The Sociology of Knowledge," *Isis* 27 (Nov. 1937): 493–503, and "Karl Mannheim's Sociology of Knowledge," *Journal of Liberal Religion* (Winter 1941): 125–47.

88. Merton to Mills, Jan. 8, 1940, UT 4B 339.

89. Merton, "Karl Mannheim's Sociology of Knowledge"; Merton to Mills, Apr. 16, 1940, UT 4B 339.

90. Merton to Mills, Nov. 6, 1940, UT 4B 339.

91. Mills to Merton, Feb. 15, 1941, UT 4B 339.

92. Merton to Mills, Apr. 5, 1941, UT 4B 339.

93. C. Wright Mills, review of *Ideas Are Weapons*, by Max Lerner, *Journal of Social Philosophy* 6 (Oct. 1940): 93.

94. Mills to "My Dear Friend," Feb. 25, 1941, UT 4B 377.

95. Mills, "Dissertation outline," UT 4B 361.

96. Becker, "Memorandum to C. Wright Mills," UT 4B 360.

97. C. Wright Mills, "A Sociological Account of Some Aspects of Pragmatism" (Ph.D. diss., University of Wisconsin, 1942), 414.

98. Ibid.

99. Mills, "Methodological Consequences," 330.

100. Alvin Gouldner, *The Coming Crisis*, 499; Pierre Bourdieu and Loïc J. D. Wacquant, *Invitation to Reflexive Sociology* (Chicago: University of Chicago Press, 1992). Bourdieu's reflexive sociology differs from that of Gouldner in important respects. While Gouldner focuses on the moral responsibilities of the individual social scientist, Bourdieu undertakes a more expansive exploration of the ways in which the basic presuppositions of social science, in objectifying the social world, structure its insights. Mills's later stress on the moral and political responsibility of the sociologist in *The Sociological Imagination* approximates Gouldner's position, but his call for the "detailed self-location of social science" in "Methodological Consequences" perhaps more closely anticipates Bourdieu.

101. Mills, "The Professional Ideology of Social Pathologists," 167.

102. Ibid., 179.

103. Ibid., 166.

104. Ibid., 170.

105. Ibid., 168 n.

106. Ibid., 165.

107. Robert Merton, "Social Structure and Anomie," *American Sociological Review* 3: 672–82.

108. On this point, see Eli Zaretsky, "Editor's Introduction," in *The Polish Peasant in Europe and America*, ed. William I. Thomas and Florian Znaniecki (Urbana: University of Illinois Press, 1984), 1–53.

109. Mills, "Methodological Consequences: Three Problems for Pathologists," UT 4B 360.

110. Ibid.

111. Ibid.

112. Ibid.

113. Kloppenberg, *Uncertain Victory*.

114. Robert Westbrook, *John Dewey and American Democracy* (Ithaca, NY: Cornell University Press, 1991).

115. Mills, "Syllabus: Contemporary Social Problems," UT 4B 353.

116. John Dewey, *The Public and Its Problems* (New York: H. Holt and Company, 1927), 180.

117. Hans Joas, "Pragmatism in American Sociology," in *Pragmatism and Social Theory* (Chicago: University of Chicago Press, 1993), 25–26.

118. Mills, "Three Problems."

CHAPTER 2. WHAT IS HAPPENING IN THE WORLD TODAY

1. Mills to Macdonald, Feb. 6, 1942, Box 34, Folder 855, Dwight Macdonald Papers, Yale University Library.

2. Mills, "On Who I Might Be and How I Got That Way" (fall 1957), in *Letters and Autobiographical Writings*, 251.

3. Mills, "A Sociological Account of Some Aspects of Pragmatism," 412.

4. Ibid., 393.

5. Ibid., 359.

6. Ibid., 372.

7. Ibid., 309.

8. Ibid., 348–49.

9. As quoted in Nobuko Gerth, *"Between Two Worlds": Hans Gerth, Eine Biografie, Jahrbuch für Soziologiegeschichte* (1999–2000): 33.

10. Joseph Bensman, "Hans Gerth's Contribution to American Sociology," in *Politics, Character, and Culture: Perspectives from Hans Gerth*, ed. Bensman, Arthur J. Vidich, and Nobuko Gerth (Westport, CT: Greenwood Press, 1982), 221–74; Hans Gerth, "As in the book of fairy tales: all alone . . ." (a conversation with Jeffrey Herf), in *Politics, Character, and Culture*, 14–49; Hans Gerth Curriculum Vitae, University Archives, University of Wisconsin at Madison; Nobuko Gerth, *"Between Two Worlds"*; Martindale, *The Monologue*.

11. See Hans Gerth, "Public Opinion and Propaganda," in *Politics, Character, and Culture*, 60–71; on the Frankfurt School, see Martin Jay, *The Dialectical Imagination: A History of the Frankfurt School and the Institute of Social Research, 1923–1950* (Berkeley: University of California Press, 1973).

12. Lewis Coser, *Refugee Scholars in America: Their Experiences and Their Impact* (New Haven, CT: Yale University Press, 1984), xi.

13. Oakes and Vidich, *Collaboration, Reputation, and Ethics*.

14. Mills, "Guggenheim Application," in *Letters and Autobiographical Writings*, 79.

15. Mills to Gerth, undated (likely early 1942), letter in author's possession; W. Lloyd Warner and Paul S. Lunt, *The Social Life of a Modern Community* (Westport, CT.: Greenwood Press, 1941).

16. Mills, "The Social Life of a Modern Community," 266.

17. Ibid., 264.

18. "Emendation and Augmentation of Outlining Done in Madison by Gerth & Mills, August 18–19, 1941," UT 4B 338; Karl Mannheim, review of *Methods in Social Science*, ed. Stuart Rice, *American Journal of Sociology* 38 (Sept. 1932): 281.

19. Gerth and Mills, "Preface" (written Aug. 1942, revised Oct. 1943), UT 4B 339.

20. Talcott Parsons, "Max Weber and the Contemporary Political Crisis," *Review of Politics* 4 (1942): 61–76, 155–72; Parsons, "Some Sociological Aspects of the Fascist Movements," *Social Forces* 21 (1942): 138–47. Parsons's analysis of the origins of fascism was similar to that of Gerth, who also emphasized that Nazi society combined bureaucratic and charismatic features. See Hans Gerth, "The Nazi Party: Its Leadership and Composition," *American Journal of Sociology* 45 (June 1940): 517–41. Parsons's attention to the particular historical situation in Germany made his essays on German fascism less vulnerable to the charge that Mills would later levy against him in *The Sociological Imagination:* that his generalized theoretical analysis was too abstract.

21. Ellen Herman, *The Romance of American Psychology: Political Culture in the Age of Experts* (Berkeley: University of California Press, 1995), 17–81.

22. Robert Merton, *Social Theory and Social Structure* (Glencoe, IL: Free Press, 1949). Incidentally, Merton wrote the laudatory foreword to *Character and Social Structure.*

23. Mills to Eliseo, Dec. 18, 1943, UT 4B 363.

24. Hans Gerth and C. Wright Mills, *Character and Social Structure: The Psychology of Social Institutions* (New York: Harcourt, Brace, 1953), 193. In formulating this conception of power, Mills was also influenced by the realist tradition in interwar American political science, as reflected in Harold Lasswell's definition of politics as a matter of "who gets what, when, how." See Harold Lasswell, *Politics: Who Gets What, When, How* (New York: McGraw-Hill, 1936). Mills took copious notes from this book, and he corresponded with Lasswell in the early 1940s.

25. As quoted in Daniel Kelly, *James Burnham and the Struggle for the World: A Life* (Wilmington, DE: ISI Books, 2001), 97. See also James Burnham, *The Managerial Society: What Is Happening in the World* (New York: John Day, 1941).

26. H. H. Gerth and C. Wright Mills, "A Marx for the Managers," *Ethics* 52 (Jan. 1942): 203.

27. Ibid., 205.

28. Gerth and Mills, "Emendation and Augmentation of Outlining."

29. Gerth and Mills, "A Marx for the Managers," 212.

30. Ibid., 210.

31. Ibid., 201.

32. Macdonald to Mills, Feb. 26, 1942, Box 34, Folder 855, Dwight Macdonald Papers, Yale University Library.

33. See Michael Wreszin, *A Rebel in Defense of Tradition: The Life and Politics of Dwight Macdonald* (New York: Basic, 1994).

34. Mills to Bell, Aug. 10, 1942, UT 4B 360.

35. Mills to Gerth, Mar. 2, 1943, letter in author's possession.

36. As quoted in Susan Stout Baker, *Radical Beginnings: Richard Hofstadter and the 1930s* (Westport, CT: Greenwood Press, 1985), 176.

37. Gerth to Mills, undated (but likely 1942 or 1943), letter in author's possession.

38. Mills, "Guggenheim Application," in *Letters and Autobiographical Writings*, 80.

39. Job L. Dittberner, *The End of Ideology and American Social Thought: 1930–1960* (Ann Arbor, MI: UMI Research Press, 1979), 314.

40. Merton to Mills, Jan. 29, 1943, UT 4B 363.

41. Lynd to Mills, Jan. 20, 1943, UT 4B 363.

42. Mills to Macdonald, Oct. 21, 1942, Box 34, Folder 855, Dwight Macdonald Papers, Yale University Library; Mills to Alinsky (undated, probably late 1943 or early 1944), in *Letters and Autobiographical Writings*, 61.

43. Mills, "Locating the Enemy," *Partisan Review* 9 (Sept.–Oct. 1942): 432.

44. H. Stuart Hughes, "Franz Neumann: Between Marxism and Liberal Democracy," Donald Fleming and Bernard Bailyn, eds. *The Intellectual Migration: Europe and America, 1930–1960* (Cambridge: Harvard University Press, 1969), 446–62; Franz Neumann, "The Social Sciences," in Neumann, et al., *The Cultural Migration* (Philadelphia: University of Pennsylvania Press, 1953), 4–26.

45. Mills, "Locating the Enemy," 432.

46. Franz Neumann, *Behemoth: The Structure and Practice of National Socialism, 1933–1942* (New York: Oxford University Press, 1942), vii.

47. Mills, "Locating the Enemy," 432.

48. Ibid.

49. There is a voluminous scholarship on the New York intellectuals. Two of the best studies are Terry Cooney, *The Rise of the New York Intellectuals: Partisan Review and Its Circle* (Madison: University of Wisconsin Press, 1986); and Alan Wald, *The New York Intellectuals: The Rise and Decline of the Anti-Stalinist Left from the 1930s to the 1980s* (Chapel Hill: University of North Carolina Press, 1987).

50. Mills, "For 'Ought,'" Sept. 19, 1953, UT 4B 390.

51. See Wald, *The New York Intellectuals*, 267–310, 344–65; Christopher Phelps, *Young Sidney Hook: Marxist and Pragmatist* (Ithaca, NY: Cornell University Press, 1997), 198–243.

52. Mills occasionally referred to himself as a "socialist" during this period, but he generally preferred the term "radical."

53. Mills to Alinsky, Dec. 18, 1943, UT 4B 363.

54. Mills to Macdonald, Oct. 10, 1943, in *Letters and Autobiographical Writings*, 52.

55. C. Wright Mills, "Pragmatism, Politics, and Religion," *New Leader*, Aug. 1942, 2.

56. Gillam, "C. Wright Mills: An Intellectual Biography," 167–68.

57. Mills to Frances and Charles Grover Mills, undated (probably Mar. 1945), in *Letters and Autobiographical Writings*, 89.

58. S. A. Longstaff, "*Partisan Review* and the Second World War," *Salmagundi* 43 (Winter 1979): 108–29.

59. Gary Gerstle, "The Protean Character of American Liberalism,"

American Historical Review 99 (Oct. 1994): 1043–73; Daniel Geary, "Carey McWilliams and Antifascism, 1934–1943," *Journal of American History* 90 (Dec. 2003): 912–34. One exception to Mills's blindness on racial issues during the war was his analysis of the Los Angeles Zoot Suit race riots of 1943. See his "The Sailor, Sex Market, and Mexican," *New Leader*, June 26, 1943.

60. Frank Warren, *Noble Abstractions: American Liberal Intellectuals and World War II* (Columbus: Ohio State University Press, 1999).

61. Randolph Bourne, "The State," in *War and the Intellectuals: Collected Essays, 1915–1919* (New York: Harper and Row, 1969), 71.

62. See Michael S. Sherry, *In the Shadow of War: The United States Since the 1930s* (New Haven, CT: Yale University Press, 1995), 64–122.

63. Mills, "Locating the Enemy," 437. Though Mills used Neumann to suggest the frightening domestic consequences of the war, in *Behemoth*, Neumann offered his explicit support for total victory by the Allies.

64. Brick, *Daniel Bell and the Decline of Intellectual Radicalism*, 78.

65. Mills, "Collectivism and the Mixed-Up Economy," *New Leader*, Dec. 19, 1942, 5.

66. Ibid., 5.

67. Ibid.

68. Ibid., 6.

69. Ibid.

70. In "Collectivism and the Mixed-Up Economy," Mills did not explore the connection of military leaders to economic and political elites, as Neumann had done and Mills would later do in *The Power Elite*. However, Mills did expand his analysis to include the military in an April 1945 piece for *Common Sense*. "The Conscription of America" was an examination of leading government and military leaders' statements on postwar reconstruction. In this article, Mills worried about a "drift toward a permanent militarized economy" that involved the "integration of big business with the military elite." See Mills, "The Conscription of America," *Common Sense*, Apr. 1945, 15.

71. Mills to parents, Feb. 1943, UT 4B 353.

72. Mills, "Collectivism and the Mixed-Up Economy," 5.

73. Mills to Gerth, undated, in *Letters and Autobiographical Writings*, 87–88; "Small Business and Civic Welfare," Report of the Special Committee to Study Problems of American Small Business, U.S. Senate, 79th Congress, 2nd Session, C. No. 135 (Washington, 1946), 3.

74. "Small Business and Civic Welfare," 1.

75. Ibid., 41.

76. As quoted in Baker, *Radical Beginnings*, 151.

77. Brick, *Daniel Bell and the Decline of Intellectual Radicalism*, 12.

78. See, for instance, Mills to Macdonald, Nov. 11, 1943, Box 34, Folder 855, Dwight Macdonald Papers, Yale University Library.

79. C. Wright Mills, "The Powerless People: The Role of the Intellectual in Society," *politics* 1 (Apr. 1944): 71.

80. On the rise of this tragic sensibility during this period, see Cotkin, *Existential America*.

81. Mills, "The Powerless People," 68.

82. Ibid.

83. Ibid., 69.

84. Ibid., 70.

85. Ibid. In part, Mills's pessimism about the ability of the independent intellectual to reach a broader audience reflected the publication history of "The Powerless People." At Robert Lynd's suggestion, Mills had originally sought to publish the essay in *Harper's,* but it ultimately wound up in *politics,* which reached a much smaller audience. "The Powerless People" thus registered Mills's fear that alienated left-wing intellectuals like himself would be able to reach only an audience of like-minded estranged individuals and hence would remain powerless to harness their intelligence to the cause of radical social reconstruction. See Mills to Lynd, undated, UT 4B 389.

86. Mills, "The Powerless People," 69.

87. Ibid., 70.

88. Ibid., 71.

89. Ibid., 72.

90. For example, Edward Said cites "The Powerless People" and holds up Mills's role as an exemplar of the role of the intellectual in *Representations of the Intellectual: The 1993 Reith Lectures* (New York: Vintage, 1994), 20–22.

91. Mills, "The Powerless People," 69.

92. Max Weber, "Class, Status, Party," *politics* 1 (Oct. 1944): 271–78.

93. The question of credit for *From Max Weber* remains controversial, since Gerth bitterly protested that Mills claimed an unfair share of credit for it. The preface states that Gerth was responsible for the selections and the translations from the German, credits Mills with the formulation of the English text, and claims that the book as a whole represents their "mutual work." The controversy over credit for this work (as well as for *Character and Social Structure*) has recently been taken up in Oakes and Vidich, *Collaboration, Reputation, and Ethics in American Academic Life.* This is a complex issue, but Oakes and Vidich seem primarily interested in bolstering the reputation of Gerth (one of the authors was his student, although he fails to mention this fact) and revealing Mills to be a shameless careerist. This argument is unpersuasive for two reasons: first, Mills's commitment to radical politics belies the notion that he was motivated primarily by career ambition; and second, as Mills well knew, his reputation as a sociologist was hardly based on the works he coauthored with Gerth. For a review that reveals Oakes and Vidich's perspective to be biased and offers a persuasive argument that Mills acted in a "reasonable, if not saintly, manner" in his dealings with Gerth, see Russell Jacoby, "False Indignation," *New Left Review* 2 (Mar.–Apr. 2000): 154–59.

94. Mills to Gerth, June or July 1944, letter in author's possession.

95. Ron Robin, *The Making of the Cold War Enemy: Culture and Politics in the Military-Industrial Complex* (Princeton, NJ: Princeton University Press, 2001).

96. Mills to Macdonald, Oct. 25, 1943, in *Letters and Autobiographical Writings,* 53.

97. Talcott Parsons, "Introduction," in *Max Weber: The Theory of Social*

and Economic Organization, ed. Talcott Parsons and A.M. Henderson (New York: Oxford University Press, 1947).

98. Hans Gerth and C. Wright Mills, "Introduction," in *From Max Weber* (New York: Oxford University Press, 1946), 47.

99. Ibid., 50.

100. Ibid., 24.

101. Ibid.

102. Ibid., 44.

103. Ibid., 70.

104. Ibid., 30.

105. Ibid., 44.

106. Weber, "Politics as a Vocation," in *From Max Weber,* 77–128.

107. Mills to Lynd, undated, UT 4B 389.

CHAPTER 3. THE UNION OF THE POWER AND THE INTELLECT

1. George H. Callcott, *A History of the University of Maryland* (Baltimore: Maryland Historical Society, 1966), 314–37.

2. Mills to Merton, July 26, 1944, in *Letters and Autobiographical Writings,* 70.

3. Mills to Fannye and C.G., undated, UT 4B 353.

4. Mills to mother, undated, UT 4B 353.

5. Seymour Martin Lipset, "The Department of Sociology," in *A History of the Faculty of Political Science, Columbia University,* ed. R. Gordon Hoxie et al. (New York: Columbia University Press, 1955), 284–303.

6. Mills to Mother and Dad, Jan. 1945, in *Letters and Autobiographical Writings,* 84.

7. Robert Lynd, "A Proposal for the Further Development of the Department of Sociology," Central Files, Columbia University Archives, Columbiana Library.

8. Merton to Davis, Dec. 4, 1944, letter in author's possession.

9. Merton to Salomon, Dec. 6, 1946, letter in author's possession.

10. Allan Barton, "Paul Lazarsfeld and the Invention of the University Institution for Social Research," in *Organizing for Social Research,* ed. Burkart Holzner and Jiri Nehnevajsa (Cambridge: Schenkman, 1982), 17–83; Jean M. Converse, *Survey Research in the United States: Roots and Emergence, 1890–1960* (Berkeley: University of California Press, 1987), 213–32, 267–304; Paul Lazarsfeld, "An Episode in the History of Social Research: A Memoir," in *The Intellectual Migration,* ed. Donald Fleming and Bernard Bailyn (Cambridge, MA: Harvard University Press, 1969), 270–337.

11. Converse, *Survey Research,* 239–66.

12. Robert Merton, "Introduction," in *Social Theory and Social Structure,* 3–18.

13. Barton, "Paul Lazarsfeld."

14. Mills conducted two statistical studies prior to joining the BASR: Mills, "The Trade Union Leader: A Collective Portrait" (with Mildred Atkinson), *Public Opinion Quarterly* 9 (Summer 1945): 158–75; "The American

Business Elite: A Collective Portrait," *Journal of Economic History* 4 (Dec. 1945): 20–44.

15. Barton, "Paul Lazarsfeld," 27. For evidence that Columbia sociologists sought a much larger subsidy, see Lynd, "A Proposal," and Lazarsfeld, "An Episode in the History of Social Research."

16. Robert Lynd, *Knowledge for What? The Place of Social Science in American Culture* (Princeton, NJ: Princeton University Press, 1939); Robert Lynd and Helen Lynd, *Middletown: A Study in American Culture* (New York: Harcourt, Brace, 1929). See also Mark C. Smith, *Social Science in the Crucible: The American Debate over Objectivity and Purpose, 1918–1942* (Durham, NC: Duke University Press, 1994), 120–58.

17. Lynd to Mills, Jan. 20, 1943, UT 4B 363.

18. Mills to Gerth, Jan. 22, 1945, letter in author's possession. In this letter, Mills describes Lynd's reply to him. Mills asked Gerth to destroy three letters in which he discussed the situation at the BASR.

19. For evidence of rifts within the Columbia Department of Sociology during this period, see Theodore Abel, *The Columbia Circle of Scholars: Selections from the Journal, 1930–1957* (Frankfurt am Main: Peter Lang, 2001), 320–21. Abel reports the comment of a colleague who referred to Merton and Lazarsfeld as "snakes in the grass."

20. Mills to Gerth, Jan. 1945, letter in author's possession.

21. Mills to Gerth, Jan. 22, 1945, letter in author's possession.

22. Mills to Gerth, Jan. 1945.

23. Mills to Gerth, Nov. 16, 1946, UT 4B 339.

24. Mills, "Reader's Report," UT 4B 389.

25. Mills to Macdonald, Feb. 5, 1945, Box 34, Folder 855, Dwight Macdonald Papers, Yale University Library.

26. Mills to Bell, Jan. 30, 1945, letter in author's possession.

27. Paul Lazarsfeld, *Radio and the Printed Page* (New York: Duell, Sloan, and Pearce, 1940).

28. Lazarsfeld, "An Episode in the History of Social Research," 279. Lazarsfeld's major study in Austria was of proletarian adolescents and unemployment.

29. Mills informed Lazarsfeld that only twenty of the two hundred major American unions had research divisions of their own and that the rest would need an outside agency such as the BASR to conduct their research. See Mills, "Memo to Lazarsfeld Re: Labor Research Division," Nov. 29, 1945, UT 4B 368.

30. C. Wright Mills, "The Politics of Skill," *Labor and Nation*, June–July 1946, 35.

31. C. Wright Mills, "The Political Gargoyles: Business as Power," *New Republic*, Apr. 12, 1943, 483.

32. C. Wright Mills, "The Case for the Coal Miners," *New Republic*, May 24, 1943, 697.

33. Ibid.

34. Nelson Lichtenstein, "From Corporatism to Collective Bargaining," in *The Rise and Fall of the New Deal Order*, ed. Steve Fraser and Gary Ger-

stle (Princeton, NJ: Princeton University Press, 1989), 122–52; David Brody, *Workers in Industrial America* (New York: Oxford University Press, 1980), 173–255; George Lipsitz, *A Rainbow at Midnight: Labor and Culture in the 1940s* (Urbana: University of Illinois Press, 1994).

35. In early 1946, Mills wrote to Gerth, "My strategy now is to back out of everything not completely essential to the Influence Study, the White-Collar Man, Character and Social Structure, and my coming teaching duties" (Mar. 13, 1946, letter in author's possession). Mills, however, spent much of the following two years working on issues related to the labor movement.

36. Mills to Gerth, undated (Jan. or Feb. 1946), in *Letters and Autobiographical Writings*, 96.

37. Hardman obituary, *New York Times*, Jan. 31, 1968. For the clearest expression of Hardman's views during this period, see Hardman, "State of the Movement," in *American Labor*, ed. Hardman and Maurice Neufield (New York: Prentice-Hall, 1951), 52–84. On labor-liberalism and its social-democratic manifestations in this period, see Lichtenstein, "From Corporatism to Collective Bargaining."

38. Mills, *The New Men of Power*, 295.

39. *Labor and Nation*, Aug. 1945, 2–3.

40. Robert Lynd, "We Should Be Clear as to What Are the Essentials and What Are the Historic Trappings of Democracy," *Labor and Nation*, Feb.–Mar. 1946, 33–39.

41. Mills, "The Politics of Skill," 35.

42. Selig Perlman, *A Theory of the Labor Movement* (New York: A.M. Kelley, 1928), 281.

43. C. Wright Mills, "What Research Can Do for Labor," *Labor and Nation*, June–July 1946, 18.

44. Ibid., 4.

45. Ibid.

46. Ibid.

47. Ibid.

48. Ibid.

49. "Bill" (William Miller) to Mills, Apr. 25, 1946, UT 4B 412.

50. Mills to Miller, undated, UT 4B 412.

51. Mills, "The Intellectual and the Trade Union Leader," UT 4B 339.

52. C. Wright Mills, "All That and—a Survey of the Left," *Labor and Nation*, Mar.–Apr. 1947, 41, original emphasis removed.

53. Mills, *The New Men of Power*, 295, 300; Mills, "Memo to Lazarsfeld."

54. Mills to Wilbert Moore, Apr. 9, 1946, UT 4B 395.

55. Mills, "The Politics of Skill," 35.

56. Macdonald, "Rebellion?—or Reconversion?" *politics* 3 (Mar. 1946): 78.

57. Macdonald, "The Root Is Man," *politics* 3 (Apr. 1946): 107.

58. Macdonald, "The Root Is Man," pt. 2, *politics* 3 (June 1946): 209.

59. Gregory Sumner, *Dwight Macdonald and the* politics *Circle*, 3. See

also Penina Migdal Glazer, "From the Old Left to the New: Radical Criticism in the 1940s," *American Quarterly* 24 (Dec. 1972): 584–603.

60. Mills to Macdonald, July 22, 1946, Box 34, Folder 855, Dwight Macdonald Papers, Yale University Library.

61. Louis Clair (pen name of Coser), "Digging at the Roots, or Striking at the Branches," *politics* 3 (Oct. 1946): 323–28; Irving Howe, "The 13th Disciple," *politics* 3 (Oct. 1946): 329–35.

62. Mills to Macdonald, undated, Box 34, Folder 855, Dwight Macdonald Papers, Yale University Library.

63. Mills to Gerth, Oct. 5, 1945, letter in author's possession.

64. Mills to Macdonald, undated, Box 34, Folder 855, Dwight Macdonald Papers, Yale University Library.

65. Todd Gitlin, "Media Sociology: The Dominant Paradigm," *Theory and Society* 6 (Sept. 1978): 208. On the origins and impact of the Decatur study, see also the articles collected in the special issue of the *Annals of the Academy of Political and Social Science*, "Politics, Networks, and the History of Mass Communications Research: Rereading *Personal Influence*," especially Peter Simonson, "Introduction," *Annals of the Academy of Political and Social Science* 608 (Nov. 2006): 6–24.

66. Paul F. Lazarsfeld, Bernard Berelson, and Hazel Gaudet, *The People's Choice: How the Voter Makes up His Mind in a Presidential Campaign* (New York: Duell, Sloan, and Pearce, 1944).

67. "Script for Slide Film Report on Opinion Leadership," Box 9, Bureau of Applied Social Research Papers, Columbia University Rare Books and Manuscripts (henceforth referred to as "BASR"); Elihu Katz and Paul Lazarsfeld, *Personal Influence: The Part Played by People in the Flow of Mass Communications* (Glencoe: Free Press, 1995).

68. Mills to Gerth, Aug. 23, 1945, letter in author's possession.

69. Mills to Gerth, June 7, 1945, letter in author's possession.

70. As quoted in Gillam, "C. Wright Mills: An Intellectual Biography," 301.

71. C. Wright Mills, "The Middle Class in Middle-Sized Cities," *American Sociological Review* 11 (Oct. 1946): 522 n.

72. "Script for Slide Film Report on Opinion Leadership."

73. Ibid.

74. Mills to Herbert Drake, June 18, 1946, Box 9, BASR. In an earlier draft of his letter, Mills also objected to associating the study's findings with a "specific commercial interest," but he apparently later dropped this objection as impolitic.

75. Lynd and Lynd, *Middletown*; Lynd and Lynd, *Middletown in Transition: A Study in Cultural Conflicts* (New York: Harcourt, Brace, 1937).

76. Mills, "The Influence Study: Some Conceptions and Procedures of Research (An Address to the American Association for the Advancement of Science in Boston 29 December 1946)," Box 9, BASR.

77. Mills and Lazarsfeld exchanged a number of letters regarding the controversy in the summer of 1947, with Merton mediating between them. See Merton to Mills, Aug. 1, 1947, letter in author's possession.

78. Unfortunately, no complete copy of Mills's discussion draft survives. There are several chapters of the report in the C. Wright Mills Papers at the University of Texas, apparently written in May 1946, as well as an undated 143-page draft (with no author indicated) of the Decatur report in the BASR papers at Columbia, which, judging by its language and style, Mills almost certainly had some part in writing. Despite occasional asides, both reports provide primarily a statistical analysis of opinion leadership in the fields of fashion, movies, consumer products, and politics using three basic criteria: gregariousness, life-cycle position (age, marital status, etc.), and socioeconomic status. In other words, there seems to be little in the drafts available in the archives that would alarm Lazarsfeld. However, Richard Gillam examined a different version of the report that no longer seems to exist. According to Gillam, Mills's draft dutifully analyzed the statistical sample to determine the characteristics of opinion leaders and opinion followers in Decatur. Much of this analysis was later taken up by Elihu Katz and Lazarsfeld in the published version of the report *Personal Influence* (1955). However, Mills did more than he was asked. Gillam writes that Mills tried in this draft "to blend empirical rigor with theoretical scope," yet "constantly overruns the limits of rigid empiricism and tips the balance toward theory." At one point, Mills explained that the draft exceeded the original aims of the study "because Wright Mills, who happened to be in charge of a first draft of this paper, just naturally wrote it this way." See Gillam, "C. Wright Mills: An Intellectual Biography," 302–4.

79. Mills to Gerth, Jan. 1945, letter in author's possession.

80. Lynd, "A Proposal."

81. Lazarsfeld, "An Episode in the History of Social Research."

82. James Coleman, "Paul F. Lazarsfeld: The Substance and Style of his Work," in *Sociological Traditions from Generation to Generation*, ed. Robert K. Merton and Matilda White Riley (Norwood: Ablex, 1980), 167.

83. Barton, "Paul Lazarsfeld," 46.

84. As quoted in David Morrison, "The Influences Influencing *Personal Influence*: Scholarship and Entrepreneurship," *Annals of the American Academy of Political and Social Science* 608 (Nov. 2006): 63.

85. Mills, *The Cultural Apparatus*, note 4, UT 4B 378. Though Mills did not list Lazarsfeld by name, it is clear that he was referring to him.

86. "The Sociology of Mass Media and Public Opinion," in *Power, Politics, and People*, 586. This article, based on the results of the Decatur study, was originally to be included in a 1950 volume of the U.S. Department of State's Russian-language publication *Amerika*, but it was censored by Russian authorities.

87. Ibid., 597.

88. Merton to Abel, Nov. 19, 1947, letter in author's possession.

89. Mills to Merton, Oct. 23, 1948, letter in author's possession; C. Wright Mills, Clarence Senior, and Rose Kohn Goldsen, *The Puerto Rican Journey: New York's Newest Migrants* (New York: Harper and Brothers, 1950). *The Puerto Rican Journey* is not an important entry in Mills's corpus, although it is interesting that it is the one instance in which he offers a sustained analysis

of race and adopts the ethnographic methods of the traditional community study.

90. Mills to Macdonald, 1947 (probably July), in *Letters and Autobiographical Writings*, 107.

91. C. Wright Mills, "Five 'Publics' the Polls 'Don't Catch': What Each of These Think of and Expect from the Labor Leaders," *Labor and Nation*, May–June 1947, 26–27; Clinton Golden and Harold Ruttenberg, *The Dynamics of Industrial Democracy* (New York: Harper and Row, 1942).

92. Brody, *Workers in Industrial America*, 173–214.

93. Mills, "Five 'Publics' the Polls 'Don't Catch'," 26.

94. Wald, *The New York Intellectuals*, 163–92; Peter Drucker, *Max Shachtman and His Left* (Atlantic Highlands, NJ: Humanities Press, 1994).

95. Mills, *The New Men of Power*, 10.

96. Ibid., 10.

97. Ibid., 3.

98. Ibid., 288–90.

99. Ibid., 155.

100. Ibid., 238.

101. Ibid., 236.

102. Ibid., 116.

103. Ibid., 120.

104. Ibid., 251.

105. Ibid., 252.

106. Kevin Mattson attributes the idea of participatory democracy (and not simply the phrase) to early New Left intellectuals such as Mills. See Mattson, *Intellectuals in Action*.

107. Mills, *The New Men of Power*, 253.

108. Ibid., 255.

109. Ibid.

110. Ibid., 260.

111. Ibid., 28.

112. Ibid., 290.

113. Ibid., 274.

114. Ibid., 291.

115. Ibid., 28.

116. Ibid., 17.

117. Ibid., 274.

118. Irving Howe and B. J. Widick, *The UAW and Walter Reuther* (New York: Random House, 1949), 290. Howe and Widick concluded their book by quoting Mills's *New Men of Power* and asking of the UAW, "Will the power be welded to the intellect?"

119. Mills to Reuther, Apr. 27, 1946, UT 4B 368.

120. C. Wright Mills, "'Grass-Roots' Union with Ideas: The Auto Workers—Something New in American Labor," *Commentary* 5 (Mar. 1948): 246.

121. Ibid., 243.

122. Mills to Weinberg, Dec. 1, 1947, UT 4B 339. The same quote appears in Mills's letter to Downing of the same date.

123. Mills, " 'Grass-Roots' Union with Ideas," 242.

124. Ibid., 247.

125. Mills, *The New Men of Power*, 291.

126. Nelson Lichtenstein, *The Most Dangerous Man in Detroit: Walter Reuther and the Fate of American Labor* (New York: Basic Books, 1995), 271–419.

127. Nelson Lichtenstein, *State of the Union: A Century of American Labor* (Princeton, NJ: Princeton University Press, 2003), 141–245; Kim Moody, *An Injury to All: The Decline of American Unionism* (New York: Verso Books, 1989).

CHAPTER 4. THE NEW LITTLE MEN

1. Mills, *White Collar*, ix.

2. Ibid., xv.

3. Ibid, xi.

4. Ibid., xv.

5. Ibid., xviii.

6. Robert Johnston, *The Radical Middle Class: Populist Democracy and the Question of Radicalism in Progressive Era Portland* (Princeton, NJ: Princeton University Press, 2003), 4.

7. Mills to Gerth, Nov. 26, 1946, letter in author's possession.

8. An excellent account of the evolution of *White Collar* is provided in Richard Gillam, "*White Collar* From Start to Finish." My account draws on Gillam's, but it also differs in several respects. Like Gillam, I see *White Collar* as an important transitional work for Mills that expressed a number of different, sometimes contradictory, impulses. However, I stress the book's roots in the social science and left-wing politics of the 1940s.

9. Mills, "Guggenheim Application" (1944), in author's possession.

10. On the turn toward social psychology and the culture and personality school, see Herman, *The Romance of American Psychology*.

11. Gerth and Mills traded chapters intermittently, particularly during the periods 1943–1944 and 1949–1950. Several factors, however, delayed the publication of the book. Most important of these was their extended conflict over the assignment of authorial credit for the work, a conflict that spilled out of Gerth's resentment toward Mills for taking what he felt to be too much credit for *From Max Weber*. Oakes and Vidich have offered a detailed account of the writing of *Character and Social Structure* in *Collaboration, Reputation, and Ethics in American Academic Life*, 57–90. One should be skeptical, however, of their claim that Mills was primarily motivated by career ambition in his dealings with Gerth.

12. However, I do not believe that *Character and Social Structure* is a "masterpiece," or that it provides a fully elaborated theory that Mills applied in all of his sociological work. For the former claim, see Oakes and Vidich, *Collaboration, Reputation, and Ethics in American Academic Life;* for the latter, see Jones, "The Fixing of Social Belief," and Joseph Scimecca, *The Sociological Theory of C. Wright Mills* (Port Washington, NY: Kennikat Press,

1977). Though it never sold well as a textbook, *Character and Social Structure* was designed for classroom use, and readers must skim through many pages of commonplace textbook observations to locate its original insights.

13. Gerth and Mills, *Character and Social Structure*, xix.

14. Ibid., 183.

15. See ibid., 32, for a diagram of their model. In the model, "character structure" was made up of person, psychic structure (or "self"), and organism. Social structure consisted of five autonomous orders (political, economic, military, kinship, and religious) and four nonautonomous spheres (symbols, technology, status, and education).

16. Ibid., 460.

17. Ibid., 95, 186.

18. Mills, *White Collar,* 356.

19. Mills to Gerth, Aug. 1946, in *Letters and Autobiographical Writings,* 99; Mills, *White Collar,* 358.

20. Mills, *White Collar,* 356.

21. Several installments of Powell's reports to Mills, along with a December 17, 1946, letter from Mills detailing instructions on what to look for, can be found in UT 4B 350.

22. Robert K. Merton, with Marjorie Fiske and Alberta Curtis, *Mass Persuasion: The Social Psychology of a War Bond Drive* (New York: Harper & Brothers, 1946), 10, 188.

23. The interview reports can be found in UT 4B 340, 341, and 342.

24. "General Instructions for the 'Everyday Life in America' Guide: *White Collar Study,*" UT 4B 401, 1.

25. Ibid., 4.

26. Mills, "Notes on the Range of Political Theory of the New Middle Class," UT 4B 365.

27. Mills, *White Collar,* 357–58. Among the works cited by Mills as influencing his analysis were: Alfred M. Bingham, *Insurgent America* (New York: Harper, 1935); Lewis Corey, *The Crisis of the Middle Class* (New York: Covici-Friede, 1935); Emil Lederer, *The Problem of the Modern Salaried Employee: Its Theoretical and Statistical Basis* (New York: WPA Project No. 165–1699–6027, 1937); Emil Lederer and Jacob Marschak, *The New Middle Class* (New York: WPA Project No. 165–97–6999–6027, 1937); Hans Speier, *The Salaried Employee in German Society* (New York: WPA Project No. 465–970391, 1939); and William E. Walling, *Progressivism and After* (New York: Macmillan, 1914).

28. Hans Falluda, *Little Man, What Now?* (New York: Simon and Schuster, 1933).

29. Bingham, *Insurgent America,* 97–98.

30. Mills, "The Defeat of Socialism 1920–1947 and the Need for Reorientation," Speech for Workers Party, Jan. 5, 1947, UT 4B 351.

31. On Western Marxism, see Perry Anderson, *Considerations on Western Marxism* (London: New Left Books, 1976).

32. Mills, *The New Men of Power,* 274.

33. Mills, "The Middle Class in Middle-Sized Cities," 521.

34. Ibid., 528.

35. Mills to Paul Lubow of UOPWA-CIO, Nov. 13, 1946, UT 4B 368.

36. Weinberg to Mills, Dec. 6, 1947, UT 4B 339; Mills to Weinberg, Dec. 10, 1947, UT 4B 339. There is no evidence that Mills actually participated in such a seminar.

37. Mills, "General Instruction for the 'Everyday Life in America' Guide," 4.

38. Mills to McCormick, July 15, 1944, in *Letters and Autobiographical Writings*, 69.

39. Mills to Frances and Charles Grover Mills, Dec. 18, 1946, in *Letters and Autobiographical Writings*, 101.

40. Ibid.

41. C. Wright Mills, "Sociological Poetry," *politics* 5 (Spring 1948): 125. Mills actually wrote this piece as a personal letter to Macdonald, not intending to have it published.

42. Mills, "Sociological Poetry," 125.

43. Indeed, many years later Elihu Katz, Lazarsfeld's collaborator on *Personal Influence,* denied a group of researchers access to the unpublished Decatur research files on the grounds that they contained "too many of Mills's private thoughts" (Katz to Meier, Jan. 12, 1969, Box 10, BASR).

44. Mills to Gerth, March 27, 1949, letter in author's possession.

45. Mills to Gerth, Dec. 1950, letter in author's possession.

46. Mills to Gerth, Feb. 12, 1952, letter in author's possession.

47. David Walker Moore, "Liberalism and Liberal Education at Columbia University: The Columbia Careers of Jacques Barzun, Lionel Trilling, Richard Hofstadter, Daniel Bell, and C. Wright Mills" (Ph.D. diss., University of Maryland, 1978).

48. Mills to Merton, Oct. 5, 1949, letter in author's possession. Merton's reply was cool and patronizing: "Dear Wright: I'm glad you wrote your note" (Merton to Mills, Oct. 10, 1949, letter in author's possession).

49. Mills to Gerth, spring 1950, letter in author's possession.

50. Merton, *Social Theory and Social Structure,* 14, 16.

51. Mills still thought highly enough of Merton's opinion, however, that he sought his advice, along with that of several other friends, when Dwight Macdonald wrote a vicious review of *White Collar* (Mills to Merton, Jan. 10, 1952, letter in author's possession).

52. Mills to Gerth, May 8, 1946, letter in author's possession.

53. Edward Shils, *The Present State of American Sociology* (Glencoe, IL: Free Press, 1948), 63 n.

54. See Ellen Schrecker, *"Many Are the Crimes": McCarthyism in America* (Boston: Little, Brown, 1998).

55. Schlesinger, *The Vital Center.*

56. Mills, Coser, and Sanes, "A Third Camp in a Two-Power World," UT 4B 363, 1.

57. Ibid., 4.

58. Ibid., 10.

59. Brody, *Workers in Industrial America,* 215–29.

60. Sanes to Mills, undated ("Sunday"), UT 4B 463; B. to Mills, Sept. 11, 1948, UT 4B 463.

61. Lichtenstein, *The Most Dangerous Man in Detroit,* 304–5.

62. Mills, "Notes on the Meaning of the Election," UT 4B 348. I quote here from separate drafts of the manuscript.

63. C. Wright Mills, "Notes on White Collar Unionism," *Labor and Nation,* May–June 1949, 19.

64. Mills, *White Collar,* 320–21.

65. See, for instance, Harvey Swados, "The UAW—Over the Top or Over the Hill?" *Dissent,* Fall 1963, 321–43.

66. "Our Story: Six Year of L & N," *Labor and Nation,* Fall 1951, 2–6, 50–54.

67. Kevin Boyle, *The UAW and the Heyday of American Liberalism 1945–1968* (Ithaca, NY: Cornell University Press, 1995), 155.

68. See Sumner, *Dwight Macdonald and the* politics *circle;* Glazer, "From the Old Left to the New."

69. Mills, Coser, and Sanes, "A Third Camp in a Two-Power World," 16.

70. Mills, "Documents," UT 4B 363.

71. See Wald, *The New York Intellectuals,* 267–310; Phelps, *Young Sidney Hook,* 198–243.

72. Mills, "Dialogs on the Left" (report of Oct. 23, 1949, meeting), UT 4B 295; Bernard Rosenberg, "An Interview with Lewis Coser," in *Conflict and Consensus: A Festschrift in Honor of Lewis A. Coser* (New York: Free Press, 1984).

73. Mills to Macdonald, Nov. 20, 1948, UT 4B 339.

74. Mills to Lambert Davis, Oct. 30, 1948, UT 4B 339.

75. Mills to Macdonald, Nov. 20, 1948.

76. See Christopher Lasch, *The New Radicalism in America: 1889–1963* (New York: Random House, 1965), 122–33.

77. Mills to Gerth, Feb. 28, 1950, letter in author's possession.

78. Mills to Sanes, Aug. 27, 1949, letter in author's possession.

79. Mills to Miller, May 30, 1949, in *Letters and Autobiographical Writings,* 136.

80. Ibid.

81. Mills, *White Collar,* 12.

82. Daniel Boorstin, *The Genius of American Politics* (Chicago: University of Chicago Press, 1953); Hartz, *The Liberal Tradition in America;* Hofstadter, *The American Political Tradition.* See also Peter Novick, *That Noble Dream: The "Objectivity Question" and the American Historical Profession* (New York: Cambridge University Press, 1988), 332–48.

83. Mills, *White Collar,* 6, 10.

84. Mills to Miller, undated (summer 1948), in *Letters and Autobiographical Writings,* 116.

85. Gillam, "*White Collar* from Start to Finish," 12.

86. Mills, *White Collar,* 286.

87. Michael Denning, *The Cultural Front* (New York: Verso, 1996), 163–99.

88. Mills, *White Collar,* 57.

89. Ibid., 63. Mills drew his statistics primarily from government sources, particularly census data. See pp. 358–63 for his explanation of how he arrived at these figures. The publisher forced Mills to cut many pages of footnotes that further supported his statistical claims.

90. For the claim that Mills viewed the new middle classes as a homogeneous category, see Johnston, *The Radical Middle Class,* 4.

91. Mills, *White Collar,* 75.

92. Ibid., 65.

93. Ibid., 75.

94. Mills, "Sexual Exploitation in White Collar Employment," UT 4B 347. Nelson Lichtenstein has noted that feminist scholars of white-collar work, such as Barbara Ehrenreich, Susan Faludi, and Arlie Hochschild, have built on Mills's insights in *White Collar.* See Lichtenstein, "Class, Collars, and the Continuing Relevance of C. Wright Mills," *Labor* 1 (Fall 2004): 109–23.

95. Mills, *White Collar,* 174–78.

96. Ibid., 77.

97. Ibid., 80.

98. Ibid., 112.

99. Ibid., xvi.

100. Harry Braverman, *Labor and Monopoly Capital: The Degradation of Work in the Twentieth Century* (New York: Monthly Review Books, 1974).

101. Mills, *White Collar,* 224.

102. Ibid., 240.

103. Ibid., 254–58.

104. Ibid., 110.

105. Ibid.

106. Ibid., 240.

107. In the acknowledgments for *White Collar,* Mills wrote, "Back of Weber, of course, stands Karl Marx, and I cannot fail, especially in these times when his work is on the one side ignored and vulgarized, and on the other ignored and maligned, to acknowledge my general debt, especially to his earlier productions" (ibid., 357).

108. Ibid., 180.

109. Ibid., 161.

110. Ibid., 109.

111. Ibid., 226.

112. Erich Fromm, *Man for Himself: An Inquiry into the Psychology of Ethics* (New York: Reinhart, 1947).

113. Mills, Untitled note, UT 4B 347.

114. Gillam makes a similar point in "*White Collar* from Start to Finish," 15–16.

115. Mills, *White Collar,* 233.

116. Ibid., 238.

117. Ibid., 236.

118. Ibid., 237.

119. Ibid., 258.

120. Paul Gorman, *Left Intellectuals and Popular Culture in Twentieth-Century America* (Chapel Hill: University of North Carolina Press, 1996).

121. See, for instance, Erving Goffman, *Asylums: Essays on the Social Situation of Mental Patients and Other Inmates* (Chicago: Aldine Pub., 1961).

122. Mills, *White Collar,* xii.

123. Ibid., 356.

124. While the "Everyday Life" study provided a source of information that Mills might have drawn on for a richer portrait of white-collar lives, Jonathan Sterne has intriguingly argued that the bureau techniques used by Mills were one cause of his excessive objectification of white-collar workers: "Mills's work is based on a massive wealth of survey research, but the surveys and interviews were done almost entirely by research assistants. Mills hardly ever spoke with the subjects of his texts, and this is one reason why his subjects rarely speak *in* his texts. The style of Mills's writing . . . reproduces the distance that he himself held from his objects of study" (Jonathan Sterne, "C. Wright Mills, the Bureau of Applied Social Research, and the Meaning of Critical Scholarship," *Cultural Studies/Critical Methodologies* 5 [2005]: 65–94 [quotation from p. 70]).

125. Mills, *White Collar,* 326.

126. Ibid., 328; Dewey, *The Public and Its Problems;* Walter Lippmann, *The Phantom Public* (New York: Harcourt, Brace, 1925).

127. Mills, *White Collar,* 325.

128. Ibid., 350.

129. Ibid., 157.

130. Ibid., 146.

131. Ibid., xx.

132. Phillip Vaudrin, Memo (Jan. 17, 1952), Box 110, Folder 6, Knopf Archives Library, Harry Ransom Humanities Center, University of Texas at Austin.

133. Wilfred M. McClay, *The Masterless: Self and Society in Modern America* (Chapel Hill: University of North Carolina Press, 1994), 240.

134. Arthur Miller, *Death of a Salesman: Certain Private Conversations in Two Acts and a Requiem* (New York: Viking Press, 1949); William F. Whyte, *The Organization Man* (New York: Simon and Schuster, 1956); Sloan Wilson, *Man in the Gray Flannel Suit* (New York: Simon and Schuster, 1955). See also K. A. Cuordileone, "'Politics in an Age of Anxiety': Cold War Political Culture and the Crisis in American Masculinity, 1949–1960," *Journal of American History* (Sept. 2000): 515–45.

135. Horace Kallen, "The Hollow Men: A Portrayal to Ponder," *New York Times Book Review,* Sept. 16, 1951.

136. Everett C. Hughes, "The New Middle Classes," *Commentary* 12 (Nov. 1951): 497–98.

137. The quote was reported to Mills and repeated by him in a letter to Bill and Bucky (Miller), undated (probably November 1951), in *Letters and Autobiographical Writings,* 158.

138. Dwight Macdonald, "Abstractio Ad Absurdum," *Partisan Review* 19 (Jan.–Feb. 1952): 114; *Letters and Autobiographical Writings,* 163.

139. David Riesman, review of *White Collar, American Journal of Sociology* 57 (Mar. 1952): 513, 515.

140. Ibid., 514.

141. Ibid., 515.

142. Mills to Riesman, Jan. 31, 1952, in *Letters and Autobiographical Writings,* 166.

143. David Riesman, with Reuel Denney and Nathan Glazer, *The Lonely Crowd: A Study of the Changing American Character* (New Haven, CT: Yale University Press, 1950).

144. Eugene Lunn, "Beyond 'Mass Culture': The Lonely Crowd, the Uses of Literacy, and the Postwar Era," *Theory and Society* 19 (Feb. 1990): 65. Most copies of *The Lonely Crowd* were sold after the release of an abridged paperback version in 1954.

145. "White Collar Seminar," Feb. 15, 1946, UT 4B 350.

146. David Riesman, "A Suggestion for Coding the Intensive White Collar Interviews," Feb. 5, 1948, UT 4B 350. See also Riesman, *The Lonely Crowd,* 47–48; and Nathan Glazer, "From Socialism to Sociology," in *Authors of Their Own Lives: Intellectual Autobiographies by Twenty American Sociologists,* ed. Bennett M. Berger (Berkeley: University of California Press, 1990), 199, 202.

147. Reuel Denney, "Not All Are Victims," *Yale Review* 41 (Mar. 1952): 476.

148. Riesman, *The Lonely Crowd,* 18.

149. Ibid., 132.

150. Ibid., 102.

151. Brick, *Transcending Capitalism,* 121–85.

152. Mills, *White Collar,* xx.

153. Ibid.

154. See the essays of Bell, Parsons, Riesman, and Hofstadter in Daniel Bell, ed., *The New American Right* (New York: Criterion Books, 1955). There was a crucial difference between the way in which these authors and Mills used the idea of status anxiety. While the authors of *The New American Right* applied the concept to a minority of Americans (particularly the followers of Joseph McCarthy), Mills believed it characterized the American middle class as a whole.

155. Richard Hofstadter, *The Age of Reform: From Bryan to F. D. R.* (New York: Knopf, 1955), 131–73.

156. Riesman, *The Lonely Crowd,* 96.

157. Jeffrey Alexander, *Twenty Lectures: Sociological Theory Since World War II* (New York: Columbia University Press, 1987).

158. See the companion volume to *The Lonely Crowd,* David Riesman, with Nathan Glazer, *Faces in the Crowd: Individual Studies in Character and Politics* (New Haven, CT: Yale University Press, 1952), 32–69.

159. Riesman, *The Lonely Crowd,* 235.

CHAPTER 5. THE POLITICS OF TRUTH

1. Mills, *The Sociological Imagination*, 13.

2. C. Wright Mills, "The Conservative Mood," *Dissent* 1 (Winter 1954) 24.

3. "Editorial Statement: Our Country and Our Culture," *Partisan Review* 19 (May–June 1952): 282.

4. Ibid., 284.

5. Frances Stoner Saunders, *The Cultural Cold War: The CIA and the World of Arts and Letters* (New York: New Press, 1999), 162–63.

6. C. Wright Mills, "Our Country and Our Culture," *Partisan Review* 19 (July–Aug. 1952): 446.

7. Ibid., 447.

8. Ibid., 450.

9. As quoted in Wald, *The New York Intellectuals*, 323.

10. Irving Howe, "This Age of Conformity," *Partisan Review* 21 (Jan.–Feb. 1954): 33.

11. Irving Howe and Lewis Coser, "A Word to Our Readers," *Dissent* 1 (Winter 1954): 3.

12. Lewis Coser, "Imperialism and the Quest for New Ideas," *Dissent* 1 (Winter 1954): 9.

13. Mills, "The Conservative Mood," 22–31.

14. Maurice Isserman, *If I Had a Hammer: The Death of the Old Left and the Birth of the New* (Urbana: University of Illinois Press, 1987), 179–223. See also Wald, *The New York Intellectuals*, 311–43.

15. C. Wright Mills, "Who Conforms and Who Dissents?" *Commentary* 17 (April 1954): 404.

16. C. Wright Mills, "On Knowledge and Power," *Dissent* 2 (Summer 1955): 201.

17. Ibid., 203.

18. Ibid., 209, 210.

19. Ibid., 211.

20. Ibid., 210.

21. Ibid., 209.

22. Ibid., 212.

23. Mills to Swados, undated (response to May 18, 1955, letter from Swados to Mills), UT 4B 411.

24. C. Wright Mills, "Why I Wrote *The Power Elite*," *Book Find News* 188 (1956).

25. Mills to Phillip Vaudrin, Sept. 17, 1951, in *Letters and Autobiographical Writings*, 155. Strictly speaking, this was a misleading characterization of Mills's work, since *The New Men of Power* was not about the American working class as such, but about American labor leaders.

26. Mills, *The Power Elite*, 364.

27. Mills to Richard Herpers, Sept. 17, 1953, Central Files, Columbia University Archives, Columbiana Library.

28. Mills, *The Power Elite*, 364.

29. Ibid., 8.

30. Gaetano Mosca, *The Ruling Class* (New York: McGraw-Hill, 1939), 50.

31. In his response to his critics, Mills claimed that he did not believe that there was any single "elite theory" as such. See Mills, "'The Power Elite': Comment on Criticism," *Dissent* (Winter 1957): 33. Mills later dismissed Pareto's work as "pretentious, dull, and disorderly." See Mills, ed., *Images of Man: The Classic Tradition in Sociological Thinking* (New York: George Braziller, 1960), 17.

32. Mills, *The Power Elite*, 18.

33. Ibid., 4.

34. Ibid., 277 n.

35. Ibid., 277; Gerth and Mills, *From Max Weber*, 47.

36. Mills, *The Power Elite*, 39.

37. Warner and Lunt, *The Social Life of a Modern Community*.

38. Matthew Josephson, *The Robber Barons: The Great American Capitalists, 1861–1901* (New York: Harcourt, Brace, 1934); Gustavus Myers, *History of the Great American Fortunes* (Chicago: C.H. Kerr, 1910); Thorstein Veblen, *Theory of the Leisure Class: An Economic Study in the Evolution of Institutions* (New York: Macmillan, 1899).

39. Mills, *The Power Elite*, 126.

40. Ibid., 125.

41. Ibid., 121.

42. Ibid., 212.

43. Ibid., 186.

44. Ibid., 276–77.

45. Ibid., 273.

46. Ibid., 283.

47. As quoted in Sherry, *In the Shadow of War*, 140.

48. Mills, *The Power Elite*, 231.

49. Ibid., 19.

50. Ibid., 285.

51. Ibid., 215.

52. Ibid., 238.

53. John Kenneth Galbraith, *American Capitalism: The Concept of Countervailing Power* (Boston: Houghton Mifflin, 1952); Riesman, *The Lonely Crowd*; David B. Truman, *The Governmental Process: Political Interests and Public Opinion* (New York: Knopf, 1951).

54. Robert Dahl, *A Preface to Democratic Theory* (Chicago: University of Chicago Press, 1956), 277.

55. Robert Booth Fowler, *Believing Skeptics: American Political Intellectuals, 1945–1964* (Westport, CT: Greenwood Press, 1978), 176–214; John G. Gunnell, *Imagining the American Polity: Political Science and the Discourse of Democracy* (University Park, PA: Pennsylvania State University Press, 2004), 220–52; Michael Rogin, *The Intellectuals and McCarthy: The Radical Specter* (New York: M.I.T. Press, 1967).

56. Mills, *The Power Elite*, 245.

57. Ibid., 266.

58. Ibid., 244.

59. Ibid., 23.

60. Ibid., 206.

61. See, for instance, Robert Dahl, *Who Governs?: Democracy and Power in an American City* (New Haven, CT: Yale University Press, 1961).

62. Mills, *The Power Elite*, 308.

63. Ibid., 246.

64. Dahl, *Who Governs?* 151.

65. Mills, *The Power Elite*, 345.

66. On Kaufman and the New Left's use of "participatory democracy," see Kevin Mattson, *Intellectuals in Action*, 193–244.

67. Mills, *The Power Elite*, 308.

68. Ibid., 198.

69. Ibid., 219.

70. Ibid., 338.

71. As a work of social analysis, *The Power Elite* stands better without the final and penultimate chapters, which were reworked versions of earlier essays that Mills did not fully integrate into his argument about the power elite. However, Mills's charge against the elite for their "higher immorality" is easier to understand if one keeps in mind the origins of this chapter. It began as an article Mills wrote for the *New York Times Magazine,* in which he argued that the causes of political and business corruption could be sought in systemic factors, not individual failings. See Mills, "A Diagnosis of Our Moral Uneasiness," *New York Times Magazine,* Nov. 23, 1952.

72. Mills, *The Power Elite,* 356.

73. Mills to Hans Gerth, undated (received Dec. 26, 1953), in *Letters and Autobiographical Writings,* 180.

74. The most important reviews are conveniently collected in G. William Domhoff and Hoyt B. Ballard, eds., *C. Wright Mills and* The Power Elite (Boston: Beacon, 1968).

75. Mills, *The Power Elite,* 364.

76. Arnold Rogow, review of *The Power Elite, Public Opinion Quarterly* (Autumn 1956): 613.

77. Mabel Newcomer, *Journal of Economic History* 16 (Sept. 1956): 432, 433.

78. Among the most important reviews of *The Power Elite* in journals of social science, see Robert E. Agger, review of *The Power Elite, Social Forces* 35 (Mar. 1957): 287–88; Robert Bierstadt, review of *The Power Elite, Political Science Quarterly* 71 (Dec. 1956); Robert Highsaw, review of *The Power Elite, Journal of Politics* 19 (Feb. 1957): 144–46; Leonard Reissman, review of *The Power Elite, American Journal of Sociology* 21 (Aug. 1956): 513–14; and Peter Rossi, review of *The Power Elite, American Journal of Sociology* 62 (Sept. 1956): 232.

79. See, for instance, G. William Domhoff, *Who Rules America?* (Eagle Cliffs, NJ: Prentice Hall, 1967).

80. A. A. Berle, "Are the Blind Leading the Blind?" *New York Times,* Apr. 22, 1956.

81. On Sweezy, see Peter Clecak, *Radical Paradoxes: Dilemmas of the American Left, 1945–1970* (New York: Harper and Row, 1973), 128–74.

82. Paul Sweezy, "Power Elite or Ruling Class?" *Monthly Review* 8 (Sept. 1956): 139.

83. Robert Lynd, "Power in the United States," *Nation,* May 12, 1956, 408–11.

84. Sweezy, "Power Elite or Ruling Class?" 146, 147.

85. Ibid., 141.

86. C. Wright Mills, "Psychology and Social Science," *Monthly Review* 10 (Oct. 1958): 204–9.

87. Robert Dahl, "A Critique of the Ruling Elite Model," *American Political Science Review* 52 (June 1958): 465. While not a direct response to *The Power Elite,* Dahl's article was clearly intended to contribute to the widespread discussion of the issues raised by the book.

88. Ibid., 469.

89. Daniel Bell, "The Power Elite—Reconsidered," *American Journal of Sociology* 64 (Nov. 1958): 248. This piece was originally presented before the Faculty Colloquium of the Columbia University Sociology Department in May 1958. It was also included in Bell's influential 1960 collection of essays, *The End of Ideology: On the Exhaustion of Political Ideas in the Fifties* (Glencoe, IL: Free Press, 1960).

90. Though a number of critics made this point, the most sustained rendering was by Richard Rovere, "The Interlocking Interlopers," *The Progressive* 20 (June 1956): 33–35. See also Dennis Wrong, "Power in America," *Commentary* 22 (Sept. 1956), 278–80.

91. Mills, "'The Power Elite': Comment on Criticism," 28.

92. Bell, "The Power Elite—Reconsidered," 243.

93. Edward Shils, "The End of Ideology?" *Encounter* 5 (Nov. 1955): 55.

94. Bell, *The End of Ideology,* 373.

95. Ibid., 370.

96. Bell, "The Power Elite—Reconsidered," 238

97. Ibid., 250.

98. Talcott Parsons, "The Distribution of Power in American Society," *World Politics* 10 (Oct. 1957): 127.

99. See Sherry, *In the Shadow of War.*

100. Bell, for instance, ignored the increasing concentration of power in the hands of the executive branch and covert organizations such as the CIA when he claimed that major decisions of national policy "are vested specifically in one individual who must bear the responsibility for the decision—the President." In fact, though, the Constitution gives Congress significant powers in foreign policy, such as the right to declare war, that were usurped by the executive branch after World War II. Parsons noted that he, too, was anxious about the "military metaphysic" described by Mills, but he went on to claim that the recent decade was a "special situation" owing to "the extremely unsettled

condition of the world at large." See Bell, "The Power Elite—Reconsidered," 243, and Parsons, "The Distribution of Power in American Society," 135.

101. See Sherry, *In the Shadow of War*, 234–36.

102. Parsons, "The Distribution of Power in American Society," 139.

103. Ibid.

104. Mills, *The Power Elite*, 26.

105. C. Wright Mills, "Two Styles of Research in Current Social Studies," *Philosophy of Science* 20 (Oct. 1953): 266–75; Mills, "IBM Plus Reality Plus Humanism = Sociology," *Saturday Review of Literature*, May 1, 1954, 22–23, 54.

106. Mills, *The Sociological Imagination*, 72; Dewey as quoted in Westbrook, *John Dewey and American Democracy*, 138.

107. Mills, *The Sociological Imagination*, 132.

108. Mills to Phillip Vaudrin, Sept. 17, 1951, in *Letters and Autobiographical Writings*, 155.

109. Mills, *The Sociological Imagination*, 33.

110. Ibid., 48.

111. The chapter of *The Sociological Imagination* in which Mills criticized Parsonian "grand theory" was originally written (though never published) as a book review of Parsons's *The Social System* (1951) for the *New York Times*. In describing Parsons's work, Mills dealt with his most abstruse and abstract book, which even many students of Parsons admitted did not render concepts useful for social research. Some of Parsons's other work was more empirical and less vulnerable to the charges Mills levied. See Mills, review of *The Social System*, by Talcott Parsons, UT 4B 389.

112. Mills, *The Sociological Imagination*, 73.

113. Ibid., 96.

114. Ibid., 101.

115. Ibid., 84.

116. Ibid., 21.

117. Ibid., 110–11.

118. As quoted in Haney, *The Americanization of Social Science*, 162.

119. Barrington Moore, "Reader's Report (May 6, 1958)," UT 4B 400.

120. Mills, "IBM Plus Reality Plus Humanism = Sociology."

121. See the responses in UT 4B 400.

122. Alvin Gouldner, "Some Observations on Systematic Theory," in *Sociology in the United States of America*, ed. H. Zetterberg (Paris: UNESCO, 1956), 34–42. See also Gouldner, "Anti-Minotaur: The Myth of a Value-Free Sociology," *Social Problems* 9 (Winter 1962): 199–213. Barrington Moore, *Political Power and Social Theory* (Cambridge, MA: Harvard University Press, 1958), esp. "Strategy in Social Science." In the *American Sociological Review*, Seymour Martin Lipset compared Moore's *Political Power and Social Theory* with Mills's *The Sociological Imagination*. "In a real sense," wrote Lipset, "these essays by Professor Moore are a more serious and dignified argument against systematic theory and rigid quantitative methodology which C. Wright Mills has developed more shrilly in his *Sociological Imagination*. The virulence and bad taste of Mills's polemic should not lead us to accept one

of a number of erroneous images put forth by Mills, namely that he is almost alone in resisting what he considers to be the dominant trends in American sociology: excessive abstraction and over-preoccupation with esoteric methodology." Lipset's quote is a good example of the dismissive contempt with which some leading sociologists treated Mills, yet in this case, Lipset had a point. See Lipset, review of *Political Power and Social Theory, American Sociological Review* 25 (Apr. 1960): 283.

123. Mills to William Miller, Mar. 14, 1957, in *Letters and Autobiographical Writings*, 230.

124. Edward Shils, "Imaginary Sociology," *Encounter* 14 (1960): 78

125. Seymour Martin Lipset and Neil Smelser, "Change and Controversy in Recent American Sociology," *British Journal of Sociology* 12 (Mar. 1961): 50.

126. Ute Gerhardt, *Talcott Parsons: An Intellectual Biography* (Cambridge: Cambridge University Press, 2002), 191 n.

127. George C. Homans, review of *The Sociological Imagination, American Journal of Sociology* 64 (Mar., 1960): 517–18.

128. William L. Kolb, "Values, Politics, and Sociology," *American Sociological Review* 25 (Dec. 1960): 966–69.

129. Lewis S. Feuer, review of *The Sociological Imagination, Ethics* 70 (Apr. 1960): 237–40.

130. Riesman to Mills, May 2, 1958, UT 4B 400.

131. Mills, *The Sociological Imagination*, 132.

132. Ibid., 4.

133. Ibid., 137.

134. Ibid., 7.

135. By using the term "sociological," Mills certainly did not mean the contemporary academic discipline of sociology, since much of the book argued that most professional sociologists lacked sociological imagination. In any case, Mills continued to believe in the basic unity of all social inquiry and the arbitrariness of disciplinary boundaries. As Mills himself admitted, the term "social science" was closer to what he meant, though he declined to use the term because of its scientistic connotations. However, Mills's use of the term did suggest the importance of sociology as "the center of reflection about social science" (22) during the period, as well as an older tradition that saw sociology as the queen of the social sciences, best able to synthesize insights from other disciplines. See ibid., 18–19 n.

136. Miliband to Mills, Apr. 26, 1958, letter in author's possession. Some commentators have also been frustrated by the expansiveness of Mills's definitions of "classic social analysis" and "the sociological imagination." For instance, Göran Therborn wrote, "Since this so-called classic social analysis is an aggregate of vastly different, mutually contradictory epistemological and substantive theoretical positions, Mills' faith must beg many questions. The idealism of Sombart or the positivism of Spencer? The social science of Comte, of Marx, or of Weber? Or perhaps some kind of synthesis ot reshuffling of positions?" See Therborn, *Science, Class, and Society: On the Formation of Sociology and Historical Materialism* (London: New Left Books, 1976), 36.

137. Russell Kirk, "Shrewd Knocks at Sociological Theories," *Chicago*

Daily Tribune, May 24, 1959; Kirk, "Freely Given Advice on Saving the World," *Chicago Daily Tribune,* Dec. 28, 1958. For a detailed account of the reception of *The Sociological Imagination,* see Haney, *The Americanization of Social Science,* 137–71.

138. Mills, *The Sociological Imagination,* 13.

139. Ibid., 5.

140. Vance Packard, *The Status Seekers: An Exploration of Class Behavior in America and the Hidden Barriers That Affect You, Your Community, Your Future* (New York: D. McCay, 1959); A.C. Spectorsky, *The Exurbanites* (Philadelphia: Lipincott, 1955); Whyte, *The Organization Man.* See also Daniel Horowitz, *Vance Packard and American Social Criticism* (Chapel Hill: University of North Carolina Press, 1994).

141. C. Wright Mills, review of *The Exurbanites,* by A.C. Spectorsky, *Saturday Review of Literature,* Oct. 29, 1955, 12. Mills also reviewed Whyte's *Organization Man,* of which he was more critical, for the *New York Times.* He clearly saw Whyte as popularizing some of the ideas he had expressed in *White Collar.* C. Wright Mills, review of *The Organization Man,* by William H. Whyte, *New York Times Book Review,* December 12, 1956.

142. Talcott Parsons, "Some Problems Confronting Sociology as a Profession," *American Sociological Review* 24 (Aug. 1959): 553.

143. Mills, *The Sociological Imagination,* 8.

144. Ibid., 118.

145. Ibid., 174.

146. Ibid., 116.

147. Ibid., 186.

148. Ibid., 190.

149. Ibid.

CHAPTER 6. WORLDLY AMBITIONS

1. Mills, "Letter to the New Left," 22.

2. "The Port Huron Statement" is included as an appendix in Miller, *"Democracy Is in the Streets,"* 329.

3. C. Wright Mills, "The Decline of the Left," *The Listener* 61 (Apr. 1959): 595.

4. Mills, "Letter to the New Left," 22.

5. C. Wright Mills, "On Latin America, the Left and the U.S.," *Evergreen Review* 16 (Jan. 1961): 115.

6. Mills, Untitled note, UT 4B 378.

7. Mills to Frances and Charles Grover Mills, Mar. 18, 1961, in *Letters and Autobiographical Writings,* 325.

8. Accounts that treat Mills and the New Left tend to focus on Mills as a theorist of participatory democracy and hence an influence on SDS, but they slight the international dimension of Mills's New Left thought: see, for instance, Miller, *"Democracy Is in the Streets,"* 78–91; Mattson, *Intellectuals in Action,* 43–96; Jamison and Eyerman, *Seeds of the Sixties,* 30–46. Such accounts of Mills feature in a common narrative of the New Left that focuses

on the campus-based white youth movement and SDS in particular. This narrative, however, has recently been challenged. On this point, see Van Gosse, "A Movement of Movements: The Definition and Periodization of the New Left," in *A Companion to Post-1945 America*, ed. Jean-Christophe Agnew and Roy Rosenzweig (Malden, MA: Blackwell Publishing, 2002), 277–302.

9. Two books that do stress the significance of international connections for the development of the New Left are Lawrence Wittner, *The Struggle against the Bomb*, vol. 2, *Resisting the Bomb: A History of the World Nuclear Disarmament Movement, 1954–1970* (Stanford, CA: Stanford University Press, 1997); and Gosse, *Where the Boys Are*.

10. Stuart Hall, "The 'First' New Left: Life and Times," in *Out of Apathy: Voices of the New Left Thirty Years On*, ed. Robin Archer et al. (London: Verso, 1989), 14.

11. Mills to Horkheimer, Dec. 15, 1952, in *Letters and Autobiographical Writings*, 197.

12. Mills to Miliband, Jan. 25, 1961, in *Letters and Autobiographical Writings*, 325.

13. Mills to Barzun, Sept. 28, 1959, UT 4B 398.

14. Mills, "Policies for Three Institutions," UT 4B 395.

15. Mills to Gerth, Nov. 8, 1956, letter in author's possession.

16. Alan Hooper, "A Politics Adequate to the Age: The New Left and the Long Sixties," in *New Left, New Right and Beyond: Taking the Sixties Seriously*, ed. Geoff Andrews et al. (New York: Palgrave, 1999), 7–25. Stressing the importance of decolonization, Fredric Jameson has similarly argued for the mid-1950s as a starting point for the New Left. See Fredric Jameson, "Periodizing the 60s," in *The 60s Without Apologies*, ed. Sohnya Sayres et al. (Minneapolis: University of Minnesota Press, 1984), 178–209.

17. Mills to Sir Sydney Gaine, Mar. 4, 1957, letter in author's possession.

18. Mills to Coser, Apr. 4, 1957, in *Letters and Autobiographical Writings*, 234–35. Mills used the phrase "pivotal year" in other letters as well. See Mills to Gerth, Apr. 8, 1957, letter in author's possession.

19. Mills to Harvey and Bette Swados, June 13, 1961, in *Letters and Autobiographical Writings*, 332.

20. On the British New Left, see Lin Chun, *The British New Left* (Edinburgh: Edinburgh University Press, 1993); Hall, "The 'First' New Left"; and Michael Kenny, *The First New Left: British Intellectuals after Stalin* (London: Lawrence and Wishart, 1995).

21. Stuart Hall to Mills, June 3, 1960, UT 4B 395.

22. Isserman, *If I Had a Hammer*, 115.

23. Norman Birnbaum, *Toward a Critical Sociology* (New York: Oxford University Press, 1971).

24. Cynthia Young, *Soul Power: Culture, Radicalism, and the Making of a U.S. Third World Left* (Durham, NC: Duke University Press, 2006), 103–4.

25. *London Tribune*, Jan. 16, 1959.

26. "Dissent—with an American accent," *London Tribune*, Feb. 13, 1959.

27. Mills, "Letter to the New Left," 22.

28. Stuart Hall to Mills, June 2, 1960, UT 4B 395.

29. E.P. Thompson to Mills, Apr. 21, 1960, UT 4B 395.

30. Miliband to Mills, June 4, 1960, UT 4B 388.

31. On Miliband, see Michael Newman, *Ralph Miliband and the Politics of the New Left* (London: Merlin Press, 2002).

32. As quoted in ibid., 67.

33. Ralph Miliband, *The State in Capitalist Society* (London: Weidenfeld and Nicolson, 1969). Like Mills, Miliband attacked liberal pluralist theory and argued that overlapping political and economic elites held concentrated political power in modern capitalist societies. Sticking closer to Marxism, however, Miliband emphasized the significance of economic elites and criticized Mills for exaggerating the autonomous role of the military.

34. Mills, *The Causes of World War Three*, 129.

35. As quoted in Stanley Pierson, *Leaving Marxism: Studies in the Dissolution of an Ideology* (Stanford, CA: Stanford University Press, 2001), 133.

36. Mills to Miliband, May 25, 1960, letter in author's possession.

37. Mills to parents, Oct. 17, 1961, UT 4B 353.

38. Many of these autobiographical letters have been published in *Letters and Autobiographical Writings*.

39. Mills, "Proposal for Comparative Sociology," UT 4B 398.

40. Mills to Hallock Hoffman, July 20, 1960, UT 4B 398.

41. Mills to Hallock Hoffman, Oct. 7, 1959, in *Letters and Autobiographical Writings*, 273.

42. C. Wright Mills, *The Marxists* (New York: Dell, 1962); Anderson, *Considerations on Western Marxism*.

43. Mills to Gerth, June 15, 1960, in *Letters and Autobiographical Writings*, 304.

44. Mills, "Letter to the New Left," 22.

45. C. Wright Mills, "Research Project on Selected Types of American Intellectuals" (Spring 1955), UT 4B 355.

46. Mills, "A Personal Note to the Reader," in *The Cultural Apparatus*, UT 4B 378.

47. C. Wright Mills, "The Man in the Middle: The Designer," *Industrial Design*, Nov. 1958, 73.

48. C. Wright Mills, "The Cultural Apparatus," *The Listener* 61 (Mar. 26, 1959): 553.

49. Ibid.

50. C. Wright Mills "The Fourth Epoch," *The Listener* 61 (Mar. 12, 1959): 450.

51. Mills, *The Cultural Apparatus*, UT 4B 379.

52. Ibid.

53. Mills, "The Cultural Apparatus," 553.

54. Ibid.

55. Mills, *The Cultural Apparatus*, UT 4B 379.

56. Jürgen Habermas, *The Structural Transformation of the Public Sphere* (Cambridge, MA: MIT Press, 1989), 249. Habermas's book was not translated into English until 1989, but it is clearly a product of the same period in which

Mills wrote. For a comparison of Mills, Habermas, and Dewey as theorists of the public sphere, see Andreas Koller, "Recovering the Road Not Taken in Social Science: Dewey, Mills, Habermas, and the Structural Transformation of the Public Sphere," unpublished paper in author's possession.

57. Mills, *The Cultural Apparatus*, UT 4B 379.

58. Habermas, *The Structural Transformation of the Public Sphere*, 159.

59. Mills, "The Cultural Apparatus," 552.

60. Ibid.

61. Ibid.

62. Mills, *The Cultural Apparatus*, UT 4B 378.

63. Hall, "The 'First' New Left," 25.

64. Raymond Williams, *The Long Revolution* (London: Chatto & Windus, 1961).

65. E.P. Thompson, *The Making of the English Working Class* (London: Gollancz, 1963).

66. *The Observer*, Jan. 25, 1959.

67. Mills, "The Decline of the Left," 593.

68. Ibid., 595.

69. Ibid.

70. Mills, *The Cultural Apparatus*, UT 4B 380.

71. Mills, "The Decline of the Left," 596.

72. Mills, *The Cultural Apparatus*, UT 4B 380.

73. John Kenneth Galbraith, *The Affluent Society* (Boston: Houghton, Mifflin, 1958); Percival and Paul Goodman, *Communitas: Means of Livelihood and Ways of Life* (Chicago: University of Chicago Press, 1947); Eric Larrabee, *The Self-Conscious Society* (Garden City, NY: Doubleday, 1960); Herbert Marcuse, *Eros and Civilization: A Philosophical Inquiry into Freud* (Boston: Beacon Press, 1955); Riesman, *The Lonely Crowd*.

74. E.P. Thompson to Mills, Apr. 21, 1960, UT 4B 395.

75. Mills to Swados, Sept. 9, 1957, in *Letters and Autobiographical Writings*, 246.

76. Wittner, *The Struggle against the Bomb*, 41–82.

77. Isserman, *If I Had a Hammer*, 127–69; Lawrence Wittner, *Rebels Against War: The American Peace Movement, 1933–1983* (Philadelphia: Temple University Press, 1984), 240–56; John D'Emilio, *Lost Prophet: The Life and Times of Bayard Rustin* (New York: Free Press, 2003), 249–62.

78. "U.S. Foreign Policy Hit by Mills," *Washington Post*, Mar. 25, 1958.

79. Mills, *The Causes of World War Three*, 8.

80. Ibid., 47.

81. Ibid., 109.

82. Ibid., 98.

83. Ibid., 96.

84. Ibid., 149.

85. "Comment on a 'Pagan Sermon,'" *Christian Century*, Mar. 26, 1958, 365.

86. Mills to Miliband, Dec. 9, 1958, letter in author's possession.

87. Mills, *The Causes of World War Three*, 153.

88. A. J. Muste, "C. Wright Mills' Program: Two Views," *Dissent* 6 (Spring 1959): 189.

89. Rev. Robert V. Woods to Mills, Apr. 23, 1959, UT 4B 420.

90. Carlton F. Brehmer to Mills, Mar. 12, 1959, UT 4B 420.

91. Senator Mike Mansfield to Jesse Gordon, June 20, 1960, UT 4B 420.

92. Richard C. Rodgers to Mac S. Albert (of Simon and Schuster), July 23, 1959, UT 4B 420. Not all the letters were positive, however. One reader, a professional solider, wrote, "To think that we gave up so much in both world wars, so that bums like your self, could write scum as that and get away with it" (William Mikula to Mills, Sept. 5, 1960, UT 4B 420).

93. Mrs. H. J. Laski to Mills, Mar. 7, 1959, UT 4B 420.

94. Dr. Alfred Jacobs to Mills, Oct. 8, 1959, UT 4B 420.

95. Dott. Paolo Calzini, undated ("June 24") to Mills, UT 4B 420.

96. Irving Howe, *A Margin of Hope: An Intellectual Autobiography* (San Diego: Harcourt Brace Jovanovich, 1982), 244–45.

97. Isaac Deutscher, *Russia in Transition* (New York: Coward, McCann, 1957); Deutscher, *The Great Contest* (New York: Oxford University Press, 1960).

98. Mills, "On Latin America, the Left and the U.S.," 110–11.

99. Irving Howe, "C. Wright Mills' Program: Two Views," *Dissent* 6 (Spring 1959): 194.

100. Ibid., 191.

101. C. Wright Mills, "Intellectuals and Russia," *Dissent* 6 (Summer 1959): 296.

102. See Miliband to Mills, June 4, 1960, UT 4B 388.

103. Mills, "Intellectuals and Russia," 296.

104. For instance, Mills wrote that Soviet industrialization involved "brutality and tyranny" and "cannot be justified by pointing out the brutality and tyranny of earlier capitalist expansion" (*The Causes of World War Three*, 72).

105. Mills, *The Cultural Apparatus*, UT 4B 380.

106. Mills, "Intellectuals and Russia," 295.

107. Irving Howe and Lewis Coser, with Julius Jacobson, *The American Communist Party, A Critical History, 1919–1957* (Boston: Beacon Press, 1957).

108. Mills, "Intellectuals and Russia," 298.

109. Mills, "On the Problem of Freedom" (Advanced Copy of C. Wright Mills' Speech; American Studies Conference on Civil Rights), Oct. 16, 1959, UT 4B 400.

110. Mills to Tovarich (summer 1960), in *Letters and Autobiographical Writings*, 314. Curiously, in this letter Mills tells a story from his adolescence that places racism at the center of the development of his commitment to social justice. According to Mills, when he was twenty, he got involved in a violent confrontation with a white stranger because Mills had helped two black men load a truck.

111. C. Wright Mills, *Listen, Yankee* (New York: Ballantine Books, 1960), 7.

112. Mills to Fuentes, Jan. 12, 1961, Carlos Fuentes Papers, Box 116, Folder 13, Department of Rare Books and Special Collections, Princeton University Library.

113. As quoted in Martin Van Delden, *Carlos Fuentes, Mexico, and Modernity* (Nashville, TN: Vanderbilt University Press, 1998), 42.

114. Jorge Castañeda, *Utopia Unarmed: The Latin American Left after the Cold War* (New York: Vintage Books, 1991), 176–85.

115. Mills, "On Latin America, the Left and the U.S.," 113.

116. Mills to Hans Gerth, July 15, 1960, in *Letters and Autobiographical Writings*, 304.

117. As quoted in Gosse, *Where the Boys Are*, 175.

118. Saul Landau, "C. Wright Mills: The Last Six Months," *Ramparts* 4 (Aug. 1965): 45–54.

119. Mills, *Listen, Yankee*, 11.

120. Audiotape of 1960 interview of Cuban revolutionaries by Mills, in author's possession.

121. "C. Wright Mills," 1962 radio documentary, at http://fromthevault radio.org/home/ (accessed on Sept. 12, 2007).

122. Mills, *Listen, Yankee*, 179.

123. Ibid., 8.

124. Ibid., 66.

125. Ibid., 152.

126. William Appleman Williams, *The Tragedy of American Diplomacy* (New York: Dell, 1962). In this second edition of his work, Appleman introduced his narrative by noting how American relations with Cuba from 1898 to 1961 symbolized the tragedy of American diplomacy. See also Williams, *The United States, Castro, and Cuba* (New York: Monthly Review Press, 1962).

127. Mills, *Listen, Yankee*, 1.

128. See Gosse, *Where the Boys Are*, 152–54, 183–87.

129. Mills, *Listen, Yankee*, 181.

130. Ibid., 43.

131. Leo Huberman and Paul M. Sweezy, *Cuba: Anatomy of a Revolution* (New York: Monthly Review, 1960), 154.

132. As quoted in Gosse, *Where the Boys Are*, 163.

133. John-Paul Sartre, "Ideology and Revolution," *Studies on the Left* 1: 7–16; Sartre, *Sartre on Cuba* (New York: Ballantine, 1961).

134. Mills, *Listen, Yankee*, 99.

135. Ibid., 122.

136. Ibid., 123.

137. Ibid., 125.

138. Ibid., 182.

139. Ibid., 183.

140. Ibid., 165, 166.

141. Audiotape of 1960 interview, in author's possession.

142. As quoted in E.P. Thompson, *The Heavy Dancers* (London: Merlin Press, 1985), 268.

143. On the Cuban Revolution, see Jules R. Benjamin, *The United States*

and the Origins of the Cuban Revolution: The Empire of Liberty in an Age of National Liberation (Princeton, NJ: Princeton University Press, 1990); Samuel Farber, *The Origins of the Cuban Revolution Reconsidered* (Chapel Hill: University of North Carolina Press, 2006); Morris H. Morley, *Imperial State and Revolution: The United States and Cuba, 1952–1986* (New York: Cambridge University Press, 1987); and Marifeli Perez-Stable, *The Cuban Revolution: Origins, Course, and Legacy* (New York: Oxford University Press, 1994).

144. Harvey Swados, "C. Wright Mills: A Personal Memoir," *Dissent* 10 (Winter 1963): 40–42; Mills, *The Cultural Apparatus*, UT 4B 379.

145. C. Wright Mills, *Escucha, yanqui: la revolución en Cuba* (Mexico City: Fondo de Cultura Económica, 1961). I thank Professor Benjamin Fraser of Christopher Newport University for helping me translate passages of this text.

146. Landau, "C. Wright Mills," 49–50; Simone de Beauvoir, *Force of Circumstance* (New York: G. P. Putnam's Sons, 1964), 589–90.

147. See Yaroslava Mills to Fannye and C. G. Mills, Feb. 22, 1962, UT 4B 353. The FBI files on Mills also offer evidence that he was disillusioned with Castro at the end of his life; see Mike Forrest Keen, *Stalking the Sociological Imagination: J. Edgar Hoover's FBI Surveillance of American Sociology* (Westport, CT: Transaction, 1999), 183.

148. Mills to "Richard," Mar. 6, 1961, UT 4B 394.

149. Mills to Mr. Obelensky, Oct. 26, 1960, Box 116, Folder 13, Carlos Fuentes Papers, Department of Rare Books and Special Collections, Princeton University Library. Mills suggested the quote as a blurb for the English translation of Fuentes's novel *Where the Air Is Clear.*

150. C. Wright Mills, "Listen, Yankee: The Cuban Case Against the United States," *Harper's Magazine* 122 (Dec. 1960): 31–37.

151. Eleanor Roosevelt, *New York Post Magazine*, Dec. 14, 1960, 3.

152. "The Siege of Cuba," *New Left Review* 1 (Jan.–Feb. 1961): 2. See also Stuart Hall and Norm Fruchter, "Notes on the Cuban Dilemma," *New Left Review* 1 (May–June 1961): 2–12.

153. Saul Landau, "Cuba: The Present Dilemma," *New Left Review* 1 (May–June 1961): 12–22.

154. Mills to Castro, Sept. 20, 1960, in *Letters and Autobiographical Writings,* 315.

155. Robin Blackburn, personal correspondence with the author, June 28, 2007.

156. Robert G. Mead Jr., "A Literary Letter from Mexico," *New York Times*, May 21, 1961.

157. Mills to Fuentes, undated, Box 116, Folder 13, Carlos Fuentes Papers, Department of Rare Books and Special Collections, Princeton University Library.

158. As quoted in Van Delden, *Carlos Fuentes, Mexico, and Modernity,* 41.

159. Carlos Fuentes, *The Death of Artemio Cruz* (New York: Farrar, Straus, and Giroux, 1964).

160. *Letters and Autobiographical Writings,* 321.

EPILOGUE: THE LEGACY OF C. WRIGHT MILLS

1. Gerth to Yaroslava Mills, undated (summer 1962), UT 4B 353.

2. Ralph Miliband, "C. Wright Mills," 19.

3. Outside *White Collar,* one of the few instances in which Mills addressed issues of gender inequality was in an unpublished 1955 review of Simone de Beauvoir's *The Second Sex.* Mills was in many ways sympathetic to de Beauvoir's perspective, but he resisted the notion that patriarchy was a fundamental cause of women's oppression, arguing instead that both men and women suffered in modern society. Clearly, this would have become a point of contention between Mills and feminists had he lived longer.

4. Mills, "The Promise (preliminary draft)," UT 4B 400, 33.

5. Mills to Carl Brandt, Oct. 26, 1960, UT 4B 390.

6. Irving Louis Horowitz, ed., *The New Sociology: Essays in Social Science and Social Theory in Honor of C. Wright Mills* (New York: Oxford University Press, 1964), iv.

7. Ibid., 19.

8. Ibid., 47.

9. Paul Jacobs and Saul Landau, *The New Radicals: A Report with Documents* (New York: Random House, 1966), 101.

10. Tom Hayden, "Radical Nomad: Essays on C. Wright Mills and His Times," 3.

11. Hayden, "Radical Nomad: Essays on C. Wright Mills and His Times," 8.

12. Ibid., 6.

13. Harold Cruse, *The Crisis of the Negro Intellectual* (New York: Morrow, 1967), 459, 467.

14. Ibid., 467.

15. Mills, *White Collar,* xix.

16. Quentin Skinner, "Meaning and Understanding in the History of Ideas," *History and Theory* 8 (1969): 52.

Index

abstract empiricism, Mills's critique of, 144, 170–74
Adorno, Theodor W., 48
Advance, The (periodical), 83
advertising, 130
Agee, James, 116
alienation, social, 106, 114, 125, 130–35, 136, 142, 160
Alinsky, Saul, 57, 60
Amalgamated Clothing Workers of America, 83
American Federation of Labor (AFL), 87, 98, 99
American Journal of Sociology, 25, 28, 33, 51, 137, 162, 174
American Sociological Review, 25, 26, 32, 114, 174
American Sociological Society (ASS), 25–26, 27, 33, 57
American Workers Party, 60
anarchism, 88, 168
Anderson, Perry, 188
anti-Communism, 6, 60, 104, 119–20, 124, 203–5
anti-imperialism, 183, 206, 210
antinuclear activism, 180, 197–201, 203
anti-Stalinist left, 8, 56, 59–60, 83, 97, 120, 124, 146, 205
antiwar stance, Mills's, 61–62. *See also* pacifism; peace movement, Mills's engagement with
apathy, political, 7, 8, 94, 115, 125, 134, 141, 161, 179, 189, 206
Arendt, Hannah, 48, 123

Aron, Raymond, 165
Aronowitz, Stanley, 10
Ayres, Clarence, 22, 24, 28

Bannister, Robert, 25
Baran, Paul, 163
Barkin, Solomon, 84
Barzun, Jacques, 117–18, 182
BASR. *See* Bureau of Applied Social Research
Batista, Fulgencio, 209
Bay of Pigs invasion, 209, 211
Beard, Charles, 13
Beauvoir, Simone de, 213, 262n3
Becker, Howard P., 26–27, 29, 32, 37–38
behaviorism, 29, 50–51
Behemoth (Neumann), 57–59, 62, 63, 64
Bell, Daniel, 11, 46, 56, 57, 62–63, 64, 66–67, 81, 118, 140, 164, 165, 166, 216, 252n100
Benedict, Ruth, 109
Berle, A. A., 163, 215
big business. *See* corporations and corporate power
Bingham, Alfred, 113
biology, social-scientific uses of, 20, 21, 28, 29, 30
Birnbaum, Norman, 183, 184
Blackburn, Robin, 214
Blumer, Herbert, 26, 28, 108, 173
Boorstin, Daniel, 126
Bottomore, T. B., 183, 218
Bourdieu, Pierre, 16, 38, 230n100
bourgeoisie, 34, 48, 113, 192–93

Text: 10/13 Sabon
Display: Sabon
Compositor: BookMatters, Berkeley
Indexer: Andrew Joron
Printer and binder: Maple-Vail Book Manufacturing Group